THE UNCHOSEN

THE UNCHOSEN

. . . for many be called, but few chosen.
MATTHEW XX:16

Charles Judah
and
George Winston Smith

Coward-McCann, Inc.   New York

Copyright © 1962 by
Charles Judah and George Winston Smith

Library of Congress Catalog
Card Number: 62-10947

Contents

The planning of a Presidential nomination is infinitely more calculated than the planning of an election; but capture of the nomination, however complicated, is a process in which the elements are subject to rational analysis and control. An election is something else again. Success or failure in the nomination can always, later, be plausibly rooted in some blunder, decision, deal, coup or treachery. With the nomination, a man is plunged into the wild, uncontrollable electoral half of the Presidential exercise; but with it, he captures control, too, of a political establishment that puts him halfway home to the White House; the nomination must be first target always.

*   *   *

In Presidential politics, one must move at the proper season of life; one hopes that the tide is right at that season. If the proper season of life comes too soon or too late in the tides of history, one remains a might-have-been—a Daniel Webster, a Henry Clay, a Henry Stimson, a Robert Taft, a Samuel Rayburn, an Estes Kefauver.

—THEODORE H. WHITE
The Making of the President 1960

Introduction

THIS is the story of nine men who sought one of the highest attainments of all—the nomination of their political party for the Presidency of the United States of America. In the end, their reach exceeded their grasp. They did not win the nomination. But the failure of such men is more interesting than most successes—men such as Lyndon Johnson, Estes Kefauver, Robert A. Taft, William Gibbs McAdoo, Benjamin Bristow, and Champ Clark. Their struggle sheds a revealing light on the awesome mystery of U. S. presidential politics, particularly on the dynamics of the national party convention—that massive power contest whose object is to produce, above all, the *right* man. The right man is by no means always the best man in terms of qualifications for the Presidency. Some of the statesmen portrayed in this book were far better equipped to lead the nation than their victorious rivals. But when a convention must choose between the best man for the job and the man who seems most likely to win it, the laurel of the nomination invariably goes to the latter. We have attempted to demonstrate the intricate process by which national conventions narrow the field of candidates to the one man who can unite the party's warring factions into a single fighting unit that can storm the White House.

In the profiles of the candidates themselves, we have explored the genesis and the nature of the presidential obsession. What are the backgrounds that cause a man to be thought of as presidential timber? How is he groomed, step by step, for the nomination? What are the forces in that background and in that grooming that mark him for success or failure at the presidential aspirant's moment of truth, the national convention? Why is distinguished service in the United States Senate a serious liability for anyone who would be President? Why are great reformers rarely nominated? To what extent do religion, marital status, and personal wealth determine a candidate's availability? What is the final influence of the presidential primary and the public opinion poll? These are some of the great imponderables of presidential politics that have absorbed us in our study of the rise and fall of the unchosen. No final answers are possible but some progress can be made toward understanding the intricacies and the logic of the American political party system as it is revealed in its leaders and its national conventions.

Throughout these contests we have also tried in some measure to reflect the evolution of the American political scene. The day of the kingmaker gives way to the power of the presidential primary; candidates, who once remained coyly in the background, emerge into the limelight of television and carry their fights onto the convention floor. And the parties themselves are seen in constant flux, moving from liberal to conservative, from isolationism to internationalism and back again, always reflecting the prevailing mood of the country and the state of the world.

For those who wish to know more about the protagonists,

biographies, memoirs, and autobiographies are available. William Thomas Hutchinson's *Lowden of Illinois* and E. Bruce Thompson's *Benjamin Helm Bristow* (in manuscript form in the University of Wisconsin library) are definitive biographies. William S. White's *The Taft Story,* Jack Anderson and Fred Blumenthal's *The Kefauver Story,* Booth Mooney's *The Lyndon Johnson Story* and J. A. Morris' *Nelson Rockefeller* are excellent. Our debt to all the above is substantial. Eugene H. Roseboom's *A History of Presidential Elections* gives a good brief narrative of all major party conventions. For a scholarly dissection of presidential nominating politics, *The Politics of National Party Conventions* by David, Goldman and Bain is unequaled.

CHARLES JUDAH
GEORGE WINSTON SMITH

THE UNCHOSEN

The Republicans

1860

THE PRESIDENTIAL nominating conventions of 1860 marked an epochal turning point in American history. The delegates of course could not know that their decision would help plunge the nation into civil war before another year had passed. Torn by the slavery crisis, unable to name a man acceptable to both North and South, the great Democratic party ruined its chances of winning the Presidency by nominating two candidates. This gave the relatively new, antislavery Republican party its first great opportunity.

As the Republicans met in Chicago on May 16 for their second nominating convention, the delegates were in a relaxed, lighthearted mood; it would still be a hard fight, but with the right man they could win. To seize the golden opportunity presented by the Democratic schism, they would have to choose a man capable of bringing all conflicting intraparty elements together.

They needed a magnetic leader—a romantic figure, an American Garibaldi who would sound a clarion call. But they had tried glamour in 1856, with the dashing John Charles Frémont, and had done well but still fallen short. A man of broader experience, of proven ability to lead, an outstanding spokesman in Congress, might be the right man to galvanize the inchoate groups into a fighting phalanx. Who but William H. Seward, the brilliant Senator from the Empire State, could do this so well? Seward was by all odds the Republican with the greatest prestige, the most strongly backed (by the New York machine of Thurlow Weed), the most striking personality and the statesman with the greatest experience. If his qualifications were considered, a nomination by acclamation seemed to be in order.

But Seward had his Achilles heel. He had made enemies throughout his years of public service, not always because of his political sins but also because his virtues had alienated those who could not agree with him. His enemies, and he had many of them, were ready to pull him down. Perhaps, for the Republicans in 1860, something less than a great crusade was in order. Perhaps a great conciliator rather than a great chieftain was needed. The right man might be right because he was less well known and more ingratiating. Perhaps he would be of the West but acceptable to the East, liked by the German immigrants but not an enemy of the Know Nothings; perhaps he would be a "solid" lawyer welcomed by businessmen, yet a man of the people; he might be agreeable to "old fogy" Whigs but spiced with antislavery opinions sufficiently to make him the choice of the free soil element in the party. Perhaps, without realizing it, as the delegates gathered in Chicago, they were ready for Abraham Lincoln.

Seward vs. Lincoln

Eminent Men Make More Enemies.
—LORD BRYCE

Don't take Seward, or we're beaten—
Take some ninny quite unknown. . . .
—CHARLES G. HALPINE, *"The New York Tribune's*
Presidential Philosophy"

CHICAGO was in a gala mood. The Wigwam at Lake and Market streets, built for the Republican party's second national convention, was decorated with patriotic bunting, evergreens and fresh-cut May flowers. Chicago was proud of the Wigwam. True, the inside was roughhewn and unplaned and the wall of an adjacent building served as its back, but garlands, blossoms and boughs hid that, and besides it was big enough to sustain a few shortcomings. It was one hundred and eighty feet long and a hundred feet wide. It would hold ten thousand people, and since there would be only four hundred and sixty-six delegates, there would be lots of room for spectators—though by no means all of the hundred thousand visitors crowding into the city. They had streamed in for days—politicians, newsmen, and the merely curious. They came by lake and on the new railroads. But if from Michigan, Maine, Missouri, or Vermont. whether a visitor bent on pleasure, a delegate with a candidate, or the emissary of a cause or interest, all were in festive mood.

One observer noted critically that the spirit was one of carnival, rather than the crusading zeal that had marked the 1856 convention that had nominated General John Charles Frémont the Republican party's first presidential candidate. Perhaps this diminution of zeal was because the Republican party was not quite the same. It had expanded, absorbed new and disparate elements, and, as is often the case, the increase in numbers was accompanied by a decrease in dedication. In Chicago it appeared that even abolition zealots were being weaned from moral zeal—reportedly many a delegate was flushed when Mayor Wentworth, for reasons never fully explained, chose to have the city's brothels raided during the convention. Or perhaps the spirit of carnival was inspired by neither cooling passion nor whiskey nor prostitutes, but rather by the heady scent of victory. With the Democrats hopelessly split over the slavery issue, Republican hopes were high. They had only to nominate the right man.

The big New York delegation arrived on Saturday, May 12, 1860. As the delegates scrambled from the grimy railroad coaches that had carried them from Buffalo in just fifteen and one-half hours they were confident that in William Seward, their state's senior United States Senator, they had the right man.

The delegation was impressive in more than size. It was able —strong in mind and muscle. Over it hovered the fragrance of European courts and the stench of the Bowery. Its chairman was William M. Evarts, lawyer and statesman. With him was John A. King, former congressman and governor of the state. In his youth King had attended Harrow in England while Lord Byron and Robert Peel were there, and the Ecole Polytechnique in Paris, where the relatives of the Empress Josephine were fellow students. A kindred spirit was George William Curtis, who had spent two years at Brook Farm.

But there were also delegates of another breed. These were "practical" politicians who smelled of booze and boodle—New York was in the throes of a traction scandal. They represented the seamy side of Babylon and did Seward more harm than good.

From top to bottom, honorable or venal, the delegation shared supreme confidence that William Seward would be nominated, and that Thurlow Weed, not a member of the delegation but nonetheless ruling it, was the man to turn the trick.

Thurlow Weed was sixty-two years old when he herded his circus of delegates from the Chicago railroad station to the Richmond House, where he established his headquarters. For over a quarter of a century he had been friend, mentor and colleague of William Seward. For at least ten years he had been grooming Seward for the Presidency. Weed was tall with broad shoulders and broad-set hazel eyes, bushy brows and white hair. He was well read; his taste was catholic, leading him impartially to travel, current history, and political writings. He assumed an air of simplicity probably modeled after Benjamin Franklin, whom he greatly admired and seemingly fancied he resembled. And maybe he did. Each made his own way from printer's devil to publisher; both were urbane men given to delivering homely advice (which neither heeded in his own life) to their readers; both were outwardly modest men who nursed far from modest ambitions, an indication that both valued the substance of power more than its trappings. Both were useful men in their own spheres. Franklin's sphere was the world of Western society, Weed's the world of New York State politics. Thus, despite similarities, there was a difference —one that quite possibly was not fully apparent to Thurlow Weed.

As a politician, Weed advocated the spoils system and openly bought votes. On the other hand, he never put his own relatives on the payroll, and bitterly resented any implication that he profited personally from the corruption that he not only tolerated but encouraged. He loved power and though usually conciliatory rather than arbitrary, he took pride in enforcing a brutal discipline if circumstances warranted it. Thus Horace Greeley had been denied a seat on the New York delegation because he had differed in some matters with Weed and Seward, with whom he had for a time enjoyed a sort of junior partnership. His followers recognized and were wary of Weed's iron fist. In April the New York convention had unanimously resolved to put forward Seward's name for the nomination at Chicago. The convention's unanimity and hysterical approval were fitting tributes to the dictatorial Weed.

In fact, Weed had been known as "The Dictator" since 1840. His friends used the title affectionately as well as respectfully. His opponents used it spitefully—and sometimes called him "the Lucifer of the Lobby."

But whether his role was that of benevolent despot or Satan, he had traveled a long way to achieve it. His father, a hard-working farmer, never prospered, and was jailed occasionally for debt. As a consequence of poverty, Thurlow received little schooling, and worked for wages from the time he was eight. He had jobs on Hudson River boats and as a blacksmith's helper, but the tide in his career that led on to fortune was his apprenticeship to a printer in Onondaga. He had found a career and an avocation; his profession was to be politics.

At twenty years of age he was foreman of the Albany *Register,* where he also wrote news stories and editorials. During the next few years he undertook publishing ventures of his own at Norwich and Manlius. Both failed. When he was twenty-seven he took a job with the Rochester *Telegraph.* The same year he was elected to the New York State Assembly. The following year, 1825, he bought the *Telegraph.* However, it was not the *Telegraph* but the Antimasonic Albany *Evening Journal* that was to bear Weed's stamp and project his voice during the coming years of power.

In 1826 one William Morgan, a Freemason of Batavia, New York, made sensational charges against the Masonic order and threatened to expose its secrets. Shortly thereafter he disappeared and was never seen again. An aroused public held the Freemasons responsible, and that an order so vicious as to resort to murder to protect its no doubt appalling secrets was inconsistent with good American principles. So the Antimasonic party was born in western New York. In the beginning it was a spontaneous popular outburst with its centers, so far as there were any, in the churches, and its platform a single plank—that a Freemason was unfit to hold public office. But it was soon rescued from this amorphous state and given shape. One of the shapers was Thurlow Weed.

In 1824, the year he was elected to the New York State Assembly, Weed had opposed William H. Crawford of Georgia, Martin Van Buren's candidate for the President of the United States. Van Buren beat him, but henceforth Weed's path was fixed. It was to meander from Antimasons to Whigs to Republicians, but it was consistent in its opposition to Van Buren, the New York Democratic machine—the famous "Regency"—and the national Democratic party.

In the fall election of 1824, Weed campaigned for John Quincy Adams, but the tide of Jacksonian democracy was already flowing. Old issues had worn thin, new ones were needed. William Morgan's disappearance was a gift—from heaven or hell; but a gift. Andrew Jackson was a Freemason; he had frequently and publicly praised the order, hence he was unfit for public office. Weed abandoned the Rochester *Register* to become publisher of the Antimasonic *Enquirer*. From the beginning, however, the *Enquirer* was as anti-Democratic as antimasonic. It supported only those candidates who were "sound" on issues other than Masonry—such as internal improvements and protective tariffs, national Republican issues. Weed was building an organization that would outlast Antimasonic frenzy.

In 1829 he was elected by the Antimasons to the State Assembly, and the same year, abandoning the *Enquirer,* he became editor of the party's newly established Albany *Evening Journal.* Meantime, in 1828, though Jackson carried New York, the Antimasons had developed such strength that they, rather than the faltering National Republicans, were the real opposition, and in 1832 Weed supported their presidential nominee rather than either the Democrat, Jackson, or Henry Clay, the National Republican candidate. However, he also guided the Antimasons into support of National Republican state candidates. Thus he was building a machine elastic enough to embrace both Antimasons and National Republicans and strong enough to combat Van Buren and the Albany Regency on even terms.

It was during the Antimasonic furor that Weed met William Seward. After that their political careers were so closely related that Seward, while serving in Lincoln's cabinet, declared, "Weed is Seward and Seward is Weed; each approves of what the other says and does."

William Henry Seward was born in Florida, New York, in 1801. (He was thus four years younger than Thurlow Weed.) Unlike Weed he suffered no hardship during his childhood and youth. He was educated in the Florida and nearby Goshen schools, and at Union College. He taught for a short time in Savannah, Georgia, to help pay his expenses in college, but this does not appear to have delayed his education unduly, since he graduated from Union in 1820 at the age of nineteen. After reading law for four years, he passed the bar and started practice at Auburn, New York. Auburn remained "home" throughout his life, though public office caused him to spend a good many years in Albany and Washington.

He entered politics almost immediately, abandoning his family Democratic Republican (Jacksonian) wing of the party for the more conservative National Republican (Adams-Clay) faction. He later explained his apostasy as being caused by a distrust of the Southern Jeffersonians—then supporting Jackson—and his support of the National Republican stand on internal improvements. In 1824 he voted for John Quincy Adams for President. However, the National Republicans were fading, and Seward joined the Antimasons in the late twenties. It was at this time that the Seward-Weed alliance was formed, though they had met casually before.

In 1834, Seward, with Weed's help, was elected New York State Senator, his first public office. In the Senate, he opposed slavery and voted to abolish imprisonment for debt, exhibiting a humanitarianism which was to consistently characterize his career.

By the 1830's the Antimason furor had subsided, and Seward joined the emergent Whig party, made up of conflicting anti-Jackson factions. The one-party "era of good feeling" was over. The country was back to a two-party system.

In 1833 Seward was defeated for re-election to the State Senate, and in 1834 as the Whig candidate for governor. From 1834 to 1837 he devoted himself to his private law practice. However, politics was in his bones, as it was in Weed's, and when Weed procured his renomination as gubernatorial candidate, he re-entered the arena. This time he won.

During his first term as governor, he began to compile the record that was to make him the as yet unborn Republican party's leading candidate for the 1860 presidential nomination. Also in this record are sown seeds of defeat.

In the campaign, his stand on slavery had been moderate. Although he favored trial by jury for fugitive slaves, he did not advocate repeal of a law permitting slave merchants in the coasting trade from landing their Negro cargo in New York and keeping the slaves there before reshipping them for sale in the Southern slave markets. However, after the election an incident occurred that put Seward among the advanced antislavery Whigs. Two New York sailors helped a slave escape from Virginia. That state's governor demanded their extradition. Seward rejected the demand. It was not a *cause célèbre*, but it did attract the attention of antislavery groups and cause them to number Seward among the "woolly-heads"—antislavery Whigs.

Of greater ultimate significance to Seward's career was his recommendation to the legislature that the state establish schools in which the teachers would be of the same faith and speak the same language as the students. He did this despite the fact that most of the immigrants, who would be the chief beneficiaries of his policy, supported the Jacksonians rather than the Whigs. The recommendation collided head on with nativist (antiforeign, anti-Catholic) sentiment that was developing. This was eventually to coalesce into the American or Know

Nothing party, but when Seward made his enlightened suggestion, the nativists were for the most part in his own Whig party. As a consequence, he was forced to retreat, although he did obtain passage for a bill providing for public schools free from religious intolerance.

This, plus further efforts in behalf of the Irish-Catholic immigrants who were pouring into the port of New York in the late forties and early fifties, earned him the enmity of the American nativists—an enmity intensified because of his ready sympathy for other unfortunate and oppressed peoples who came to America. He was especially eager to help the Magyars fleeing from Hungary after the failure of the 1848 revolts. He introduced a resolution in the Senate denouncing the Russian and Hungarian governments, and suggesting the possibility of "setting apart a portion of the public domain to be granted, free from all charges, to the exiles of Hungary already arrived, and hereafter to arrive, in the United States, as well as to the exiles fleeing from oppression in other European countries."

This resolution exhibited not only Seward's interest in Europe's persecuted peoples but an eagerness to dispose of the public lands, a policy he consistently championed. He believed that rapid settlement would accelerate internal improvements and ultimately, through strengthening the North, make disunion more difficult. Thus he anticipated the Republican policy on homesteads, and their 1860 campaign appeal to "vote yourself a farm."

Internal improvement was always foremost in his thoughts. During his first term as governor he initiated an elaborate and expensive program of such improvements in New York and continued to support it even in the face of "hard times." Although consistent with his party's position, the program's cost resulted in a 20 percent decline in price of New York State bonds and laid him open to charges of extravagance and financial irresponsibility. Nonetheless, he was re-elected governor in 1833—and in 1848 to the United States Senate. Thus Seward arrived on the national stage at a time when partisan and sectional conflicts were so intense that in the next decade they were to split and destroy old political parties, bring new ones into being and eventually plunge the country into civil war. It was a time when it was becoming more and more difficult to avoid commitment on deeply divisive issues—a time when an aspiring politician might be better served by obscurity.

What sort of man was William Seward when he took his seat in the United States Senate? His biographer, Frederic Bancroft, describes him as "a slight, wiry man of scarcely medium height," whose head "viewed from the side . . . appeared to be large, for it was long and narrow." He had a "thin beardless face" and "small, clear blue" eyes. His prominent Roman nose was almost beaklike in profile, his thick hair was reddish brown "and at the end of the forties was beginning to show a slight sprinkle of grey." His full-face expression was one of shrewdness and mental activity.

Seward was industrious and quick-witted. His manners were "dignified, but not courtly"; his "easy and unpretentious address was very pleasing." He was well read: "Old and standard authors he preferred to any literary novelties. He would devote his spare moments, for a week or two, to some poet, philosopher, or historian, and then take up another. Chaucer, Ben Jonson and Ariosto were among his favorites. Of English essayists he liked Sidney Smith, Macaulay, Mackintosh, Jeffrey and Carlyle. Prescott's histories he read as soon as they came out. . . ."

Although Bancroft found Seward's public speeches less eloquent than Webster's, Clay's, or Beecher's, he admitted that the "speeches of no political orator of the period were so popular and effective, or attained so high an average of excellence" as his.

Whatever his capacities as an orator, Seward delivered two of the most noteworthy speeches of his age. Both were to have a profound effect on his career.

The first was on March 11, 1850. The occasion was a debate brought about by the problem of slavery in the territories acquired from Mexico by the Treaty of Guadalupe-Hidalgo. John C. Calhoun had delivered what amounted to an ultimatum in behalf of the South: so far as the new possessions were concerned the South must have equal rights with the North. He might have stopped there, but instead he chose this occasion to lay down the terms upon which the South would remain in the Union. The Fugitive Slave Law must be enforced; the North must cease to agitate against slavery; there must be a constitutional amendment guaranteeing "equilibrium" between the North and South—this despite, and indeed because of, the North's ever-increasing majority of the total population. Only thus could the South protect itself against aggression.

Seward accepted Calhoun's challenge. Point by point he rejected the Southerner's demands. Because government could not change the moral conventions of its people, antislavery agitation would continue; because it was abhorrent to the North the Fugitive Slave Law could not be enforced; slavery would not be permitted in the newly acquired territories. And it was at this point that he uttered words that were to plague and haunt him: "There is a higher law than the Constitution which regulates our authority over the domain. . . ." Finally he hurled the gauntlet flung down by Calhoun back into the Southern champion's face: "Emancipation is inevitable and is near . . . whether it shall be peaceful or violent depends upon the question whether it be hastened or hindered; . . . all measures which fortify slavery or extend it tend to the consummation of violence, all that check its extension or abate its strength tend to its peaceful extirpation."

The speech made Seward a national figure overnight, acclaimed by angry antislavery men of the North and cursed in the South. But it was premature. During the great debate over slavery in the territories, Henry Clay, the Great Compromiser, extended himself to win his last compromise. Daniel Webster, after sitting grim and silent for weeks as the debate raged, threw himself and his great influence on the side of pacification.

Before the compromise measures passed, Calhoun was dead, Clay was through and Webster damaged politically. But they did pass. It was the last effort of the giants of the middle years of the Republic, those men who had entered public life as "War Hawks" clamoring for, and getting, the War of 1812, and who left it sacrificing what remained of their lives and careers, trying, each in his own way, to preserve civil unity and peace. Eighteen-fifty marked the end of their era. A new generation was taking over—one bred to sectionalism, controversy, and even hate. Among its Northern leaders was William Seward.

Despite his 1850 opposition to Clay's compromise, Seward made no effort to prevent the Whigs from endorsing it in the 1852 party platform. This may have been a mark of Weed's influence. Weed believed in following rather than leading public opinion, and judged rightly that the majority of Northerners did not welcome talk of emancipation. Seward refrained from further antislavery agitation and waited for an unmistakable call from the public.

The call came as a consequence of the Kansas-Nebraska Bill. Introduced into the Senate on January 4, 1854, by Stephen A. Douglas, aspirant for the Democratic nomination for the Presidency, the bill provided that the inhabitants of each territory determine by popular vote if slavery should be permitted. Douglas hoped that this principle of "popular sovereignty" would unite Northern and Southern Democrats—and bring him the Presidency. No doubt he also sincerely believed that his solution would close the widening breach between the North and South. Logically he may have been justified in his calculations. Had the measure been accepted by both sides, it might possibly have prevented the Civil War at the cost of the prolongation of slavery. But neither North nor South was in the mood for logic. The Kansas-Nebraska Act detonated an emotional explosion that was to blow the country further in the direction of war.

A great many people, particularly in the West, seemed ready

to fight. Indignation meetings were held in churches and school-houses throughout Michigan, Wisconsin, and Ohio, and spread into Illinois and Indiana.

Seward was still content to watch and wait. Although he spoke in the Senate against the Kansas-Nebraska Bill, he did not rush to the forefront of the attack. The call to battle was not yet clear. The Whigs, expiring elsewhere under the blows of anti-Nebraskans, Know Nothings, and Democrats, were still strong in New York, and it did not appear expedient to change horses with the 1854 senatorial election in the offing. Seward was re-elected, however, and in the fall of 1855 joined the Republican party, one of the last Whig leaders of national reputation to abandon the sinking ship. In a sense, then, his justification of his act was a requiem for the dying Whigs:

> Now there is neither Whig party nor Whig south of the Potomac. Let, then, the Whig party pass. . . . The Republican organization has laid a new, sound and liberal platform. Its principles are equal and exact justice; its speech open, decided and frank. Its banner is untorn in former battles, and unsullied by past errors. That is the party for us.

Of course, Weed went with Seward, or Seward with Weed, and in a sense the pair did not join the New York Republicans so much as annex them, for with them went the rank and file of the Whig "woolly heads" and the superb Whig party organization. Thurlow Weed was still "The Dictator."

Seward was in a receptive mood for the Republican presidential nomination in 1856, but Weed, believing neither party nor candidates to be quite ready, opposed the idea and supported John Charles Frémont. Seward cheerfully accepted the decision to wait until 1860, and campaigned for the "Pathfinder."

Eighteen fifty-six was a crusade:

> Arise, arise ye brave, and let your war cry be
> Free speech-, free soil-, free men-,
> Frémont in victory.

But the crusaders, notwithstanding a creditable showing, were beaten. Weed was right again. The Republicans were not yet ready, though in New York, fighting with the deadly precision of professional party troops, they elected John A. King governor and won a majority in the State Assembly.

In 1857 Weed continued to strengthen the party machinery while Seward forged to a position of acknowledged leadership among the Republicans in the United States Senate. In 1857 came Seward's second memorable speech. The issue was the Dred Scott decision in which Chief Justice Taney of the United States Supreme Court held that Congress had no power over slavery in the territories, thus throwing them open to slavery and slave competition with free labor.

The response was immediate and violent. Abolitionists screamed that the Constitution so interpreted was a covenant with hell, and burned copies of it in the streets of Boston. In Illinois, from whence his voice was beginning to be heard, Abraham Lincoln counseled patience. The decision should be accepted for the time being for what it was—a political decision which politically made could be politically reversed.

But William Seward, although he did not join in the shrill hue and cry of the abolitionists and supported neither nullification nor secession, was not patient. In a speech delivered in Syracuse, New York, he made a frontal attack not only on the Dred Scott decision but also on the "slave power" of the South. The slaveholders, a minority of around three hundred and fifty thousand (383,637 in 1860), owned more than 3,950,000 slaves and riveted their rule on the remainder of the population. And their evil power extended beyond the confines of the South. It chose thirty United States Senators, two hundred and thirty-three members of the House of Representatives; it cast ninety-five electoral votes. The President of the United States, James Buchanan, was an ally of the slaveholders. Five of the nine justices of the United States Supreme Court were from slaveholding states. The national civil service was dominated by proslavery henchmen. But opposed to this formidable power was the North—expanding in population, in industry, and in agriculture. Then came the fatally quotable words: A clash between the two systems was not "the work of interested or fanatical agitators and therefore ephemeral . . . it is an ir- repressible conflict between opposing and enduring forces."

Later he attempted to withdraw from the extreme position he had taken at Syracuse. Thus, in a speech on the admission of Kansas to statehood his tone was conciliatory, and he con- demned John Brown's raid at Harper's Ferry. Abolitionists cursed him and radical Republicans repudiated his leadership. The poet Whittier flung him into the dump heap with the fallen angel Webster—another Ichabod. Still, the earlier image created by the evocation of the higher law and the prophecy of an irrepressible conflict did not entirely fade out. It was clear- est in the South but it lingered in the North, too. Seward was no longer on the extreme left wing of his party, but he was on the left.

In 1859 he visited Europe. He said publicly that what he saw there would help him to solve problems in America. Sew- ard's biographer, Bancroft, suspected that he wanted to "know and be known among the great public men of the world." Others, in a period when the fiction that the office seeks the man was still scrupulously observed, suspected that a can- didate was merely assuming a conventional attitude of detach- ment on the eve of decision.

Whatever the reason for the European tour, it was an un- qualified success. In England Queen Victoria invited him to be presented at her court; he met Palmerston, Lord John Russell, Gladstone, the historian Macaulay; in France, he became ac- quainted with the Minister of State and the poet Lamartine. The King of Belgium invited him to a state dinner; the Pope granted him an audience; he had interviews with Victor Em- manuel II and Cavour. In Austria he called on the Minister of Foreign Affairs.

Upon his return from Europe in December of 1859 he was

greeted in New York as a great American returning home.
New York City feted him, crowds along the railways cheered
him.

In the winter and early spring of 1860 he avoided political
controversy in the Senate, but utilized the opportunity to lavishly entertain his colleagues and friends. When Congress adjourned he went home to Auburn. To wait. Sometime in early
May he had the cannon on the lawn of his home loaded—ready
to be discharged upon the reception of the news that the Chicago convention had nominated him as the Republican party's
candidate for the Presidency of the United States.

William Seward was ripe now—and ready.

In Chicago, at his Richmond House headquarters, Thurlow
Weed was sure of it. Not without reason. Seward as a candidate
for major office had carried New York in four elections; he was
obviously a man who could win. In the Senate he had compiled
a record that could well stand as the Republican party platform. He was an internal improvement advocate; he was sound
on the protective tariff; he had supported the Homestead Bill
of 1859. Above all, he represented Republican opposition to
the extension of slavery. But issues alone are not enough. A
candidate's name must be familiar to voters throughout the
country; he must appeal to the emotions as well as the reason
of the electorate. Here, too, Seward was not wanting. No Republican, save Horace Greeley, was so well known. People
crowded into the Senate to hear him speak; the country's
newspapers published his views; multitudes throughout the
North regarded him as the symbol of the Republican party.
And Seward on the eve of the convention had more in his favor
than a distinguished name and popular favor—he had pledged
votes. New York, Michigan, Wisconsin, California, and about
half of New England were for him on the first ballot. Other
states would follow when favorite sons were disposed of.
Finally, in Weed, Seward had the best of managers. Putting it

together, there was no doubt about it. William Seward was way out ahead. He was the man to beat; it was Seward against the field.

But there was a field, and he was not invulnerable. Although his assets were substantial, his liabilities were heavy. Foremost was the antagonism of the Know Nothings, who had not forgiven him for championing immigrants and Catholics. They had supported Frémont in 1856, and the Republicans needed their votes in 1860, particularly in Pennsylvania, New Jersey and Indiana, which were regarded as key states, and where nativism was strong.

Secondly, Seward's strong stand on slavery had angered many voters—and his belated efforts to retreat to a more conservative position cooled the enthusiasm of the extreme antislavery wing of the party.

Less important, but nonetheless grist for anti-Seward mills, were blemishes acquired in his role as New York State politician. The charge of financial irresponsibility, first made when he was governor, would not quiet down; he was identified with Weed and allegedly corrupt state contracts. At Chicago this aura of evil was given substance by reports of the conduct of the New York delegation. A daily paper printed the following lurid portrait:

> The New Yorkers here are of a class unknown to Western Republicans. They can drink as much whiskey, swear as loud and long, sing as bad songs, and "get up and howl" as ferociously as any crowd of Democrats you ever . . . heard of. They are opposed, as they say, to being "too d——d virtuous." . . . At night those of them who are not engaged at caucusing, are doing that which ill tutored youths call "raising h——l generally."

Still another handicap was Horace Greeley, sometime member of the Weed-Seward-Greeley triumvirate, and probably the best-known Republican in America. Although his New York *Tribune* could not properly be called the official organ of the Republican party, it voiced the sentiments of the rank and file, tens of thousands of whom waited anxiously to see what Horace Greeley was saying.

Like Weed and Seward, Greeley had been a staunch Whig, and like them a somewhat tardy comer to the Republican party. Like Seward he opposed slavery which he attacked in the *Tribune* as a moral evil. Nevertheless, although defending editorially the irrepressible conflict speech, he had questioned its wisdom privately, and did not himself, at this time, press for emancipation.

Despite his 1859 boast that he had never sought Seward's advice and had no wish to advance his fortunes, Greeley had, since 1840, supported Thurlow Weed's organization and its candidates, including Seward for both governor and Senator. As early as 1854, however, he seemed unhappy in the partnership, apparently feeling that he was not accepted on equal terms with the others. Finally, corrupt jobbing in Albany, which Weed tolerated if he did not promote, troubled Greeley, although seemingly not so greatly as he publicly proclaimed.

But either it took Greeley a long time to make up his mind regarding Seward for the Presidency, or he was avenging himself for fancied ill treatment by playing cat and mouse with his former friends and colleagues. In January, 1859, he praised Seward editorially and continued on friendly personal terms with the Senator even while disagreeing with him in the columns of the *Tribune*. Weed assumed that this indicated support and assured Seward, on the eve of his departure for Europe, that although the *Tribune* editor had been acting coolly, he was now reconciled. Consequently, when on December 26, 1859, the *Tribune* announced that Seward did not have sufficient strength to warrant support, it must have been a severe blow.

In opposition to Seward, Greeley had no chance whatsoever to go to the Republican national convention as a member of the New York delegation. When, however, he was asked to fill a vacancy on the Oregon delegation he promptly accepted—and at Chicago proved to be one of Thurlow Weed's major problems.

With the leading candidate vulnerable, there was sure to be opposition. It was Seward against the field, but the field was large. It included Fessenden of Maine, Hale of New Hampshire, Wilson and Banks of Massachusetts, Pennington and Dayton of New Jersey, Cameron and McLean of Pennsylvania, Salmon P. Chase of Ohio, Edward Bates of Missouri, and Abraham Lincoln of Illinois. Of these, Bates and Lincoln were the most formidable.

Bates was the leading candidate of the right. Greeley, although he had reservations as to his capacities and detested his views on the Fugitive Slave Law, supported him as the candidate who if elected would be most able to mediate between the North and South. On the eve of the convention Weed regarded him as Seward's chief rival; Lincoln's managers, though chiefly occupied with Seward, did not neglect to tear down Bates.

Abraham Lincoln occupied the center. His debates with Douglas in 1858 had given him national stature and fixed him in the public mind as a firm opponent of the extension of slavery, while his sympathy for and understanding of the Southerners' "problem" attracted Northerners—especially in Indiana, Illinois and Ohio—who had economic and family ties with the South. And he was regarded as "safe" by the conservatives of the East. Thus he was a Westerner acceptable to the East; he was stronger in his opposition to slavery than Bates, but less reckless in his opposition than Seward; he had not offended the Know Nothings; his Whig past was as orthodox as that of his principal opponents; his pleas for the recognition of the dignity and economic worth of labor made him popular with the workers. So, on the whole, Lincoln was not unacceptable anywhere outside the South, and the South had few delegates at Chicago.

Prior to the convention neither Horace Greeley nor Thurlow

Weed regarded Lincoln as a formidable opponent. Greeley, though admitting that on a recent journey he had found "Honest Abe" popular in the West, believed that at best he was a possibility for the Vice-Presidency. Weed, even more deluded, was almost condescending to the Illinois delegation, graciously inquiring if its candidate might be available for second place on the ticket. Judging from the subsequent activities of Judge Davis and his cohorts, this was about as sensible as being gracious to hungry crocodiles.

The convention opened promptly at noon, May 16, Seward's birthday. North and South Carolina, Tennessee, Arkansas, Louisiana, Alabama, Mississippi, Georgia and Florida did not participate. Although Texas had failed to cast a single vote for Frémont in 1856, six delegates, five residents of Michigan and a Canadian, were admitted as its representatives. The border slave states, Missouri, Kentucky, Maryland, Virginia and Delaware, had sent a scattering of delegates. All of the Northern and Western states as well as Kansas and Nebraska territories and the District of Columbia answered the roll call.

Wherever they were from, the delegates had been under pressure since they arrived in Chicago. At the Seward headquarters, Weed and the New York delegation were lavish with food, drink, good-fellowship and promises. Seward would be nominated, and with him as the nominee there would be plenty of money not only for the presidential campaign but for state campaigns as well. And money was necessary to win elections. Such arguments, plus Seward's front running position, were so effective that some members of even the Illinois delegation were shaken, and proposed that it might be prudent for Lincoln to accept second place.

Horace Greeley, too, was discouraged. He wired his paper that he doubted if Seward could be stopped. He did not give up, however, but kept on urging that Bates of Missouri was the man who could unite all sections of the country and factions of the party. Seward was admittedly a good man for whom he, Greeley, would gladly work if only he believed he could be

elected. But he did not believe it. Former Know Nothings, conservative Whigs, and dissident Democrats would not vote for
him. This would result in the loss of the border slave states to
Bell, nominee of the recently founded Constitutional Union
party, and the Northern border states to the Democrats. And
so the most damaging charge that can be made against a candidate (*Bob Taft can't win; polls show Nixon can't carry New
York, Pennsylvania,* etc.) was leveled at Seward. Ironically,
Thurlow Weed had used it to block the nomination, and probable election, of Henry Clay in 1840.

Greeley himself believed, or pretended to, that here, as when
speaking editorially in his paper, he was expressing rather than
shaping opinion. Whether this was true or not, the view he
was expressing impressed even Seward supporters, and on
Tuesday, May 15, a meeting was held that may have determined
the nomination more than twenty-four hours before the convention was officially in session. At this meeting a committee
representing Seward delegates from New England conferred
with representatives from Illinois, Indiana, Pennsylvania and
New Jersey, and informed them that while they wanted
Seward, they wanted even more to win. If the delegates from
the key states felt that Seward could not be elected, and could
unite on another candidate, New England would join them.
This meant that Seward would have to show overwhelming
strength on the first ballot and win on an early one or his
strength would dissipate. But the New England position was a
challenge as well as a promise. The anti-Seward forces must
find a candidate upon whom to unite.

Greeley thought he had such a candidate in Bates; the Lincoln managers disagreed. The strategy of the latter was relatively simple. They believed that Illinois, Indiana, Pennsylvania and New Jersey would, if they combined, determine the
nomination. They must be persuaded to combine for Lincoln.
Not on the first ballot—it was hopeless to try for that—but on
the second or third, or even later. Every effort, then, must be

made to win over key men who, when the time came, would push Lincoln as second choice. Such an effort was made. No arguments were neglected, and few demands rejected. Lincoln himself complained: "They have gambled me all around, bought and sold me a hundred times. I cannot begin to fill the pledges made in my name."

Nonetheless, when the convention was called to order, the anti-Seward forces had failed to combine behind either Bates or Lincoln, and no other candidates had shown signs of strength. Weed had reason for continued confidence. This confidence was increased when a motion requiring a two-thirds majority for nomination was presented by the anti-Seward forces—obviously fearing a Seward majority—and defeated. Friends of Seward seemed to be in control. After organization was completed, the convention was adjourned until the following day.

On Thursday, the platform was adopted. It demanded statehood for Kansas, a homestead act, river and harbor improvements, and a daily overland mail; it opposed any change in state or national naturalization laws. On Slavery, the party stand was less militant than in 1856. The Dred Scott decision was condemned as was the extension of slavery, but so was John Brown's raid, and the right of each state to order and control its domestic institutions (slavery) was upheld. Neither the Fugitive Slave Law nor slavery in the District of Columbia was mentioned. There was a mildly worded plank favoring a protective tariff.

The Seward supporters were elated with the platform, feeling that it fitted their candidate perfectly. He had favored protective tariffs, internal improvements, a homestead act, and the stand on naturalization—aimed at the German vote—was consistent with his sympathy for immigrants. Indeed, the homestead and naturalization planks were called the "Dutch planks." Inasmuch as he had retreated from the stand taken in the irrepressible conflict speech, even the relatively mild stand on slavery was regarded as favorable.

After the unanimous adoption and acclamation of the platform, the convention's first significant incident occurred. With the majority rule for nomination in effect and a platform favorable to their candidate adopted, the Seward forces were ready to vote. Their opponents, however, recognizing the strength of Seward's position and wanting to undermine it while they built up their own candidates, were violently opposed.

Lacking votes to adjourn, they resorted to a trick. It was announced that the tally sheets for recording the vote were not ready. It was late, and the delegates were hungry. In the confusion that followed, the convention was adjourned.

What "might have been" had something else been different is one of the most fruitless of speculations; it is also one of the most irresistible. Would Seward have won if the balloting had begun on Thursday? He was probably at the flood tide of his strength; anti-Seward elements had not united on another candidate; the Lincoln managers had not yet staged their offensive of the night of May 17–18. On the other hand, there was no reason to believe that Seward could have won on the first ballot, and as it was late, a second roll call might not have followed. In any event, Seward supporters, although disappointed, did not appear downhearted or apprehensive. They would have liked to win on Thursday, but Friday would do. The New York delegates returned to the Richmond House to entertain Seward men and drink champagne to their approaching victory.

The Lincoln forces went to work, or rather—recognizing that the crisis was at hand—redoubled efforts that had already reached such proportions that Lincoln had sent word from Springfield: MAKE NO CONTRACTS THAT WILL BIND ME. The response was uniform and revealing:

> DUBOIS: "Damn Lincoln."
> SWETT: "I am very sure if Lincoln was aware of the necessities . . ."
> DAVIS: (Lincoln's manager): "Lincoln ain't here and don't know what we have to meet, so we'll go ahead, as if we hadn't heard from him, and he must ratify it."

They went ahead.

The crucial states were Illinois, Indiana, Pennsylvania and New Jersey. Illinois was safe for Lincoln from the beginning, although Weed did make a perfunctory effort to win them with an offer of the Vice-Presidency. Following the Thursday adjournment, Pennsylvania and Indiana met in the Cook County courthouse to consult. Both states had favorite sons, but were reconciled to the probability that the race was between Seward, Lincoln and Bates. Missouri, aware of the meeting, sent Frank Blair to address it on behalf of Bates. He did so, advancing the stock Bates argument that he was the man to unite the party. News of the meeting was sent by an Indiana delegate to Lincoln headquarters at the Tremont House. Judge Davis dispatched aides to attack Bates and plead Lincoln's cause. They carried out the assignment so effectively that Blair's work was undone.

Following the courthouse meeting, Indiana caucused, and as a result sent private word to Davis that Indiana was safe for Lincoln. Asked how the state had been won, Charles Ray replied simply that they had yielded to the demands of the Indiana leaders. A cabinet post and Indian Commissioner had been asked.

The Pennsylvania delegation had a harder time. Simon Cameron, a long-time boss, was the favorite son; although he had dickered with Weed he had not pledged himself or the delegation to Seward. Andrew G. Curtin, of Pennsylvania and Cameron's rival, was opposed to Seward; he arrived in Chicago favoring Bates. Thaddeus Stevens stubbornly insisted upon Judge McLean. Lincoln had little front-line strength, and no serious drawbacks. After hours of wrangling, the delegation adjourned Thursday night without reaching a decision. Friday morning it was agreed to cast a first-ballot vote for Cameron. Then on a crucial vote regarding second-ballot support, Lincoln led Bates by four votes. Governor Curtin, tenaciously fighting against Seward, had swung to Lincoln. And Lincoln's emissaries themselves had been hard at work. Among other things Cameron had been promised the Treasury Department.

But Lincoln's victory was not unqualified; Seward was not quite out of the picture. It was agreed that if Lincoln failed to show on the second ballot that he had a fighting chance, Pennsylvania would swing to Seward.

Meantime, New Jersey had reached a decision. Weed had offered William Dayton, the state's favorite son and Frémont's 1856 running mate, another vice-presidential nomination. Judge Davis countered with the promise of a good diplomatic position—he was appointed minister to France—but more effective than promises was the argument that the Republicans could not win without Illinois, and that only Lincoln could carry the state against Douglas, the Democratic nominee. Whatever the reasons, sometime during the night New Jersey resolved to cast a first ballot for Dayton and then swing to Lincoln.

The meetings Thursday night and Friday morning had two important consequences. Bates was virtually eliminated, and the anti-Seward forces had gone a long way toward meeting the New England challenge. When the balloting began on Friday, it was Seward versus Lincoln.

On the first ballot, Seward received 173½ votes, Lincoln 102, Cameron 50½ (47½ from Pennsylvania), Bates 48, Salmon P. Chase of Ohio 49, other candidates a handful. Two hundred and thirty-three votes were needed to win. Weed, in an anteroom of the Wigwam, where he had installed himself, did not appear to be disturbed. Seward, only sixty votes from nomination, had a comfortable lead. But on the second ballot the earth shook, and he was on the brink of catastrophe. When the roll call was complete Seward had gained only eleven votes, Lincoln 79. The score stood Seward 184½, Lincoln 181. There was a moment of silence in the Wigwam, followed by a wild outburst from the Lincoln-packed galleries. The New York delegation sat stupefied and unbelieving. When Missouri, abetted by Horace Greeley, sent a messenger proposing that they stop Lincoln by throwing Seward strength to Bates, Weed, although he declared it too late, agreed. It was a desperate remedy, giving Bates a trial run, and presumably counting on Bates's support for Seward if the run fell short. But, as Weed had known, it was too late. Even while they talked the third ballot was under way, and the Lincoln bandwagon was rolling. At the end of the roll call Lincoln needed 1½ votes for nomination. Ohio switched four from Chase, and it was all over.

Pandemonium broke loose in the convention hall and over-flowed into the streets as the news spread. Impromptu torchlight parades formed to acclaim the victory of "Honest Old Abe."

Thurlow Weed said little, and was reported to have wept as the dream spun in the course of over twenty years of patient labor faded away. Although his own candidate had also lost out, and although he was persistently to deny personal animosity toward Seward, Greeley smiled broadly when Lincoln's nomi-nation was announced. The cavalier treatment of Horace Gree-ley had been avenged.

The reaction of Seward, waiting in Albany—where the can-non on the front lawn would not be fired—is not on record. But if he, too, wept, and he may have, for his ambition appears to have been compulsive, he recovered. Beaten and disap-pointed, he was not embittered. The years were to show that if he could not be President he could serve Presidents. Lincoln was to have no colleague more distinguished or more loyal.

After a hundred years the verdict of history is unmistakable, and as nearly undeniable as such verdicts can be. Abraham Lin-coln was the right man as a candidate, and incomparably the best man for the Presidency. But was this apparent in 1860? As a two-term governor, Seward possessed administrative ex-perience; Lincoln had none. Seward was an acknowledged leader of the United States Senate; Lincoln's one term in the Congress had been lusterless. Seward, since at least 1850, had been a national figure whose speeches were awaited and views debated by millions; Lincoln had not emerged from relative obscurity until 1858. Either could stand on the party platform without discomfort, but it fitted Seward somewhat better than Lincoln. All in all, then, it would appear that in 1860 Seward was the man best qualified for the job. But Lincoln was nominated.

Eugene H. Roseboom, in an able study of presidential elections, says:

"To believers in the hand of Providence in American history, the Chicago nomination must afford an amazing example of its mysterious ways. Midnight conferences of liquor-stimulated politicians, deals for jobs, local leaders pulling wires to save their state tickets, petty malice and personal jealousies—a strange compound, and a man of destiny emerges."

This is very well for "believers in the hand of Providence," but for one seeking a more rational explanation it will scarcely do. It is possible that a hundred years were to pass before a candidate's convention managers were to be as ruthless and effective as those of Lincoln in 1860. Their promises were prodigal, even in the face of their candidate's protests; their physical energy was prodigious, and their strategy was impeccable. They were to be found armed with arguments and baited hooks wherever delegates could be reached. They left no stone unturned, even that of forging tickets of admission to the Wigwam so that the galleries would be filled with Lincoln supporters. To discount the importance of all this activity would be absurd, and it is quite possible that inept or less determined managers might have failed to capitalize on their candidate's assets. But the thesis that the contest was a battle of wits between David Davis and Thurlow Weed, and that Davis brought his entry from behind to victory through superior maneuvering, is an oversimplification. Thurlow Weed was not a novice. He was an experienced and highly successful politician who had elected more candidates to more offices than all the Lincoln managers put together. Although he was overconfident until too late, he was not idle. He, too, made promises and offered jobs; he had campaign money to offer and offered it lavishly. There is no evidence that he was either outwitted or out-promised. But Davis had the candidate with the best chance of winning the election, and to a politician, a candidate's avail-ability is judged first of all by his chance of winning. If the party is in the happy position of being sure it can elect anybody, any-body is likely to be nominated—witness the overall quality of nominees in "one-party" states—but if it is faced with a fight, the test of availability becomes rigorous, and from the stand-point of those responsible for choosing a nominee it is better to win with the right man than to lose with the best one—no matter how loud the trumpets call or how high the banners fly as the latter goes down to defeat. In 1860, though he might have been elected, Seward was a decidedly risky candidate.

James Bryce, in discussing "Why Great Men Are Not Chosen President," wrote:

> . . . Eminent men make more enemies, and give those enemies more assailable points, than obscure men do. They are, therefore, in so far less desirable candidates. . . . Other things being equal, the famous man is preferable. But other things never are equal. . . . No man stands long before the public and bears a part in great affairs without giving openings to censorious criticism. Fiercer far than the light which beats upon a throne is the light which beats upon a presidential can-didate, searching out all the recesses of his past life. Hence, when the choice lies between a brilliant man and a safe man, the safe man is preferred.

Lord Bryce could have been speaking of Seward. As gover-nor, he had alienated the nativists, and in 1860 nativism was still a factor to be reckoned with. The conservatives, especially strong in the Northeast, also found Seward's record disturbing. As governor he had been accused of financial irresponsibility; as Senator he had aligned himself with the spenders; his ir-repressible conflict speech was rash. In short, he was too radical. Ironically, as Secretary of State under Lincoln and Johnson, he was to be a conservative influence—but that was later. In 1860, the timid and the privileged regarded him as something of a firebrand. His stand on slavery, particularly his reference to emancipation, alienated voters in the Northern border states who had economic or sentimental ties with the South. These were the vital states in any Republican blueprint for victory. On the other hand, his subsequent attempt to modify his position angered the abolitionists.

So in the end, it was his own career and, to the extent that his career was the product of his ambition to be President, his own ambition that doomed Seward. Greeley's lethal chant, "Seward can't be elected," spelled out the doom.

Thurlow Weed never forgave Greeley, and fought him until Greeley's death. Raymond of the New York delegation declared Greeley ten times more effective than Seward's other enemies, and John Defrees, another delegate to the convention, was even more emphatic: "Greeley slaughtered Seward and saved the party." But this, as in the case of the hand of Providence and the activities of Judge Davis and his henchmen, is an oversimplification. By tramping from delegation to delegation voicing his forebodings, he hurt Seward. But had Greeley been absent from the convention, it is almost certain that Lincoln still would have been nominated. Not Greeley, though he was the hatchetman for the occasion, but Seward made Seward unavailable, and 1860 was not the first or the last time that a recognized party leader has been defeated because his public career has left him too much exposed. This has been particularly true of members of the United States Senate. Although many have tossed their hats into the ring, not one *front rank* leader of that body has been elected President. Political arithmetic, not maneuver, malice or deals, was the basic cause for Seward's rejection.

Abraham Lincoln was the right man—of all the candidates he was the most available. He was inexorably opposed to the extension of slavery, but, though expressing the conviction that the house could not remain divided, he had at no time expressed himself as in favor of emancipation within the Southern states. So he was acceptable to the free-soil Republicans, and was no more feared than any other member of his party by Old Whigs, or Old Democrats. His expressions of sympathy for the South's "problem" reassured those Northern voters who themselves sympathized in varying degrees with the South. He had pleased conservatives by saying the pre-eminent task was to save the Union. He had not offended the nativists, on the one hand, nor joined them on their witch hunts on the other. German immigrants could vote for him in good conscience. His career as an Illinois politician had alienated no national party leaders. Eastern ironmasters did not suspect him of being a freetrader. Finally, although of lesser importance, the phrase "Honest Abe" had some significance at the Republican convention of 1860. An image was emerging—the image of a raw-boned angular figure, whose very lack of grace somehow symbolized unimpeachable honesty. This contrasted to Lincoln's advantage with the polished world traveler, Seward—protégé of Thurlow Weed and the ring that ruled New York from Albany.

These qualities of availability gave Lincoln advocates their opportunity; they exploited it faultlessly. Weed, too, could and did promise, but without the convincing promise of victory other promises lack substance.

The Republican convention of 1860 nominated the right man—that is, the man with the best chance to win. Inadvertently it also chose the best man.

The Republicans

1876

IN *1876 the Republican party was in trouble. The halcyon days of 1872 when Grant had won the Presidency in a popular and electoral college landslide were gone. "Grantism" as a synonym for corruption had entered the American vocabulary; the "bloody shirt," wave it as party orators might, could not make voters forget the dirty linen. Even the North was sick of radical reconstruction. It was ready to leave the South to wrestle with its problems in peace. Worst of all, an industrial depression had laid hold of the country three years before and had not yet loosened its hungry grip.*

In the congressional elections of 1874 the resurgent Democrats had captured the national House of Representatives for the first time in sixteen years, and although he was not yet nominated they had in Governor Tilden of New York, who had broken the Tweed ring in New York City, the perfect antidote

47

to Grantism. Not just any Republican could beat him. The party must choose wisely and unite behind the right man.

But the Republicans were badly divided. There were the Stalwarts among whom were numbered most of the President's closest advisers and friends. They were unreconstructed radicals determined to build a strong Republican party in the South on a foundation of Negro voters. This was the substance and end of their radicalism. On other social and economic issues they were conservative, and they professed to believe that the cries of corruption that filled the air were raised by hypocrites intent on building their own political fortunes on the ruins of the Republican party and Grant's reputation. They would have liked Grant for four more years, but the third term tradition, plus scandal, plus hard times, was too heavy a burden for even a national hero to bear. Senators Oliver Morton of Indiana and Roscoe Conkling of New York were the Stalwarts' next best choices.

The Half-breeds occupied the party center. They did not defend the corruption of the Grant administration but neither did they publicly condemn it, and they regarded Republicans who did as disloyal to the party. Naturally they were not unreservedly loved by the President and his circle and were looked upon coldly by party reformers. But they represented the attitude of the average American voter who does not approve his party's crimes and misdemeanors but can't bring himself to admit their gravity. The Half-breed leader was Senator Blaine of Maine. Blaine was the most popular politician of his time, but corruption had spotted him, and other Half-breeds were at hand to assume his mantle—and presidential aspirations—should the need arrive. Among the shrewdest of these was Governor Rutherford B. Hayes of Ohio who clearly foresaw and foretold the possibility of a deadlock between Blaine and his right- and left-wing opponents and held himself ready to profit from it.

The reformers constituted the party's third faction. As the radicals were radical only on reconstruction so the reformers *were reformers only on the issue of good government. They demanded civil service reform and an end to corruption. In other respects most of them were conservative. For the presidential nomination they had hitched their frail wagon to Benjamin Bristow's shooting star.*

Bristow vs. Hayes

It is very much as if a good bishop were selected to perform a great work of engineering, and yet we are justly thankful for it.
—*New York* Sun

The intensest feeling I had was that it [the presidential nomination] should not go to Bristow. . . . I hate to hate but I am in danger of that feeling now.
—MRS. JAMES G. BLAINE

WHEN Benjamin Bristow was borne to national view on a cresting wave of whiskey, he was forty-three years old. An impressively big man with broad shoulders, he had a high forehead and sharp piercing eyes. His round, close-cropped beard was surmounted by a drooping mustache. He disdained the flowing locks of many of his contemporaries for short-cut, carefully brushed hair. The total impression was that of a neat, meticulous individual, who might well be exasperatingly efficient.

He was not a great man. He lacked imagination. He was neither demagogue nor statesman; he was not a master politician in either the best or the worst sense: he did not entrance or enthrall the masses. He did not bind his followers to him with strong thongs of loyalty. He lacked the gift of good fellowship; he was hypersensitive, suspicious, complaining, possessed of certitude rather than certainty. He lacked charity and was incapable of concession or even compromise. Yet, for a year or two it seemed possible that he might become President of the United States. In the end he did not come within a hundred votes of even the nomination, but he stopped the apparently unstoppable Blaine, and if in 1876 he was neither the best man nor the right man he appeared to be in some respects his party's logical candidate for the Presidency. This because he had one shining gift to offer a people who—though their stomachs were as strong as at any time in American history—were nauseated by the stench of graft. He was an honest man. A reform candidate, his strength lay in the popular reaction against Grantism. No major party has ever nominated for the Presidency a candidate whose chief claim to support lay in opposition to his own party's corruption; Benjamin Bristow's precipitous rise and decline followed the classic trajectory of the reform candidate and his fate.

It was "stewing hot" in Cincinnati in mid-June, 1876. The Republicans were gathering for their sixth national convention.

"What can I tell you about Cincinnati?" James Russell Lowell, delegate from Massachusetts, was to write. "It was very interesting to meet men from Kansas, Nevada, and California, to see how manly and intelligent they were, and especially what very large heads they had. They had not the manners of Vere de Vere, perhaps, but they had an independence and self-respect which are the prime elements of a fine bearing. I think I never (not even in Germany) sat at meat with so many men who used their knives as shovels, nor with so many who were so quiet and self restrained. . . ."

Delegates were everywhere. Men of national repute and party power conferred on the merits and availability of Morton, Conkling, Blaine and Bristow.

Oliver Morton's strength was rooted in the Civil War and the worst of its fruits. He had been a vigorous and capable war governor, and, after the war, a radical leader in the United States Senate where he supported every harsh reconstruction measure, and voted for the impeachment of President Johnson. No one waved the bloody shirt more flamboyantly, and few as effectively. He controlled Indiana's Republican party with an organization built on patronage and spoils. He was strong with state and national veteran groups, and had carpetbagger and scalawag support in the South. He counted on backing from Grant, but although his expectations were not unreasonable, they were not realized. Grant men at Cincinnati preferred Conkling.

Aside from a good record as a war governor, Oliver Morton was mostly wrong. But his wrongness was rooted in his convictions. He used them in his interests but they were real. In respect to the public interest Roscoe Conkling had no convictions. He was the most colorful politician of his day, but the colors were of unhealthy hue. He was a tall, handsome man with red hair and a red beard. His dress was that of a dandy; rumor whispered of his successes with women. He was arrogant, shallow, superficial, selfish. He was feared rather than liked. But he defended Grant and Grantism waspishly and without apology and was the Stalwart leader in the Senate. He also was boss of New York's Democratic organization. He hated James G. Blaine.

The Blaine-Conkling feud started in 1866 when both were members of the United States House of Representatives. They disagreed over a minor matter of patronage. Conkling had attacked Blaine in a speech heavily laden with sarcasm. Blaine replied in kind, saying what many of his colleagues who had cowered under the New Yorker's tongue-lashings had been wanting to say for a long time.

"The contempt of that large-minded gentleman is so wilting, his haughty disdain, his grandiloquent swell, his majestic turkey-gobbler super-eminent, overpowering strut has been so crushing to myself and to all men of this house, that I know it was an act of the greatest temerity for me to venture upon a controversy with him."

Blaine's gibes were to haunt Conkling as long as he lived, and after he was dead he was remembered as the statesman with the turkey-gobbler strut. Yet it's possible that Blaine lost the most by the day's exchange. He may have lost the Presidency.

James G. Blaine possessed personal magnetism and ability. He served as Speaker of the House of Representatives, in the Senate, and as Secretary of State. His strength and his weakness lay in his devotion to the Republican party. Men, even Republicans, might make mistakes; the party could do no wrong. He had been a Republican since the party's birth, and as a Maine newspaper editor supported it vigorously. He attended the first Republican National Convention. He was a Lincoln man, first in the Maine legislature and then in the United States Congress. He hated slavery wholly and honestly; he regarded secession as undiluted treason, and had difficulty in believing even Northern Democrats could be anything but fellow travelers. The end of the war did not alter his views very much. Republicans remained the defenders of the faith and the Union; Democrats—by reason of innocence or malice—were subversive. The very simplicity of his faith, eloquently expounded, made him popular. Voters do not like hard choices; they do not like to have to distinguish between shades of gray. They like black and white, right and wrong, easy decisions based on uncomplicated emotions. Blaine made Republicans white, Democrats black; Republicans right, Democrats wrong; Republicans admirable, Democrats contemptible. This made politics comfortable.

Next to the Republican party, Blaine believed in wealth and the men who were making it and using it to develop America. He was candid about it, even naïve. "But I like rich people," he once protested, and he voted in their interest with a clear conscience. The only thing better than a Republican was a rich Republican. He served the country's financial interests out of conviction, and saw no reason why they should not serve him. Although honest by his own lights (he refused to accept a two-thousand-dollar bonus the house voted itself, and kept clear of the graft surrounding Grant) he saw no reason for rejecting a loan of sixty-four thousand dollars, secured by almost worthless stocks, from the Little Rock & Fort Smith Railroad. Nor did he repay the money. All this at a time when he was Speaker of the House and the railroads were asking for and getting favorable legislation. This got him into trouble.

In 1876, two months before the Republican convention, supporters of rival presidential aspirants spread the story of his railroad transactions throughout the country. He denied wrongdoing and demanded a congressional investigation. The House complied; he defended himself so well before the committee that he was exonerated. However, just when trouble seemed to have been averted, a man named Mulligan appeared with letters purporting to prove not only the original charges but other shady deals, including the sale of railroad bonds to Maine constituents at a commission of something over 100 percent. Once again Blaine rose to the occasion. Obtaining possession of the Mulligan letters, he read an apparently edited version to the Senate, and dramatically demanded, and was accorded, vindication. It was a magnificent performance, and the country as a whole applauded. But the reformers were unconvinced. The whole melodrama was heightened a few days later when he collapsed from fatigue and strain, frightening his adherents and giving hope to his adversaries. But as the delegates gathered at Cincinnati, Blaine, in spite of his illness, was the solid favorite for the nomination. A month earlier Governor Hayes had written:

> I still think Blaine is so far ahead in the number of delegates he has secured and is securing that his nomination is not improbable . . . with two or three hundred delegates in his favor will not all the loose odds and ends gravitate to him? It so seems.

Benjamin Bristow was born at Elkton, Kentucky, June 20, 1832. His paternal grandfather was a carpenter and lay preacher who violently opposed slavery; his father, Francis Bristow, was a lawyer and successful Whig politician. His mother came from a distinguished Kentucky family, Southern in tradition and sentiment. Thus, he was a son of the border with the border's divided loyalties, and the heir to two blood-streams. One was that of Archibald Bristow, who had crossed the mountains in 1790 to farm, preach the Bible, and curse slavery; the other came from Captain Thomas Helm, who had founded amidst the riches of the Blue Grass one of Kentucky's proudest families. And he was the product of his heritage. From Archibald Bristow he inherited unassailable integrity and crusading zeal, from Captain Helm stately bearing, aristocratic manners, a sense of public responsibility and an innate conservatism that was to make him acceptable as a presidential candidate to New York bankers as well as reformers.

At the age of nineteen he graduated from college, and two years later joined his father in the practice of law. Soon thereafter he married Abbie Briscoe, the adopted daughter of a wealthy planter, who died a few years later, leaving the young couple an estate valued at a quarter of a million dollars.

Elkton was too small for Bristow's ambition. He moved to Hopkinsville, a larger town twenty miles away. Hopkinsville was the county seat of Christian County, which was sharply divided between small farmers and wealthy slaveholding planters. As in the South as a whole, the latter, although a minority, controlled the wealth, the press, and the county government. Bristow, by virtue of family, education, property and wealth, belonged to and associated with the elite, and was in no sense a popular leader interested in broad social or economic reform. Nonetheless, bred to his father's principles, he passed from the Whig to the Republican party, was a strong Union man, and opposed the extension of slavery. Thus, on the eve of the Civil War, he was happily married, wealthy, launched on a promising legal career, and a leader of the Republican and pro-Union forces in his part of the state.

Kentucky was probably as bitterly divided over secession as any other state. Committed to slavery and Southern in kinship and sentiment, it was part of the Ohio Valley and had strong geographic and economic ties with the North. So as war approached and the necessity of decision became imminent, apprehension increased, and the debate mounted in intensity. Benjamin Bristow was in the midst of the struggle. He and his father stumped Christian and Dodd counties arguing, as Lincoln did, that the issue was not slavery but the Union.

Kentucky did not secede. Instead, though recognizing the authority of the national government, it declared itself neutral in the war. The position was a legal absurdity and a psychological impossibility. Kentuckians were neutral neither in spirit nor in act—least of all Benjamin Bristow who, after the neutrality stand was abandoned, raised a Union regiment, the 25th Kentucky Infantry, and went into battle with it at Fort Donelson.

Bristow emerged from a potentially disgraceful incident at Fort Donelson as a man of passionate honesty. A Chicago paper charged that the 25th Kentucky had not only fled the field, but fired into an Illinois regiment. Bristow's reaction was prompt and characteristic. "A baser, more villainous and unmitigated *lie* never escaped the lips of man or devil." It was invented by a "hired scribbler" to excuse "the precipitate flight of his own masters." But even while screaming persecution, Bristow remained honest. He admitted that a captain and fifteen or twenty privates of his regiment had joined the Illinoisans in flight—as a matter of fact they were retreating after having exhausted their ammunition—and confessed to his wife that the miscreant captain was one of his own relatives.

At Shiloh a shell knocked him unconscious, and though his injuries did not prove to be serious, he was carried from the field. His regiment was so decimated in the battle that it was consolidated with the 17th Kentucky at the end of the second day of fighting. Thus, when he recovered from his wounds, he had no regiment, and spent the summer of 1862 recruiting another—this time cavalry. Throughout the fall and winter he led his new troops against irregular marauders, and in the summer of 1863 participated in the pursuit and capture of John

Hunt Morgan and his raiders. This virtually ended his military career as he was elected to the Kentucky Senate in the late summer.

In the State Senate Bristow was a leader of the "unconditional" Union men. Like Lincoln he saw the war as one for the preservation of the Union. His attitude toward slavery was consistent with his principles. He was always deeply to believe in and defend property; nevertheless, although he himself was a slaveholder, he insisted that if abolition was to be the price of preserving the Union, the price must be paid. When the Thirteenth Amendment came before the Kentucky legislature, he was among the minority that voted for it.

After the war ended, Bristow resumed the practice of law. In November, 1865, he was appointed Assistant United States District Attorney for Kentucky, and promoted to District Attorney six months later. In the prosecution of the duties of his office, he waged war on the Ku Klux Klan and, prophetically, was zealous in pursuit of violators of the internal revenue laws.

Early in 1870, he resigned as United States District Attorney and joined the Louisville law firm of Harlan, Newman, and Bristow. John M. Harlan was destined to be Bristow's friend, counselor, ally, and, in Bristow's eyes, Judas Iscariot. Harlan wrote of this friendship:

> In 1870 . . . I invited him [Bristow] into our [law] firm. . . . In the same year, partly through my influence, he was appointed Solicitor General, and during his absence [in Washington] we held almost daily confidential correspondence. . . . No two men were ever more intimate than we were . . . there was nothing I would not have done in order to advance him.

The Solicitor-Generalship which Harlan referred to was offered Bristow in October, 1870. He accepted, regarding it as a possible steppingstone to the United States Supreme Court. However, he was not happy in Washington, where the pillage and the traffic in jobs offended him. Moreover, he regarded his chief, Attorney General Amos T. Akerman, as "the most unmixed ass now at large." Never one to suffer silently or feel loyalty to a superior whom he regarded as an ass, he threatened to resign, but Harlan, reminding him of his ambition for a Supreme Court appointment, dissuaded him.

However, he was not resigned and continued to complain, eventually carrying his complaints to the President, and urging that Akerman be replaced by Harlan. Akerman was eventually forced to resign, not because of Bristow's activities, but for refusal to give a favorable opinion on a contemplated raid on the public lands by Gould, Harrington, and other financiers. George H. Williams of Oregon, rather than Harlan, was appointed to succeed him.

Bristow was unhappy again. This time he sent a letter of resignation to Grant, but the President persuaded him to withdraw it. However, he continued to "look around," and when Tom Scott, a railroad magnate, sought him as a legal adviser to the Texas and Pacific Railroad and president of its subsidiary, The California and Texas Construction Company, he accepted. November 15, 1872, he resigned as Solicitor General.

The years in Washington were not unrewarding. He had practiced before the Supreme Court of the United States and made a favorable impression; he had frequently substituted for the Attorney General at cabinet meetings; he had impressed President Grant favorably. He left office on good terms with nearly everybody except the Attorneys General under whom he had served.

Tom Scott had gone to work as a station agent for the Pennsylvania Railroad when he was twenty-seven years old. He was a division manager at twenty-nine, general manager of the line at thirty-five and first vice-president at thirty-eight. He knew all about railroads—how they were built, how they operated, and how they were profitably wrecked. He also knew the indispensable role of influence in the raids that the railroads were making, legal of course, usually through Congress, on the United States Treasury. That was where Bristow could be used. That such a role might be incompatible with the prickly pride and pricklier conscience of an honest man would not even occur to Tom Scott, who, like the libertine who believes all women are harlots at heart and finds a surprising number who are, was accustomed to making good offers and finding few who rejected them. On the other hand, Benjamin Bristow, clothed in flowing robes of virtue, would not find it credible that anyone would attempt to seduce him. So it took him a little over seven months to understand what kind of company he was in. The final disillusionment came when he was asked to aid in the disposal of worthless stocks. July 1, 1873, he resigned and returned to Louisville to practice law.

Bristow returned to Louisville in July of 1873. In June the following year he returned to Washington, not as Attorney General or Justice of the Supreme Court, positions for which he was eminently qualified, but as Secretary of the Treasury, for which on the surface he was not qualified at all. But qualifications for office never bothered Grant very much, and there were other things in Bristow's favor: as a hard-money man he was acceptable to Eastern bankers; he was influential in Kentucky where the Republican party needed strength; he had powerful friends who were pushing him; the reformers were beginning to be a nuisance and his appointment would be a bone to quiet them.

He was not particularly eager for the job, but friends urged him to accept, pointing out that the Treasury might well be a steppingstone to the Supreme Court, and (fateful, fatal words) even the Presidency.

Bristow's appointment was well received. He had fought the cause of the Republican party in Kentucky; Grant had approved of him as a soldier at Fort Donelson and Shiloh, and as Solicitor General; as anticipated, the reformers were mollified if somewhat bewildered. "It is very much as if a good bishop were selected to perform a great work of engineering, and yet we are justly thankful for it," the New York *Sun* editorialized. At about the same time, the *Sun* also said that the Treasury

Department was an "abyss of corruption and immorality." Bristow descended into the abyss, cleaning it up, and emerged a presidential candidate.

One of his first acts was to order that all employees not doing the job for which they were paid be taken off the payroll. Eighteen resigned the day the order was issued. Before he was through, some eight hundred followed. For those who remained, civil service rules were established. Altogether his reorganization of the department saved the government three or four million dollars a year. But this was mere administrative reform and, vital though it is, administrative reform is not the stuff that attracts much public attention and thrusts a man into the forefront of presidential possibilities. It doesn't make good copy.

Bristow was not the first to expose the graft-riddled Grant administration. Grantism was too flamboyant, too contemptuous of the public, for concealment. The reformers had been denouncing it; congressional committees had censored it; the Senate had upon occasion rejected confirmation of its apostles. But, somehow, it had all added up to little more than a nuisance, and Grant himself, overwhelmingly re-elected in 1872, saw no evil, heard no evil and spoke no evil. He really didn't believe very much in the existence of evil, and the magnanimity that he had shown the fallen enemy at Appomattox was as a cloak of immunity to the "friends" who surrounded him in Washington. These friends, who betrayed him every day, were greedy, unscrupulous and cynical. Annoyed congressmen could be handled; honest officials (and there were some) could be cowed or disposed of, reformers were gnats to be brushed aside.

But Benjamin Bristow was not a gnat; he was a ram to batter down the strongholds of wickedness; he was the New York *Sun*'s "good bishop." Maybe, as his enemies protested, he was an ambitious man newly infected by the presidential virus; if so, it only increased the fever of his zeal. And if he was not the discoverer of Grantism, he blazoned it across the sky in letters so large that men all over the country—too busy with their own affairs to read or want to read—still must read. In doing so, he became the symbol of reform. Roscoe Conkling might sneer at "snivel service" reform; fellow cabinet members might seek to undermine him; Babcock, Grant's trusted private secretary and the evil genius of his administration, might attempt to destroy him; the President himself might willfully shut his eyes to the writing in the sky, but for almost three years the people read until they came to see Benjamin Bristow, tall and strong, a Galahad on a white horse in quest of the Grail. Which he wasn't at all. He was intolerant; he tried to poison the President's mind against colleagues; he whined; he returned malice for malice and sometimes initiated the exchange. But he was an honest man with a job to do, and he was getting it done in the face of obstacles that defeated other honest but less determined men within the Grant administration. From 1873 to 1876 this one compelling virtue dazzled the public, and concealed behind a curtain of rectitude all Bristow's shortcomings.

His early battles included the safe burglary conspiracy, the seal lock frauds, the New York warehouse contract scandals, the fraudulent cotton claims, and the attack on the District of Columbia ring. All these and others were not mere administrative reforms, they were battles in an unrelenting war on the organized gang that was looting the United States Treasury. And the war was on the thieves as well as the thieving. Men went to jail.

Naturally this made enemies of the whole fraternity of thieves. It also aroused the wrath of the Republican Stalwarts —Grant men who, though not necessarily sharing in the spoils or even approving of the spoilsmen, felt nonetheless that the greater sin was giving sustenance to Democrats and ammunition to the reformers. Moreover, Bristow's treachery was the more odious because he had eaten of their bread. They had lifted him to the high places from which he now attempted to cast them down. For he did not confine his orgy of reform to his own department, but carried tales to Grant concerning the misdeeds of others. Worst of all, he was the center of a conspiracy to capture the President himself, and his administration. This design called for the total surrender of Grant's inner circle of advisers, and the reorganization of the cabinet around Bristow and the "better element." The stables would then be cleansed and Bristow would be in line for the Presidency of the United States.

Of course the Stalwarts fought back. The counterattack was so unrelenting that Bristow considered resigning, but his friends, now seriously grooming him for the presidential nomination, dissuaded him. This was the situation when the Whisky Ring scandal exploded with a force that for a time threatened to deliver the Republican party into the hands of the reformers—and Benjamin Bristow.

In 1869 a Missourian, General John McDonald, who had served without distinction in the Civil War and turned to speculation in war claims when it was over, came to Washington. His purpose was to get a letter from Grant commending him to the master speculators of the age, Jim Fisk and Jay Gould. Grant refused his request but, inasmuch as he was looking for a man to oppose Carl Schurz and his reformers in Missouri, promised him a federal appointment if he would go back home and take on the job. McDonald agreed, and upon his return to St. Louis, he was appointed Supervisor of Internal Revenue for Arkansas and Missouri and given a free hand to reorganize Missouri's Republican party. In turn he promised to raise money for carrying on party work. These arrangements completed, he turned to the task of organizing his campaign of pillage.

The first step was to persuade treasury and distillery employees that crime would not only pay but be safe. To do this he made it appear that President Grant himself was cognizant of, and perhaps a participant in, the racket. Thus, he let it be known that when in Washington he was an intimate of the President, visiting and dining at the White House. And he ostentatiously presented Grant with a fine team of horses and a carriage, expensive harness and a twenty-five-dollar whip to match. (The President later paid for the horses.) He also cultivated and made an accomplice of Babcock, Grant's secretary. This latter was not difficult; it would have been far more difficult to keep Babcock's snout out of the public trough than to get it in.

Orville Babcock was a West Point graduate. He served in the Civil War with distinction, advancing on merit from second lieutenant to brigadier general, and earning the praise of all the commanders under whom he served. Grant was among these latter, and when he was elected President he appointed him as his private secretary. From this vantage point he established a kingdom of graft.

His role in the Whisky Ring was to counteract any rumors as to what was going on that might reach the President, and prevent action on the part of the Treasury or Attorney General, or, if this proved impossible, to give warning of any impending peril. In return for his services he received thousands of dollars, gifts of jewels and, according to the cryptic telegraphic correspondence, female flesh. Even so, if measured by the profits of the ring, his price was not exhorbitant. But, after all, he could afford moderation. The Whisky Ring was only one of his many sources of revenue.

Having secured his Washington base, General McDonald was ready to open his campaign. The objective was to divert a large part of the whiskey tax from the government treasury to himself. Its success depended upon corrupting public officials —in Washington and the field—and distillery employees. If he could do this the scheme was relatively simple. Bristow's agent, Boynton, described the operation in 1876.

> The law regulating the collection of the whiskey tax would be effective against fraud if the officers charged with its execution were honest. A dishonest store-keeper at a distillery could allow two quick fermentations in the time the law prescribed for one, and permit the distiller to so keep his books as to show but half

or even less proportion of his real production. A gauger at a rectifying-establishment could allow entries of spirits never received to be made on the books, and refrain at will from cancelling stamps upon lots ready for shipment. And when the collectors and supervisors, and their chief deputies and assistants, not only winked at such neglect, but made the tenure of subaltern officers conditional upon them, the facilities for fraud were practically unlimited. . . .

One house was found where fifty-three thousand gallons were put on the market by false stubs, in a single week; and another house testified that it manufactured two hundred and twenty-five thousand gallons a month, and half its entire annual output was "crooked."

From the best estimates made up to the present time, the ring at the date of its capture, was defrauding the government at a rate little, if at all, below three million dollars annually.

As early as 1874, Bristow suspected the whiskey frauds and proposed transferring the supervisors of the Bureau of Revenue's collection districts. McDonald, scheduled to be transferred to Philadelphia, hastened to Grant with the complaint that his departure would weaken the Republican organization in Missouri. The argument prevailed; Bristow was checked; the ring had triumphed. But in February, 1875, Bristow received unanticipated support. George Fishback, the publisher of the St. Louis *Missouri Democrat*, wrote a Washington correspondent that if he were given the support of the Treasury Department he could expose the Whisky Ring. The offer was presented to Bristow and promptly accepted. The man Fishback had in mind backed away, but Myron Colony, Secretary of the Cotton Exchange and commercial editor of the *Missouri Democrat*, stepped into the breach. Fishback came to Washington and with Bluford Wilson, Solicitor General of the Treasury Department, and Bristow himself, drew up plans for the attack.

It was all very secret. In Washington, Bristow, Wilson, and the newspaper correspondent, Boynton, were the only ones to know, and in St. Louis the preliminary investigation was to be under the direction of Fishback and Colony. Even President Grant was kept in ignorance until the time for action. He was then informed and gave his approval. However, willfully misled or willfully blind, he apparently did not at first realize that McDonald and other government officials as well as distillers and their employees were involved.

Ten weeks, during which the investigation spread from St. Louis to Milwaukee and Chicago, were spent in collecting evidence. Then, on a night in early May, the "great raids" were staged. Distilleries and rectifying houses were seized. There had been rumors in Washington that something was afoot, and McDonald had received and passed on warnings, but they were too vague and too late. In St. Louis, Milwaukee, and Chicago culprits were caught red-handed. Two hundred and thirty-eight indictments, including distillers, rectifiers and revenue officials, followed. Other treasury agents fled the country. McDonald made preparations for a visit to Europe.

Bristow was the man of the hour. The public cheered him; the press praised him. Grant wrote, "Let no guilty man escape." Even the Stalwarts climbed on the bandwagon, and tried to make political hay by attributing the raids to the President.

Let no guilty man escape. Bristow accepted the command literally, pressing the prosecutions of the guilty and purging the revenue department of the careless and incompetent. These latter were political appointees, and the screams of Republican bosses could be heard throughout the land—particularly in Washington. Grant was shaken and, though he had undoubtedly been sincere in his order, when his personal secretary Babcock was indicted his doubts increased. And Babcock did not flee. He fought back. The attack on him, he insisted, was an attempt on the part of Grant's enemies to discredit the President and his administration. The Stalwarts, taking heart from Grant's growing hostility to Bristow, climbed off the bandwagon and closed ranks. "Bristow's ambition involves Grant's ruin" was their new battle cry. Nor was the attack on

Bristow confined to undermining his influence with the President. Private detectives were hired to gather evidence that might blacken his reputation. They came up with stories ranging from fraudulent traffic in mules to robbing a store in his youth. No proof of these or any other charge was forthcoming, however, and Bristow, far from being intimidated, widened the scope of his activities, dismissed more treasury officials and pressed the prosecution of those indicted. Most of these latter were convicted, but Babcock, aided by a character testimonial from Grant, was acquitted. This was hailed in presidential circles as a victory for the Republican party, but the press and public at large viewed it as a miscarriage of justice and continued to acclaim Bristow as the "relentless prosecutor." He merited the title. According to Boynton in an article published October, 1876, in the *North American Review* some two hundred persons were indicted; about a hundred pleaded guilty and a dozen fled the country.

This continuing zeal did not endear Bristow to Grant, who considered demanding his resignation, but it brought him to the forefront as a presidential candidate of the reform wing of the Republican party. On May 15, 1876, a reform meeting was held at the Fifth Avenue Hotel in New York City. Both Republicans and Democrats attended. The purpose was to consider means of nominating reform candidates for both parties. The leader was Carl Schurz; others attending were Charles Francis Adams, Mark Hopkins, James Freeman Clark, Theodore Roosevelt, Sr., and William Cullen Bryant. Altogether there were some two hundred participants. The New York *Tribune* called them "the saving element in American politics." No candidates were endorsed by name but there was no doubt that sentiment was for Bristow for the Republican nomination. Thus a month before the convention, he emerged as the recognized choice of the parties' reformers.

He had other support, too. The "old" conservatives—the last of the Hamiltonians, who recognized the obligation of a propertied governing class to conduct itself in a seemly manner, and distrusted the new breed of graceless, ruthless capitalists spawned by industrialism—approved of him as honest and efficient. They liked his hard-money and tariff views and saw in him, a Kentuckian, an instrument for reinstating responsible leadership in the South—one that would restore profitable commercial relations between the sections. Thus reform clubs for Bristow were often rosters of the "best people." John Amory Lowell and George Thayer were active in Boston, Joseph Choate, John Jay and John Jacob Astor in New York. Membership in other cities was equally impressive. In the Middle West, Bristow support included conservative business interests and German and Scandinavian liberals—the Schurz following; in the South conservatives who hoped he would end carpetbag-Negro rule were for him. He could count on the solid support of Kentucky.

Thus as the delegates streamed into Cincinnati, Benjamin Bristow's following was broadly based and his position as a serious candidate firmly established. In March Rutherford B. Hayes had written in his diary:

> His [Bristow's] war on the whiskey thieves gives him prestige as the representative of reform. I am not sure but he would be the best candidate we could nominate. I am sure I prefer him to any other man.

But Bristow also had his weaknesses as a candidate. He was hated by Grant's circle, which continued to send agents to Kentucky charged with digging up some sort, any sort, of scandal with which to knock awry his halo of virtue. During the spring preceding the convention it was publicly reported that he had received $50,000 for prosecuting a fraudulent mule claim while Solicitor General, accepted bribes for compromising liquor suits, leaked cabinet secrets for speculative purposes and had an affair with a "scarlet" woman.

While there is no evidence that Grant participated in these attempts at character assassination, he did become convinced that Bristow was trying to win the Presidency by discrediting him and his administration, and he grew more and more hostile to his Secretary of Treasury as the prosecution of the Whisky Ring continued. The relations between the two finally became so strained that Bristow privately notified Grant of his resignation from the cabinet to take effect June 20—after the Republican convention.

While the attacks on him failed to damage Bristow with the public, they did undoubtedly hurt him with convention delegates who wanted a candidate who could unite all elements of the party. However, he might win without the Stalwarts if he could get the support of the Half-breeds. These latter were for Blaine, but might be persuaded to accept Bristow as second choice if their favorite failed to muster a majority. Recognizing this, Senator Hoar of Massachusetts tried to get Bristow and Blaine together. He describes his effort in his autobiography:

> For a good while it seemed as if the rival aspirations of Blaine and Bristow might exist without ill-feeling, so that when the time came, the supporters of either might easily give their support to the other, or agree without difficulty in the support of some third person. I gave a banquet at Wormley's in the spring of 1876 which I hoped might have some tendency toward this desired harmony. . . . They talked together, as I sat between them, during the whole evening in the most friendly and delightful way . . . I do not believe there was at that time in the heart of either a tinge of anger against the other.

But anger developed. As a good party man Blaine could not approve of Bristow's public exposure of Republican graft and maladministration. Then came the Mulligan letters. Although Bristow himself was not involved, Blaine rightly suspected that the Bristow camp had a hand in their disclosure. Finally, an obscure Kentucky newspaper published a scurrilous attack not only on Blaine but on his wife as well, casting reflections on the latter's virtue. Neither Bristow nor his supporters had anything to do with this, but for Mrs. Blaine it was the last straw. The depth of her resentment may be measured by a confidential letter written on June 4th. After referring to the ordeal she and her husband were passing through because of the Mulligan affair she turns to Bristow's candidature for the presidential nomination: "Why should the great Republican party play into the hands of Confederates whether they hail from farther South or from Kentucky? The intensest feeling I had was that it [the presidential nomination] should not go to Bristow. . . . I hate to hate but am in danger of that feeling now." Her resentment exploded into the open a week later. On June eleventh Blaine collapsed from strain caused by overexertion in defending himself from the Mulligan charges, or perhaps from a sunstroke. Bristow, hearing of his rival's sickness, hurried to the Blaine home to express his sympathy. Mrs. Blaine, meeting him at the door, accused him of responsibility for her husband's condition and unceremoniously turned him away.

The incident was telegraphed to Bristow's manager at Cincinnati and, according to Senator Hoar, served to drive the Bristow and Blaine forces further apart. Not that they were ever close together. Bristow was among the least conciliatory of men, while Blaine, wise in the imperatives of politics, did not fear a rival who lacked the support of party leaders and party organizations. His fear was of another sort. He described the phantom that haunted him to Jeremiah Black. Black wrote:

> . . . He had no fear of Morton, who did not "represent a single sure electoral vote," nor of Bristow, whose support was not organized, nor of Conkling, whose candidacy was "an absurdity," since he could not even carry his own state of New York. "Is there anybody you are afraid of?" asked Black. "Yes," replied Blaine . . . "the Great Unknown."

Was he seeing an as yet immaterial specter, or was he unwilling to utter the name of the Great Unknown, who was even then waiting—patient, quiet, benign, as dangerous a dark horse as was ever expertly groomed for the presidential stake race?

At Cincinnati, Bristow's headquarters were set up at Pike's Opera House. Harlan, who was in charge, had brought a large number of workers from Kentucky; Walter Q. Gresham brought supporters but no votes from nearby Indiana; George William Curtis and Carl Schurz represented the reform movement. Supported by the Cincinnati papers, the *Commercial* and *Gazette*, rallies for "Bristow and Reform" were staged. They were well attended, noisy. Delegates were cornered, buttonholed and warned that if the Republicans were to win in November the Augean stables must be cleaned. Benjamin was the destined Hercules for the job. The cause was good, the workers, as reformers are wont to be, were zealous. The word to Bristow was encouraging.

Of course, there were obstacles. They had little money and, as Blaine had shrewdly observed, no organization worthy of the name. Aside from Kentucky, they did not have the support of a single state machine. And, though during the months immediately preceding the convention Bristow had been approached, he had steadfastly refused to make "deals" for support. The crusade was to be unsullied by the dirt of politics.

The convention was called to order on the morning of June 14th. In the afternoon the Bristow forces made their first move. George William Curtis got the floor to read a message from the New York Reform Club. It was in effect an ultimatum warning the delegates to nominate a reformer—Bristow, though his name was not mentioned—or face the defection in November of the reform wing of the party. A resolution was then offered to adopt the letter as representing the sentiment of the convention. John ("Black Jack") Logan of Illinois, a Stalwart among Stalwarts, took the floor. He contemptuously rejected reform; he rejected reformers as not even being Republicans. A Republican convention should be controlled by and express the views of Republicans. Other speakers followed. The resolution lost. It had been a bold attempt to get Bristow endorsed before he or anyone else had been nominated. Its most significant result was to emphasize the breach between Stalwarts and reformers. The middle looked like an increasingly favorable position. Bristow wasn't in the middle.

The nominating speeches were made late in the second day. The overlong exhortations of contemporary conventions were happily not yet in vogue, but the days when Lincoln could be put in nomination in twenty-seven words and Seward in twenty-six were gone. The speeches were short, but they were speeches. His friend Harlan nominated Bristow. His theme was reform and his candidate's able administration of the Treasury Department. It was a good speech, eloquently delivered and well received.

It was Robert Ingersoll's turn. His man was Blaine. Fresh from the defense of members of the Chicago Whisky Ring, he disliked Bristow even more than he loved Blaine. He was the most famous orator of his time, and although it lasted only five minutes he made one of his most famous speeches. The alchemy of his eloquence transformed James G. Blaine of Mulligan letter fame into the Plumed Knight. He waved the bloody shirt as high and as effectively as it was ever waved. Republican was made a synonymn for patriot: ". . . If any man nominated by this convention cannot carry the state of Massachusetts, I am not satisfied with the loyalty of Massachusetts." And by implication the loyalty to the Union of all Southerners was suspect, and any Southerner (Bristow), even though he had fought and bled for the North, was presumptuous to aspire to the Presidency. Certainly such a candidate should depend on more than "a certificate of moral character signed by the Confederate Congress." Then emerged James G. Blaine, the "Plumed Knight," his shining lance fixed "full and fair against the brazen forehead of every traitor to his country."

It was magnificent. The delegates loved it; they laughed and cheered; some wiped their eyes. Even Bristow supporters joined in the applause. Had the vote been taken immediately, Blaine might conceivably have been nominated—though the tribute was more to Ingersoll than to Blaine. But there were others to be nominated, and by the time this was done the frenzy had subsided. Moreover, it was late in the afternoon and the chairman was informed that it was not safe to use the hall's gaslights. The convention adjourned until the next day. Seven candidates had been nominated. Besides Bristow and Blaine these were Oliver Morton of Indiana, Roscoe Conkling of New York, Rutherford B. Hayes of Ohio, John Hartranft of Pennsylvania, and Marshall Jewell of Connecticut. The latter two were strictly of the favorite-son variety.

The balloting started at the opening of the third day. The result of the first roll call was Blaine, 285; Morton, 124; Bristow, 113; Conkling, 99; Hayes, 61; Hartranft, 58; Jewell, 11; William A. Wheeler—who was to be chosen for the vice-presidential nomination—3. Blaine was within a hundred votes of winning; Bristow was 172 votes behind Blaine and 265 from the nomination. In addition to the size of his lead, an analysis of the vote appeared to favor Blaine. Conkling and Morton, representing the Stalwarts, had between them 223 votes; Bristow and Hayes, 174. Combined, this was enough to defeat Blaine. But how could they combine? To the Stalwarts the reformers were sniveling hypocrites, disloyal to the party if not to the country; to the reformers the Stalwarts represented all the forces of corruption. So the Half-breeds had but to hold firm for Blaine until one of the wings crumpled and fell into their laps.

The Blaine forces did hold firm. So did Bristow's, who, though only gaining one vote, had moved into second place after the first ballot. During the first five ballots the only significant trend was the decline of the Stalwarts—Morton and Conkling losing 46 votes between them—and a corresponding gain for Hayes, who went into third place with a 43-vote increase.

The Blaine managers knew their candidate could not stand a prolonged deadlock. They had tried—without success—to deal with both Hayes and Bristow for support in return for the vice-presidential nomination. Now they resolved to call upon their reserves. As a consequence Blaine, who, like Bristow, had gained only one vote in five ballots, began to move up. When Michigan was reached on the roll call, its vote was crucial. The delegation had been cannily splitting its ballots, awaiting the strategic moment when its influence would be most felt, and the ensuing gratitude the most rewarding. If it waited longer it might be too late. Bristow had been getting eleven votes, Blaine five, the rest were scattered. A solid vote for Blaine might be decisive in pushing his bandwagon over the finish line; on the other hand if cast for Bristow it might conceivably start a swing toward him. Howard, chairman of the Michigan delegation, dragged himself—he was crippled—to his feet. The convention was quiet.

"There is a man in this section of the country who has beaten in succession three Democratic candidates for President in his own state, and we want to give him a chance to beat another Democratic candidate for the Presidency in the broader field of the United States. Michigan, therefore, casts her twenty-two votes for Rutherford B. Hayes."

Although by no means stopped, the Blaine advance had been slowed down and the anti-Blaine forces of all stripes joined in a noisy demonstration. Even Bristow delegates were on their feet cheering. But they were dancing on their own coffin. Bristow's goose was cooked. Hayes had moved into second place and if Blaine, now only seventy votes short of the nomination, was to be stopped, only he could stop him.

Rutherford B. Hayes, a native son of Ohio, was, in 1876, fifty-four years old. Admitted to the bar in 1845, he was practicing law in Cincinnati at the outbreak of the Civil War. He served in the Union army and left the service in 1865 a major general. He was in the United States Congress from 1865 to 1867, where, avoiding controversy and factional commitment, he compiled a record that was without blemish and without distinction. After one term, he returned to his law practice and Ohio politics.

In the following decade he was elected governor three times, proving himself his state's best vote getter. As a public official he was competent, unassailably honest and conservative. He was faithful to the Republican party, and though completely aloof from its scandals, he refrained from criticism of the Grant administration. A "Westerner," he opposed postwar inflation and was thus acceptable to the business interests of the East.

Although sometimes spoken of as a dark horse, he was not one. For over a year he had carried on correspondence with friends concerning his chances for nomination. His candidacy was carefully planned and nurtured. His role was that of a compromise candidate, should such a need arise. He offended no one, spoke well of all rivals, and refrained from seeking delegates outside of Ohio. He used Bristow as a stalking horse. In April, two months before the convention, he wrote to a newspaper correspondent who had lavishly praised him and criticized Bristow:

> . . . Also your articles . . . too laudatory and friendly. You must also see that, as I well know, some of my best friends are Bristow men. If others lose temper we must not.

So, strictly according to plan, at the end of the sixth ballot Hayes was around—unloved and unhated, without a halo, but unsullied, robed in availability. Stalwarts could abide him; most reformers (but not James Russell Lowell) could stomach him; Half-breeds could not find fault with him. Had he been given to dramatic utterances—which he was not—he might have said as another candidate for the presidential nomination was to say some eighty-four years later, "I am ready."

As the roll call for the seventh ballot began, the Blaine men, knowing it was now or never and seeking to stampede the convention, were on their feet shouting, cheering, stamping. Alabama, Arkansas, Georgia, Illinois, responded with new votes for the Plumed Knight; the crucial moment had arrived; the anti-Blaine forces had to unite or be skewered on his shining lance. The Stalwarts held the key; New York and Pennsylvania withdrew to opposite sides of the hall for consultation, knowing it was either Hayes or Blaine.

Then the break came, not away from Blaine but from all other candidates to Hayes. Indiana withdrew Morton's name and cast its votes for Hayes; Conkling and Hartranft withdrew, relinquishing New York and Pennsylvania to the Ohio governor; Harlan, who had already made a deal committing himself when the time was ripe, surrendered Kentucky (thereby earning a seat on the United States Supreme Court) and, as he himself later said, "the fate of Blaine was doomed." At the end of the roll call, Blaine, with 351 votes, was just a heartbreaking 27 votes short of a majority; Hayes, with 384, was the nominee; 21 die-hards had stuck with Bristow to the bitter end.

The incredible had occurred. Roscoe Conkling had helped nominate a candidate reportedly receptive to "snivel service" reform; Oliver Morton had come to terms with a man not opposed to a policy of conciliation in the South. Hayes had been nominated by a combination of the "best" and "worst" elements of the Republican party. Grantism and reform had bred a candidate. Their bedding had not been from fondness; how had it occurred?

There probably has been no political convention in which there were so many cross currents of bitterness as in the Republican convention of 1876. The feeling between reformer and Stalwart was more than disagreement on policy or principle; they regarded one another with something akin to the loathing that an honest man might feel toward a thief, or a loyal one toward a traitor. And there were animosities that went beyond the more or less impersonal ones arising between factions. Personal outrage and dislike were involved. Roscoe Conkling had never forgiven Blaine for making him ridiculous as the man with the turkey-gobbler strut, and no one could nurse a more monumental grudge than Roscoe Conkling. Mrs. Blaine, though she might "hate to hate," hated Bristow as the author of calumnies directed against her husband and herself, and though the Senator may not have shared his wife's feeling, at least in degree, many of his followers did. For his part, Bristow after his ignominious dismissal from their doorstep had no love for the Blaines. By the time the convention was called to order, Grant's mind had been so thoroughly poisoned against Bristow that he later declared that had his Secretary of the Treasury been nominated, he would have campaigned against him. Bristow insisted that he was loyal to the President, but he never forgave injuries, real or fancied, and the attacks on him by Grant's circle had been real.

Only Hayes, standing benign above the sea of anger, escaped the battering of its waves. And he undoubtedly benefited from this immunity. But this alone would not have been enough. Although they may have contributed, personal conflicts did not determine the nomination. Conkling could control New York's votes but not those of Stalwarts elsewhere, yet the Stalwarts from other states chose Hayes rather than Blaine. Grant was still a national hero, beloved by the populace, but as a retiring President his influence on hard-bitten politicians was slight. Bristow had no power at all. His following had selected him to bear the banner of reform, and as their presidential candidate he was their creation, not their leader. When they deemed it expedient they would abandon him, and they, not he, would choose where they went. The Blaine followers remained loyal to the end, so the hates or loves that might have influenced them on a second choice were of no consequence.

Pure politics, unsullied by personal animosities, undoubtedly dictated the choice of most of the Stalwarts. With Morton and Conkling failing to win support, they had lost—for the time being—the Presidency, but if they could retain control of the party machinery and of Congress they might continue to live fatly while awaiting another convention and a fairer day. But with Blaine President, their prospects were poor. He was a veteran statesman skilled in all the arts of politics. No man knew Congress better than he. He had a large, devoted national following. Add to these assets the great powers accompanying the Presidency and he would undoubtedly be able to take over the party, lock, stock, barrel and—most appalling thought—patronage. Lean Stalwart harvests would ensue. With Hayes there was hope. Less tested in political battle and with no following outside his state, they might capture him as they had captured Grant, or roll over him as they had rolled over Johnson. And at worst, he didn't seem too bad. His record in Ohio had been one of honest administration, but if that was a blemish (and even to most of the Stalwarts it wasn't) it was the only one. He had rejected overtures to identify himself with the hated reformers, he had not raised his voice against corruption in the national government. A Half-breed rather than a reformer, he was a more acceptable Half-breed than Blaine. As such he was the best the Stalwarts could get. They were practical politicians. They took him.

But what of the reformers and their man Bristow whose name had been in the papers for three years as the archfoe of corruption? If there was, indeed, a knight in the Republican party tilting a lance for the pure and the helpless, it was he, not Blaine. Why had he been so easily unhorsed? For five ballots he led Hayes, almost doubling the latter's vote for four of them. Then the bubble burst. That was the trouble. It had always been a bubble. A candidate for the presidential nomination whose chief claim to popularity has been earned by exposing his party's shortcomings is not popular with party politicians. Bristow was such a candidate. Exposure of Grantism was his only real claim to the nomination, and in staking out that claim he had made too many enemies. Among these were not only thieves and spoilsmen but also party loyalists who, although honest themselves, put party reputation and success above strict party integrity, and rationalized their position by telling themselves that washing dirty family linen should be a private family affair. Bristow had not only washed the very dirty Republican linen in public, but had hung it across the sky, as visible as the sun and the stars, to dry. For this, neither Half-breed nor Stalwart would forgive him. Only a political eunuch, a "snivel

service" reformer, could love him. And even they had few illu-
sions regarding his success. Lowell was to write: "I had little
hope before I went [to the convention] of Mr. Bristow's nomination." Lodge had told Carl Schurz that the odds were a thousand to one against anyone who had so many enemies being
nominated. The reformers used him to stop Blaine, as did
Hayes. He was expendable and, unaware of his mission, he ex-
pended himself without stint. Then, wisely, they threw him
aside.

And while Stalwart and reformer beat their candidates into
the ground in stopping Blaine, Hayes waited until the "appro-
priate" time. That would be when virtue and politics were wed.
In a diary entry of May 19, 1876, Hayes had written:

> It is only in the contingency of a union between those who
> look for availability in the candidate and those who are for
> purity and reform in administration, that I am a probable
> nominee.

The union took place a month later. As he had foreseen,
Hayes was the nominee.

Blaine's political sun was to continue to shine and burn even
brighter; Bristow's was quenched forever. His decline as a national figure was even more precipitous than his rise. Hayes,
anxious to unite the party, would not risk Stalwart and Half-
breed displeasure by recognizing any claim he might have for
office, or even an unofficial place in party councils. "Bristow
men" went into the cabinet but not Bristow. When a Supreme
Court vacancy occurred, it was Harlan, Bristow's closest friend
and Cincinnati manager, rather than Bristow who was appointed. (And there ended a beautiful friendship.) For twenty
years his ghost was to continue to walk and wail, but after the
sixth ballot in Cincinnati, Ohio, June 17, 1876, Benjamin Bristow was politically dead.

Blaine was probably the best man. He had political experience, political skill and wide knowledge of public affairs. That

he profited financially by unethical deals with the railroad interests and then lied about it appears to be a fact. However, it was the single blemish in an otherwise long and useful public life that spanned a period when the ethics of the business community were at the lowest level in America's history, and it is perhaps unrealistic, if not hypocritical, for a people who tolerate and even applaud making a "fast buck" in business to hold its nose when it is done in politics. When the communications media and the business and professional and labor community —doctor, lawyer, merchant, chief—turn lily white, politicians will probably turn pure. In any event, Blaine paid the price for his lapse. But for it, he might have been President of the United States.

Hayes was the right man. A few Republican reformers bolted to Tilden, the Democratic candidate, but most of them, as did Blaine and his Half-breeds, supported Hayes. Conkling sulked during the campaign, pretending to be ill. Otherwise the Stalwarts went along. The election of 1876 is the most controversial in American history and—although there is no doubt that Tilden got the most popular votes—no one will ever know who was elected on election day. Hayes was eventually declared President, and it's difficult to quarrel with success. The Cincinnati convention, despite the scandals of Grantism, had picked a winner.

Bristow was neither the best man nor the right man. Although his term as Secretary of the Treasury indicated that he was an able administrator, and his subsequent career as one of New York's leading corporation lawyers was to prove him a man of considerably above-average ability, he had little experience and apparently little interest in broad problems of public policy. Moreover, he was stubborn, hypersensitive, and unwilling or unable to compromise. He could not confess himself to be wrong or his critics to be either right or honest. He could never have gotten along with Congress; he might well have suffered the fate of Andrew Johnson, even to the point of impeachment.

But he was safe from that fate. He could never have been elected. The Stalwarts, including Grant, would have campaigned against him or knifed him; few Half-breeds would have wholeheartedly supported him; the reformers were mostly inept politicians with no organization. He had taken a road that never has, and probably never will, lead to the Presidency. Exposure of governmental corruption is necessary if democracy is to work. No deed is more noble. But selfishly considered it is best for an aspiring politician to leave it to the other party. It is the path not to office but to martyrdom.

The Republicans

1880-1888

NO DECADE in American history has produced a series of such close elections as that of the 1880's. In 1880 James G. Garfield defeated General Hancock by 9,464 votes. In 1884, Cleveland beat James G. Blaine by 23,005. In 1888 Benjamin Harrison won in the electoral college although Cleveland had a lead of 100,456 popular votes. Thus in these three elections the total difference in the popular vote of the two parties was 132,-925, or about the same as between President Kennedy and Richard Nixon in the "cliffhanger" election of 1960.

One might suppose that such close races would be characterized by dramatic clashes between candidates for nomination or election, and that the electorate would be rocked with partisan rivalry. Such was not the case. The emotion-charged issues that had stirred Americans for half a century—slavery, the right of secession, reconstruction—were now settled, the corruption that had shocked the nation during Grant's two administrations had been reduced by President Hayes and the new social and economic issues bred of industrialism were still in gestation.

In the 1880's the ruling powers of both parties accepted the doctrine of wealth. They paid lip service to democracy but acted as the agents of plutocracy. Egalitarianism existed chiefly in the belief that all men had an equal right to get rich, and that those who managed to do so were equal. In no other decade of American history have both major parties been more subservient to property. Under such circumstances issues between the parties or factions within the parties were neither very important nor very dramatic. They differed on tariff schedules and monetary policy; leaders fought for power and office. The electorate remained largely unmoved—stirred more by the past than the future. Southerners voted against Yankees and reconstruction; Northerners responded to the appeal of the "bloody shirt."

It was on such a stage that the politicians played their part. The play was as drab as the setting. The Republican party still had its Stalwarts, Half-breeds and reformers, but the issues that divided them had little meaning. Each wing had its candidates but the objective was primarily office rather than policy. The actors were worthy of the play and scene. Except for Grant, who appeared in one final act, none is well remembered. Garfield because of assassination is recalled as a martyr. What he was a martyr to would be hard to say, and he has little further claim to fame. James G. Blaine was the one man of the decade who could arouse genuine mass devotion. But although Blaine towered above other Republican statesmen of the era he could not rise above his milieu and missed greatness.

Blaine's only rival in service to his party and persistence in his quest for the Presidency was another Half-breed, Senator John Sherman of Ohio, a perennial aspirant. But there were others also—such as Benjamin Harrison—lurking in the shadows, ready to seize the standard if he faltered.

Sherman vs. Garfield,
Blaine, Harrison

Mr. Sherman represents the principles of the Republican party from its beginning. He has never wavered in his allegiance to the party.

—JAMES G. BLAINE

Too late Victor immovable. Take Trump and Star.
—ANDREW CARNEGIE to SENATOR ELKINS

FEW MEN have wanted the presidency worse for a longer time than John Sherman of Ohio—or have been frustrated so often. His is the story of the plodding tortoise who—contrary to fable —was passed by light-footed hares, and in the end even by another tortoise. He was never defeated in an election. He served in the cabinets of two Presidents. But the presidential nomination though within his reach was always just beyond his grasp. The time was never quite ripe until it was overripe. Twice he marched up the hill leading to the Republican nomination and marched down again before the issue was resolved. The third time he remained resolute and was shot down.

John Sherman was born in Lancaster, Ohio, May 10, 1823. His father died six years later leaving a wife and eight children. The burden was too heavy for the widow—she was forced to scatter the family. John fell to the lot of a cousin who lived in Mt. Vernon. As a child he was lively and a trial at home and at school. At fourteen he quit school to work on a state canal project, a job which he lost three years later when the Democrats carried Ohio. It was the only political job he was to lose in a career that stretched over almost half a century. After a few months of idleness he entered a law office in Mansfield, Ohio, to read law. He was admitted to the bar in 1844.

In August, at the age of twenty-five, he married Margaret Stewart, the daughter of a prominent Mansfield lawyer. The same year he attended his first national political convention, that of the Whigs. He was also a Whig delegate to the 1852 Whig convention, but his role was insignificant. He was still young and probably had little interest in a party that was in a state of advanced decay.

But the repeal of the Missouri Compromise and the passage of the Kansas-Nebraska Act swept him into the vortex of the political storm that was bursting over America. He became an ardent anti-Nebraska man, and as such was elected to the United States House of Representatives in 1854. The next summer he helped to organize the Republican party in Ohio. He was to serve it and it was to serve him until he retired from politics in 1898. Thus for forty-three years he held office continuously as Representative, Senator or cabinet member. His record is the more remarkable in view of the fact that during these years Ohio, a doubtful state, elected four Democratic governors and three Democratic Senators. Yet though in the same period it sent three Republican Presidents to the White House John Sherman remained unchosen.

In the House he made a reputation as a staunch though moderate partisan. He was a member of the congressional committee that investigated conditions in "bloody Kansas," and wrote the majority report. He flayed the Democrats but not severely enough in the eyes of critics. In his own Ohio the abolitionists attacked him.

In 1859 he was a candidate for Speaker of the House, but after two months of maneuvering and deadlock he chose to withdraw rather than continue the fight. This defeat was caused in part by Southern opposition to his rather offhand endorsement of Hinton Helper's *The Impending Crisis of the South,* a book that Southern planters hated as much and feared more than *Uncle Tom's Cabin*. In 1860 he campaigned hard for Lincoln. In 1861 he was chosen by the Ohio legislature to fill the United States Senate seat vacated by Salmon P. Chase, who was entering Lincoln's cabinet. In the Senate he was a member of the Finance Committee on which he was to serve so long with distinction. From the beginning he advocated economy and sound money policies. His one aberration was in support of greenbacks, but he explained this on the grounds that they were necessary to finance the war, and that America's economy would eventually grow up to the expanded currency. In this last prophecy he was correct.

When the war was over he favored conciliation, and after Lincoln's death, defended President Andrew Johnson's effort to carry out a moderate reconstruction policy. Nonetheless, and though Johnson was his personal friend, when it became evident that the radicals not only controlled Congress but also had the support of Northern voters he knuckled under, voting for every radical reconstruction measure, and even for the impeachment of Johnson. When the impeachment was defeated it may have been the thin whisper of conscience that prompted him to say that he was entirely satisfied.

This compliance with expediency was dictated by ambition as well as party loyalty. Opposition to the ruthless radical leadership would unquestionably result in prescription in the Senate, and quite possibly loss of his seat. In a corrupt age John Sherman was an honest man, but the voice of ambition was always to be louder than that of his personal convictions in determining his stand on political issues. And the voice of the party was loudest of all. He did not bow his neck to the yoke of party regularity; he wore the yoke proudly. To the extent that reconstruction was a means of building the Republican party in the South he could support it with clear conscience. A dominant Republican party was in the interest of the nation.

During the Grant administration Sherman emerged as a Half-breed, one of that group of Republicans who though loyal to the party and opposed to reform that might endanger pa-

tronage were nonetheless distressed by corruption. Among the
leaders of this company, in addition to Sherman, were Blaine
of Maine, Garfield of Ohio, Hoar of Massachusetts and Allison
of Iowa. They were able men and good public servants. That
every one of them was at one time or another put in nomination
for the Presidency attests to the fact that they also possessed
shrewd political judgment. If further proof is needed it may be
noted that although the Stalwarts might control patronage and
some of them collect boodle, Half-breeds had the longer political life expectancy, and were elected President. Reformers were
compelled to be content with the consciousness of their own virtue.

In the Senate, Sherman was interested in many issues including the tariff, but throughout his career government finance
and fiscal policy was to be his first love and the chief source of
his reputation.

In 1876 Sherman was one of the Ohio politicians who successfully master-minded Rutherford B. Hayes' presidential nomination. The autumn election was more difficult. Tilden, the
Democratic nominee, was in Sherman's own words, ". . . a
man of singular political sagacity, of great shrewdness, a
money making man. . . . He had taken an active part in de-
feating the corruption of Tweed in New York politics. He had
been elected governor of the State of New York, as the candidate of reform and honesty in politics." To make the situation
more difficult, Hayes was a colorless candidate and not very well
known. His election would be a hard nut to crack. Nevertheless, the Republicans cracked it, and John Sherman played an
important role in the cracking. He campaigned vigorously, not
dwelling on fiscal policy, corruption or the tariff, but on the
past and future subversive activities of Democrats:

> . . . The election of Mr. Tilden would result in the virtual
> nullification of the constitutional amendments, and amount to
> a practical restoration to power of the old Democratic party.
> The revival of the rebel claims, the refunding of the cotton tax,

and the damages done to rebels, were fully commented upon, as were the outrages committed upon Freedmen . . . the organization of the Ku-Klux Klans, and the White League, and the boldness with which the laws were disregarded in the south.

Here is the self-portrait of a tough, seasoned campaigner who knows that an appeal to the voter's emotions is a surer way to his favor than one to his reason, and regards a political campaign as a duel to death or victory rather than an opportunity to discuss national problems. And although he was not campaigning for himself it helps to explain why he was never defeated in an election. The hustings transformed the rather dry Washington statesman into something akin to a fiery demagogue.

But valuable as his contribution during the campaign may have been, his greatest service to Hayes was yet to come. He himself recorded that the result of the election of 1876 was very doubtful; it has remained very doubtful ever since. That Tilden got a majority of the popular vote has never been questioned, and the unofficial count as reported from the states immediately after the election indicated he had won a majority in the electoral college.

The Republicans were claiming fraud in Louisiana, South Carolina and Florida. If these claims should be upheld by the state returning boards Hayes would win by one vote. As a member of a group of Republicans sent by Grant to New Orleans to witness the official Louisiana canvass Sherman was involved in the decision made in that state. The group did not go merely to witness the count; its actual mission was to influence the board. (The Democrats were engaged in a similar attempt.) Under the Louisiana law the returning board verified the election count and certified the winner. There was no appeal from its decision. The board was undoubtedly corrupt. This, however, does not prove that its decision to throw out more than 12,000 Tilden votes—enough to give Hayes the election—was the wrong decision. It does indicate that the Republicans bid higher than the Democrats for a favorable verdict. Part of the price was paid by Sherman when as Secretary of the Treasury, he gave members of the Louisiana board good jobs.

The South Carolina and Florida electoral boards also found sufficient evidence of Democratic fraud to reverse the decision given at the polls. Hayes had won his one-vote electoral college majority.

But the crisis was not over. Throughout the country voices were raised charging that the election was being stolen. There was even talk of armed resistance and protest marches on Washington. Congress resolved to appoint a commission to review the whole affair and, in effect, to supplant the electoral college in deciding who had been duly elected President.

Sherman opposed this as unconstitutional but was outvoted. The commission was supposed to be judicial, basing its rulings solely on evidence. Apparently evidence looked different to Republican and Democratic eyes. Every decision was reached by a strict party vote. There was one more Republican than Democrat on the commission, so Hayes won.

The protesting voices were not stilled. The Republican leadership, though not afraid of actual violence, was anxious that Hayes should not begin his administration amidst cries of corruption. Further compromise was in order. After weeks of discussion an agreement was finally reached at a meeting held just six days before the inauguration. The Republicans promised that Hayes would withdraw the troops from the South—abandoning the carpetbaggers and freedmen—in return for a Democratic pledge not to further oppose the Hayes' claim to the Presidency. The deal was made between moderate Republicans who had had enough, and sensed that the voters had, of the "Southern Problem," and Southern Democrats more interested in regaining state control than winning the Presidency. Informal and unofficial, it was nonetheless effective—ending as satisfactorily as the circumstances permitted the most controversial election in American history.

From first to last John Sherman played an important role in the 1876 election. He had helped nominate Hayes, campaigned for him and been a representative of the Republicans in Louisiana. In the final negotiations for Democratic acceptance of Hayes' election he acted as the new President's spokesman. For his services he was appointed Secretary of the Treasury. The cabinet was a step upward. Having served in Congress for twenty years he had little more to gain as a Senator, but as Secretary of the Treasury he could claim administrative as well as legislative experience. This may not be a major consideration in winning votes, but a man who wants to be President cannot afford to overlook possibilities.

It is doubtful if the years at the Treasury did further his ambition. Government financial operations are seldom glamorous, and with the exception of Benjamin Bristow, whose popularity was as a crusader against corruption rather than as a government official, no Treasury Secretary has ever become a popular hero. But they are occasionally cast as villains—Hamilton in the eyes of Jeffersonians. Mellon after the 1929 crash. And in a mild way John Sherman.

Sherman supported resumption of specie payments from conviction, and carried on refunding so vigorously that August Belmont called him "the noblest son of the noble state of Ohio." But debtors all over the country, caught in the squeeze of a deflationary policy, called him other things. At a gathering in Toledo he was booed and accused of robbing widows and orphans to make capitalists rich. This was only a year before the 1880 Republican National Convention.

In matters of department personnel he was more spoilsman than reformer. He completed Bristow's task of cleaning out the thieves, but his own appointments were confined to deserving party workers. In a fight between Hayes and Conkling over New York patronage, which involved the latter's challenge to presidential leadership, he threw the whole weight of the Treasury on the side of the President. Hayes won and was grateful, but

Sherman had alienated the Stalwarts without winning over the reformers and he was second to Blaine in the hearts of the Half-breeds.

Nonetheless, in the spring of 1880 he was recognized as one of his party's leaders and as such was ready for his first try for the presidential nomination. Although not the favorite in the race, his chances were good if the favorites should cancel out each other.

Grant had written in August preceding the convention that he was not a candidate for public office but he had added equivocally: ". . . nor would I hold one if it required any maneuvering or sacrifice to obtain." It would take both, of course, but not on the General's part. Stalwart politicians, lean after four hungry years, stood ready to undertake the maneuvering, while the public interest would constitute a fitting sacrifice. And although the tradition against a third term was an obstacle, the ex-President had a good chance to hurdle it. The stench of Grantism had largely dissipated during the four years since he had left office, and the image of the national hero remained clear. He was unquestionably the most popular man in America. Politically, too, the situation favored him. The abandonment of radical reconstruction had put an end to Republican hopes in the Southern states, but though unable to elect a candidate or deliver an electoral vote they still sent delegates to the national party conventions, and these, recalling the lush days under Grant, were easily brought into his fold. In the North the Stalwarts were led by Conkling of New York, "Black Jack" Logan of Illinois and Don Cameron of Pennsylvania. If each could deliver his state, Grant would be in striking distance of the nomination. A little management, a few deals, would cover the remaining ground.

If Grant faltered Blaine was ready. Barely defeated for the nomination in 1876, he was second only to Grant in the affections of Republican voters, and in the eyes of many politicians he would be easier to elect than the General because of the third-term liability and the certainty that the Democrats would revive the issue of corruption. But Blaine, too, had weaknesses. The reform wing of the party could not forget or forgive the Mulligan letters, and the Stalwarts, especially Conkling, were hostile to the Maine Senator.

And if Blaine faltered, who but John Sherman? He planned carefully along lines successfully followed by Hayes four years earlier. This called for hanging off the pace until Grant and Blaine ran each other into the ground. Such strategy seemed particularly sound since no other compromise candidate was in sight. Of course there was always the "unknown" that Blaine had feared on the eve of the '76 convention, but that possibility was not great. Franklin Pierce had been the only legitimate "unknown" to be nominated for the Presidency in the history of major party politics. Besides a plan—in an era when an aspirant was compelled by custom to stand aloof—a capable convention manager was of the utmost importance. Sherman wanted James A. Garfield for the job, but it took some angling to get him.

Garfield, eight years younger than Sherman, was born in a log cabin in Ohio. His youth was in the classic pattern of the poor boy bound to rise. He worked as a carpenter, teacher and farmer while saving enough money to go to college. After graduating he took a position as professor of ancient languages and literature at Western Reserve Eclectic Institute. A year later he was its president. But his ambition was not for academic distinction; he entered politics. Unlike Sherman, Garfield had the gift of personalizing politics. He was warm, handsome and genial, and an effective speaker whose rich voice fairly exuded moral fervor.

He entered politics as an antislavery, anti-Nebraska man. When the Civil War broke out, although he had just been admitted to the Ohio bar he volunteered and served with distinction, fighting at Shiloh and Chickamauga. Elected to Congress in 1863, he resigned from the army with the rank of major general.

His record in Congress was that of all successful Republican politicians of the period. He supported the war and, when it was over, radical reconstruction. He advocated the confiscation of Southern property and joined in the Wade-Davis Manifesto which condemned Lincoln for being too soft toward the South. Although not among the spoilsmen who surrounded Grant, he was accused of being involved in the Crédit-Mobilier railroad scandal. He appealed his case to the voters and was acquitted.

Like Sherman he was a member of the Ohio delegation that put Hayes over in 1876, and like Sherman he was sent to Louisiana after the election. In addition he was a member of the commission that decided the election in Hayes' favor. When Sherman was named Secretary of the Treasury, Garfield wanted to succeed him in the Senate, but Hayes dissuaded him on the grounds that he was needed as administration leader in the House. He bowed to party need and served successfully for four years.

Thus by 1880, aside from Hayes, who having pledged himself to one term was about to pass into the limbo reserved for most ex-Presidents, and Sherman, Garfield probably was Ohio's most distinguished Republican. As such he let it be known that although he was not a candidate for the presidential nomination he was available as a dark horse should the need arise. It was in part to render him still darker that Sherman wanted to commit him to his own cause.

Once again Ohio had a senatorial vacancy and Sherman offered to support Garfield for the seat in return for aid at the forthcoming national convention. Garfield rejected the proposal and let it be known that when he did decide whom to support, Sherman's attitude would be a factor in the decision. Trapped, Sherman was forced to support Garfield while the latter remained uncommitted. The Ohio legislature elected Garfield, who still refused to endorse Sherman.

But Ohio was for Sherman and Garfield's ear was close to the ground; in early spring, unable to resist the tide, he capitulated. It was now Sherman's turn. In order to commit Garfield so

deeply that he could not decently retract, he asked him to nominate him and act as his convention manager. Garfield, who had
earlier described Sherman as one who "studied the popular
current, floated with the tide and drifted with the wind of public opinion," asked what personal characteristics Sherman
wanted emphasized in the nominating speech. The reply was
that "the chief characteristic of his life from boyhood up had
been courageous persistence in any course he had adopted."
Both descriptions may be accurate. Having determined upon a
course Sherman was persistent and courageous, but he unquestionably studied the popular currents before making a decision.

The 1880 Republican convention was held in Chicago. The
Grant forces came with a campaign plan. This called for the
election of Cameron as convention chairman. He would use
the power of the chair to ram through the unit rule binding
each state delegation to cast its whole vote according to the
wishes of the majority. It was sound strategy, as Grant had
strong but not unanimous support in a number of delegations.
If these could be marshaled as units the General might well
sweep the convention.

But the Stalwarts reckoned without Garfield who, assuming
leadership of not only the Sherman but the whole anti-Grant
faction, was immediately on his feet. Urging compromise in the
interest of unity, he presented the name of Senator Hoar for
chairman. The convention supported him. Conkling, realizing
that with the loss of the chairmanship his group had also lost
the unit rule, changed tactics. To counteract the claim that
Grant's nomination would result in a party bolt by the reformers, he presented a resolution that the delegates bind themselves by an oath of loyalty to whomever the convention might
nominate. Garfield was again eloquent in opposition. He said
that on his record no one could deny that he was a loyal Republican, but that the right of the individual to act according to his
conscience must be respected. The convention applauded and
rejected the motion.

Roscoe Conkling was called many things during his long

career but no one denied that he was politically astute. He wrote, "I congratulate you on being the dark horse," across the top of a newspaper and passed it to Garfield. What Garfield thought is not on record, but when the time came for him to nominate Sherman he made a remarkable speech. It described Sherman in eloquent phrases, but to many who listened and others who were to read it in the light of subsequent events its fascination lay in the fact that it described James A. Garfield quite as well as it did John Sherman. Conkling's dark horse was beginning to glow.

The first ballot was unsurprising. Grant led, Blaine was a close second, Sherman a distant third. There was a scattering of votes for favorite sons. The roll calls then proceeded for two days, setting the longest record in Republican party history. In the beginning it was the situation that Sherman as the leading compromise candidate had hoped for, but as ballot followed ballot and the delegates failed to break to him his position worsened. A compromise candidate to whom during a long deadlock no one turns is doomed.

The break came on the thirty-fourth ballot. Wisconsin switched from Blaine—but not to Sherman.

Its sixteen votes were cast for Garfield.

It was a tense moment. Garfield stood up. Would he employ his eloquence, his famed sincerity, to forswear ambition—to withdraw and urge delegates friendly to him to support Sherman? He began to speak words which, had he continued, might have become a renunciation of the Wisconsin delegates' support. But Senator Hoar, convention chairman, took pity on him and ordered him to sit down. Garfield had been dauntless in battling Conkling and the Stalwarts but now, withholding the last measure of support to John Sherman, he submitted to the chair's ruling. Meek as any lamb he sat down after an indecisive protest. On the next ballot Indiana voted for him.

Sherman, waiting in Washington, received the word and marched down the hill. "Whenever the vote of Ohio will be likely to assure the nomination of Garfield, I appeal to every delegate to vote for him. Let Ohio be solid," he wired. His delegates responded with alacrity. Blaine's followed. On the thirty-sixth roll call Garfield was nominated. Proving the adage that the Old Guard dies but never surrenders, Grant received two more votes on the last ballot than on the first.

Sherman himself attributed his defeat to nine recalcitrant Ohio delegates who had supported Blaine from the beginning. He underestimated his weakness. In judging his pre-convention position he later reminisced: "My strength and weakness grew out of my long service in the House, Senate and cabinet," and admitted somewhat wistfully in speaking of Blaine, ". . . his brilliant and dashing manner . . . made him a favorite with all the young and active politicians. . . ." This was more perceptive than his post-convention analysis. Garfield was not Blaine, nor was his manner brilliant and dashing, but he was ingratiating and was the first—but not the last—Republican orator to use moral earnestness as a curtain to conceal occasional lapses in moral character. His guilt of actual perfidy has been a matter of speculation. Sherman did not think so in 1880, but later in life he developed some doubts. The historian Rhodes concludes that "apparently the thought of his trust was overpowered with the conviction that the prize was his without the usual hard preliminary work." But, loyal or treacherous, it is virtually certain that, though he may have risen to the Presidency on Sherman's corpse, he was not the murderer. For thirty-four ballots Sherman was available. In all that time he failed to attract appreciable strength. This was not Garfield's fault. It might be argued that during that time Garfield did not work very hard for the man he was managing—did not make promises or enter into deals as David Davis had done for Lincoln, as Mark Hanna was to do for McKinley, but the strategy of a compromise candidate is to offend no one by trying to steal his votes and wait patiently for the break. For Sherman the break never came.

So Garfield was nominated and elected, and went on to the White House and assassination; and John Sherman took the Senate seat which the victor had vacated without ever filling.

As the 1884 Republican National Convention drew near, Blaine towered above the party. Garfield was dead; Grant was dying; President Arthur, although a candidate and assured of a substantial block of votes from the now rotten boroughs of the South which were wholly dependent upon presidential patronage, had failed to gain recognition as the party's leader. Of course there were the Sherman brothers—and Blaine, gun-shy after being nosed out twice by a rival who had appeared coy, was keenly aware of their presence. He is supposed to have said that he preferred to be defeated by the General than conquered by the Senator. Since he undoubtedly preferred neither, this may have expressed the priority of his fears rather than of his preferences. As a politician he could oppose another politician with a politician's armament—his record as a statesman, his loyal party bosses and phalanxes of party workers, his way with men—but what can a mere politician do when faced by the national idolatry of a war god? Aware of his peril, he carefully tested the ground, personally urging the General to accept the nomination. The latter said no, that he did not want to damage his brother's chances. Blaine must have been relieved but his enemies in the party—and he still had them—continued to push General Sherman, who thus remained a sword of Damocles dangling over his head.

Meanwhile John Sherman was waiting, not hopefully but not altogether without hope. He was to recall in his memoirs that he had said in a statement published throughout Ohio that he was not a candidate and would not try to gain even an Ohio delegate's vote. This was true, but not quite the whole truth. In the spring of 1884 he had written to his brother:

> I have made up my mind to be silent and neutral, and I think that is your best course. . . . I would gladly take it [the nomination] as an honorable closing of thirty years of political life, but

I will neither ask for it, scheme for it, nor have I the faintest hope of getting it. . . .

By May 4th the presidential itch was a little stronger. In a letter in which he is trying to be completely candid with William Tecumseh he is not quite successful. There is an undertone of impatience. One feels that what he really wants to say is, "If you don't want it for heaven's sake get out and give me a chance—poor as that chance may be." He writes:

> It is certain that if Blaine is not nominated in the early ballots a movement will be made for your nomination, and if entered upon will go like wild fire. Someone should be authorized to make a definite and positive refusal if you have concluded to decline the nomination if tendered. My opinion is still that while you ought not to seek, or even beforehand consent to accept a nomination, yet if it comes unsought and with cordial unanimity you ought to acquiesce. . . . If desired by me I could have the solid vote of Ohio but I see no prospect or possibility of my nomination.

General Sherman took his brother's advice. He did not seek the nomination, and when the convention convened made a definite and positive refusal. This was on June 3rd. On June 5th, he did it again with a second telegram. This one had the same precise efficiency that he had exhibited when marching his army to the sea: I WILL NOT ACCEPT IF NOMINATED AND WILL NOT SERVE IF ELECTED. It was to become a classic that no other reluctant candidate has seen fit to repeat. Having sent the wire, the General wrote his brother explaining that he had acted so that the convention might be free to turn to John in the event of a deadlock between Blaine and Arthur. There is no reason whatsoever to question either his word or his motive. It is, however, possible that he actually lessened the likelihood of a stalemate. As long as he was in the background anti-Blaine delegates might hold off, hoping to wear the leaders down until the crucial moment for the presentation of the hero's name arrived. With the hero fleeing the field there was no bastion around which to rally.

The convention was called to order June 3rd. In a contest over the election of a temporary chairman the Blaine adherents were defeated, demonstrating that as in 1880 there were enough anti-Blaine delegates to beat him if they could agree on a rival. On the 6th the candidates were put into nomination, and in spite of his disavowal of any hopes Sherman allowed his name to be entered. Joseph Foraker, a rapidly rising Ohio politician, made a nominating speech so equivocal that one listener fancied that though Sherman was the subject, he detected Blaine's white plume waving in the background. Unkind critics speculated that Foraker might be cultivating Blaine supporters so that he might be their second choice should their favorite falter. Others placed in nomination were President Arthur, Logan of Illinois, with whom it was reported Blaine had already made a deal involving the Vice-Presidency, and Senator Edmunds of Vermont.

On the first roll call Blaine led and Arthur was second. Sherman had only thirty votes, and after two more ballots he released his delegates. Blaine was nominated on the next roll call. Logan, as predicted, was given second place on the ticket.

Sherman, as he always did, campaigned hard for the party, but the reformers deserted to Cleveland and the Plumed Knight—called by the Democrats the "tattooed [by graft] man"—though at last chosen remained unanointed. Grover Cleveland was elected President and after twenty-four years of exile in the wastelands of defeat the Democrats were once more in possession of the White House. It is the longest period that any major American party suffered such banishment and survived.

It is difficult to envisage as devoted a party man as John Sherman being anything but dismayed at such a catastrophe. Yet his chagrin must have been tempered by the voice of ambition reminding him that if Blaine had won he would almost certainly have been renominated in 1888, but with Blaine defeated the road was open for another Sherman bid. It would be the last one, for he was already sixty-one years old. He might ignore the enveloping shroud of years a little while longer—say until 1888—but by 1892 it would be impossible. He might remain on the scene as an elder statesman, but the Presidency would be out of the question.

In 1885 Sherman was elected to the Senate for the fifth time. This was unprecedented in Ohio history. Before he was chosen he told his brother that to win would fulfill his ambition and leave him content to "take a tranquil and moderate course." On his return to the Senate he was chosen president pro tempore, and three years passed as tranquilly as he could have wished. But as 1888 approached he plunged once more into the deepest of political whirlpools—his final try for the Presidency.

Sherman still believed that his failure to win nomination in 1880 was caused by the lack of a solid Ohio vote. Consequently when in 1888 he was urged to become an active candidate, he replied that he would not do so unless he had the endorsement of the state convention and the pledged support of a united delegation. He received the former when the state convention met almost a year before the national convention. This was all he needed. He was "out and running." Never before had he worked so hard and so openly.

In the late summer he and his brother made a seven-thousand-mile junket to the Pacific Coast. It was no little advantage to be seen with General William Tecumseh Sherman, and there was opportunity to become acquainted with state and local politicians.

The Ohio state elections were to be held in November. By September, Sherman was on the stump for the state and congressional ticket. He praised Republicans, attacked Democrats and once again ran up the bloody shirt. The tenderfoot too young or too soft to use the word rebel was ridiculed. Cleveland had suggested returning Confederate battle flags captured during the war to the South. Sherman was outraged that "we must surrender our captured flags to the rebels who bore them, and our Grand Army boys, bent and gray, must march under the new flag, under the flag of Grover Cleveland."

By November, without abandoning the Civil War as an issue, he was turning his attention to growing prohibition sentiment. "Is there not a choice between that [Republican] party and the Democratic party, which has always been the slave of the liquor party . . . I trust that when that good time comes our Prohibition friends and neighbors who stand aloof from us will come back and join the old fold and rally around the old flag. . . ."

Foraker was elected governor and the Republicans won control of the state legislature. The following April the state party convention was held. A solid Sherman delegation to the approaching national convention was chosen. Among its members were Foraker, William McKinley and Mark Hanna, a Cleveland industrialist who was elbowing his way into the inner circle of Ohio Republican politics.

Sherman now felt that "I might fairly aspire to the nomination. Mr. Blaine had declined it on account of his health, and no one was named who had a longer record of public service than I." Of course there was dissent. Some Ohio newspapers attacked him and Mrs. Sherman begged him not to run. And naturally there were rivals. Without a Republican President to throw the weight of patronage and presidential prestige into the scales the race was wide open.

Blaine was still the greatest menace. In 1887, accompanied by his wife and daughters, he had left America for an indefinite stay in Europe. He attended Queen Victoria's garden party, dined with the British nobility and played skittles with Andrew Carnegie at Carnegie's Scotch castle. During the autumn he visited Germany, Vienna and Budapest; winter found him in Florence from whence he wrote the chairman of the Republican National Committee that his name would not be presented to the approaching party convention. He reaffirmed this stand from Paris in April and again in May. And yet he remained a menace. Unlike General Sherman, he had not said he would not run if nominated. And his supporters insisted that he would. Even when he refused to return to America in time for the convention, going instead for another visit with Carnegie in Scotland, Blaine talk continued. After a few roll calls the Republicans would turn to their great and beloved leader.

Although, except for Blaine, Sherman had no outstanding rivals, there was no lack of competition. Almost every state seemed to have a candidate. Indiana had two: Walter Q. Gresham and Benjamin Harrison.

Walter Q. Gresham was the reformers' candidate. As a federal judge he attained national fame by deciding the Wabash Railroad receivership case against Jay Gould and for defrauded investors. Consequently he was opposed by the railroads and other speculative elements in the relatively new world of big business. Chauncey Depew of the New York Central Railroad quipped that, if nominated for President, Gresham would "Wabash all of us." It was not one of the wit's better quips, but it expressed a heartfelt sentiment.

Indiana's other entry, Benjamin Harrison, had the right background for a presidential candidate. His great-grandfather had signed the Declaration of Independence; his grandfather, William Henry Harrison, was enshrined in American history as Old Tippecanoe, who had defeated the tribe of the wily Indian chief Tecumseh in battle and the wilier Van Buren, the Red Fox of Kinderhook, for the Presidency. But Benjamin Harrison had more to recommend him than distinguished ancestry. Born of parents of very modest means, he was a self-made man, happily married, an elder and for many years Sunday school teacher in the Presbyterian Church, and a Westerner so staunchly conservative that he was acceptable to the East. He had been a general in the Civil War. And he possessed a further virtue that was not inconsiderable after Blaine's defeat in a campaign in which he had been featured by Democrats as the "tattooed man." Harrison was scrupulously honest. True, he was far from being the ideal candidate. Small, neat, balding and somewhat rotund, his appearance was not impressive. He was not an outstanding orator. His manner, except with intimates, was cold, sometimes supercilious. But somehow he got votes. In Indiana, a pivotal state, he had been elected United States Senator. He was not making an active campaign for the presidential nomination, but his supporters were quietly pushing him as a second-choice possibility.

Two other candidates were of a relatively new breed in American politics. Heretofore the increasingly powerful business interests had been content to be represented by career politicians who shared their views and served their interests. Now a few industrial barons were wetting their own feet in political waters.

Chauncey Depew, lawyer, railroad president and United States Senator, was probably too wise and too witty to take his candidacy very seriously. Nonetheless he was a candidate, and when in the spring of 1888 Sherman went to New York in search of votes he found that Depew had them cornered.

Russell Alger of Michigan did take his candidacy seriously. A lumber magnate, known as the Match King, he came to Chicago determined to get the nomination if money could buy it. He opened headquarters that had the heady accents of a millionaire's hangout, and promised if nominated to spend $5,000,000 on his campaign and make it up by a higher tariff on matches.

It was improbable that such a candidate could win, but neither could he be ignored. And there were other candidates. Some were nationally known. Others were at best favorite sons, but they would get votes and their managers would have some bargaining power. Never had a Republican convention been so unpredictable as to outcome.

In 1861 a young minister, Russell Conwell, delivered an address that he was to repeat in churches, town halls, college auditoriums and on the chautauqua circuit all over the United States. It came to be the best-known sermon in American history. It proclaimed the gospel of wealth. He called it "Acres of Diamonds," and its message was that people could find diamonds (dollars) in their own backyards. He who failed in the quest did so by reason of his own unworthiness.

> I say you ought to get rich, and it is your duty to get rich . . . to make money honestly is to preach the gospel . . . let me say here clearly, and say it briefly, though subject to discussion that I do not have time for here, ninety-eight out of one hundred rich men in America are honest. That is why they are rich . . . let us remember there is not a poor person in the United States who was not made poor by his own shortcomings. . . . It is all wrong to be poor, anyhow.

Conwell, although it was only 1861 and he was only nineteen years old when he first delivered his sermon, had a vision of the dawning Gilded Age—and that vision encompassed its politics:

> Young man, won't you learn a lesson in the primer of politics that it is a *prima facie* evidence of littleness to hold office under our form of government? Great men get into office sometimes, but what this country needs is men who will do what we tell them to do . . . if you only get the privilege of casting one vote, you don't get anything that is worth while. Unless you control more than one vote you will be unknown. . . . This country is not run by votes. Do you think it is? It is governed by influence. It is governed by the ambitions and enterprises which control votes.

That was in 1861, a year after the Republicans had held their second national convention in Chicago, and during the next twenty-eight years the party and the city adopted Conwell's gospel and advice. In 1860 Chicago's population of 109,000 had ranked it ninth among the cities of America; in 1888, with over a million, it was second. In 1860 there were "miles of wooden houses of the meanest kind that must be removed . . . leagues of wretched, bottomless streets that must be filled"; by 1888 the Great Fire had attended to the wooden houses and civic enterprise had found a bottom for the streets. But Chicago

had done more than dig itself out of the mud. It had found its
diamonds, though its richest acres looked and smelled more
like a pigsty than fields of gems. The city, boasted the *Colum-
bian Exposition Graphic* two years later, exported over 44,000,-
000 pounds of canned and almost 10,000,000 pounds of salted
meat. It manufactured dry goods, iron goods, clothing, boots,
shoes, paper goods, jewelry and watches. It published 34 daily
and 250 weekly newspapers. Nor was culture neglected. There
was a city library with 175,000 volumes and an art institute.
There were 317 churches.

Although the gaudy mansions with marble fronts located
just north of the Chicago River still housed multimillionaires,
the new generation of the apostles of wealth had begun to move
far south to Prairie Avenue where they lived in heavy massive
residences—some in Norman Romanesque revival style, of
rough granite ashlar, pierced with narrow slits of windows.
They were for the most part hard working; they went to Protestant churches, voted Republican, and made and respected
money. In demeanor they were a little grimly sober and respectable as if they were aware of a mission to live down the
city's earlier, lustier days. Yet they were not far removed from
those days in either time or spirit.

The Auditorium in which the Republican National Convention of 1888 was held was a measure of how far Chicago had advanced since the day when Abraham Lincoln was nominated
in the Wigwam; and Louis Sullivan who designed it symbolized
the dynamic quality that characterized the rising city.

Although its great theater, seating 4,250, was ready for use,
the Auditorium was not yet completed in 1888. Made of huge
granite blocks, it would be a city in itself: hotel, office building, theater, and surmounted by a great tower of solid masonry.
Like Chicago the Auditorium was unfinished, but it was massive, impressive and growing.

The Republican party had changed even more than Chicago. In 1860 it was a party of protest, urging revolt against the
commercial and planting interests that had dominated the

Whig and Democratic parties. Abraham Lincoln had praised labor as of greater worth than capital. The Republican party of 1888 was dedicated to capital. It had united with the great corporate interests. Depew and Alger were at Chicago as candidates; Elkins, representing coal and railroads, Wanamaker for commerce and Mark Hanna for iron were there as delegates. Far away in Scotland the party's titular leader was keeping in touch with the convention; a transatlantic cable at one hand— Andrew Carnegie at the other. To paraphrase Calvin Coolidge, who would have felt at home in Chicago in 1888, the business of the Republican party was business, and business was keeping a firm hold on its party.

Next to business, patriotism was the dominant note of the convention. The Civil War was fought again. Frederick Douglass, the venerable Negro abolitionist orator, begged, "Be not deterred from duty by the cry of 'bloody shirt.' Let that shirt wave so long as blood can be found upon it."

But although the city and the party might change and new forces materialize, climate and man repeat themselves. The weather was hot and sticky; the rank and file of the delegates were good-natured and noisy. Political clubs led by bands paraded in the streets, supporting their favorite with the blare of trumpets and the roll of drums. In crowded rooms in the Palmer House and Grand Pacific Hotel, the activities were neither so noisy nor so innocent. Positions and men were being probed; deals were being discussed; votes were being bought.

Sherman, or at least his cause, was involved both for good and for evil in the latter activity. He wrote in his *Recollections*, "I believe and had, as I thought, conclusive proof that the friends of General Alger substantially purchased the votes of many of the delegates from the southern states who had been instructed by their conventions to vote for me." Sherman quotes no figure but the reported price was fifty dollars a head. The means by which these votes were "substantially" bought were simple and safe. All delegates were given tickets to the visitors' gallery. It was these which were bought. If the sellers thereafter voted for the buyer's candidate it could not be proved to be more than coincidence. Governor Foraker, to explain the bad feeling that existed in the Ohio delegation—and incidentally to contrast his own virtue with Hanna's vice and gloss over his own equivocal behavior as a Sherman delegate—gave a detailed description: "A great many colored delegates from the South, as is their custom, had tickets to the Convention which they desired to sell. They brought their tickets to our rooms at the hotel, and Mr. Hanna, in the presence of us all, bought them. I protested against such methods, saying it would bring scandal on the entire delegation and hurt Sherman's cause. Mr. Hanna and I had a spirited discussion over the matter, and it resulted in my leaving the rooms and seeking apartments on another floor." Other convention delegates confirmed Foraker's charge that Hanna was buying convention tickets.

The convention was called to order on June 19th. The Chairman of the National Committee in the opening address emphasized the tariff as the chief issue of the campaign. The temporary chairman then followed with a speech that must have sent chills down the spines of Sherman supporters. After picturing Abraham Lincoln, Ulysses Grant, John Brown and "Black Jack" Logan—all of whom were dead—as marching side by side "along the highway of the nation's Glory," he turned to James G. Blaine who was by no means dead—even though it might be fairly said that his ghost haunted the convention. (He was the Chicago bookies' favorite at 2–1.) Blaine was pictured as that "gallant leader, that chevalier of American politics, the glory of Republicanism and the nightmare of Democracy, our Henry of Navarre . . . our uncrowned King. . . ." Despite the hyperbole it was the sort of thing that could be said about James G. Blaine. To say it about Sherman would be to make him ridiculous.

On the second day of the convention, oratory, including memorials, was still in order. The deaths of ex-President Arthur and Roscoe Conkling were duly noted and regretted. Conkling was "the peerless statesman and citizen" whose death was "a calamity to the cause of Republican principles and the interest of the nation." He would have loved it.

The honored dead being disposed of, the platform was brought in by William McKinley. It supported a high protective tariff, opposed immigrant contract labor and Democratic efforts to demonetize silver, supported the public school system, civil service reform and pensions for the G.A.R. It was a platform Sherman or any other Republican could run on, and was strengthened in the eyes of the righteous by an additional plank adopted on the floor: "The first concern of good government is the virtue and sobriety of the people and the purity of their homes. The Republican party cordially sympathizes with all wise and well directed efforts for the promotion of temperance and morality."

On Thursday, the third day, the pace quickened. Word came from Scotland; a rumor spread throughout Chicago; avowed candidates were nominated.

The word from Scotland was a message from Andrew Carnegie which appeared in Chicago newspapers: Blaine would accept a draft. So, although Blaine's name would not be placed in nomination he was still very much in the picture, and his image grew clearer with a rumor that was whispered wherever there were delegates to listen: Governor Foraker had been offered the Vice-Presidency on a Blaine-Foraker ticket. Of course it was only gossip and no one would say for sure that Foraker had accepted, but it was food for thought. Especially on the part of those who recalled 1880.

Nominations were the official business of the day. Sherman was nominated by General D. H. Hastings of Pennsylvania, and was given a bigger, longer, noisier ovation than any other candidate. It was climaxed with everyone singing *"Marching Through Georgia,"* which, considering that most of his pledged delegates were from the South, seems something of a paradox. Nine men were formally placed in nomination. Before the balloting ended, eleven more were to receive votes.

The balloting began on Friday. On the first roll call Sherman got 229 votes, over a hundred short of the 416 necessary to win. Depew, Alger, Harrison and Allison were bunched with between seventy and a hundred votes apiece; Blaine, despite his insistence that he was not a candidate, got thirty-five; the rest were scattered.

Sherman picked up twenty votes on the second roll call. No one else did much better, although Alger went into second place with a total of 116. The third ballot showed no significant trend, but ominously Sherman lost five votes. After three ballots the convention adjourned until evening. At the evening session the only interesting incident was the withdrawal of Depew. This was of no importance so far as Depew was concerned—no one had regarded him seriously—but where New York's vote would go was important. There was no roll call Friday night.

On Saturday morning William McKinley earnestly—and he could be as earnest as any man alive—disavowed ambition. McKinley's star was rising; he was regarded as a rival of Foraker for party leadership in Ohio. Not a candidate, he had nonetheless received a few votes on each of the first three roll calls. Interrupting the fourth, he stood up. Unlike Garfield eight years before, he did not sit down before he had finished what he had to say. He climbed on his chair so that he might be heard better. He spoke clearly and forcibly. He loved his state Ohio, and Ohio was pledged to John Sherman. He himself was pledged to John Sherman; he was not a candidate; he wanted no votes. It was an appealing performance. The convention applauded. It was impressed, but not necessarily converted. McKinley continued to get votes.

Although the fourth and fifth ballots resulted in no breakthrough there were significant changes. Gresham faded from 123 on the third ballot to 87 on the fifth ballot; Alger moved up a little but was still far back of Sherman whose vote had declined from a high-water mark of 249. But Harrison was really moving. He was in second place, only eleven votes behind Sherman on the fifth roll call.

The Blaine hopefuls could not risk a further Harrison advance. They requested and got a recess until evening, and then got an adjournment of the evening session until Monday. The time for bedrock bargaining had arrived.

When the convention adjourned Saturday afternoon, Sherman's position was still good. He was ahead and the situation was fluid. Harrison had come up but he was a long way from majority, and had lost four votes on the fifth ballot. He might have run out of steam. The real threat still appeared to be Blaine. His supporters had easily engineered the recess and now had Saturday night and Sunday to organize their push. And Foraker was attempting to abandon the ship. Late Saturday night he issued a statement to the press that from now on he was going for Blaine. He claimed that this was not disloyalty to Sherman on whose behalf he had done all he could but who he was now convinced could not be nominated. The apology was worse than the defection; if the chairman of Sherman's own delegation declared his cause hopeless other supporters were not apt to be more optimistic. Then the situation changed with dramatic suddenness. Foraker had hardly issued his statement when a cable from Blaine arrived. The Paris decision stood. He was not a candidate.

This deflated the Blaine balloon before it got off the ground. He was to get a few die-hard votes to the very end but he was out of the race. And now John Sherman who had stood in Blaine's shadow—in the House, in the Senate, and most of all as a presidential candidate—emerged into the sunlight. No other candidate, perhaps no other living Republican, could claim such long, distinguished, faithful party service. None of his remaining adversaries had his experience, none was as well known. He himself was confident: "On Monday, the 25th of June, I did not anticipate a change on the first ballot from the last one on Saturday. I did expect, from my dispatches that the nomination would be made that day and in my favor."

That's the way it looked to Sherman in Washington. In Chicago Foraker scrambled off the limb he had just crawled out on

and became a Sherman man again. And in a room in the Grand
Pacific Hotel a meeting was held. Aldrich, high priest of high
tariff and a power in New England, was there. So were Platt
of New York, Quay of Pennsylvania, Clarkson, an Allison manager, and Elkins of West Virginia, an erstwhile Blaine man.
They would probably have united on Blaine had they received
the right word, but the word had not been right. They had to
look further. There is no incontrovertible evidence what they
decided, and presumably they did not decide anything conclusive at that moment. They would wait a little. But what is incontrovertible is that the climate of the meeting was not favorable to Sherman.

General Sherman wrote his wife that the convention was in
a muddle on Sunday morning.

A cable from Andrew Carnegie did a lot to clear it up. It was
in his own code. TOO LATE VICTOR [Blaine] IMMOVABLE. TAKE
TRUMP [Harrison] AND STAR [Phelps of New Jersey]. The lid
to Blaine's coffin, by his own wish, was nailed down, and his
successor named by the "rich people" that he liked so much.
The cable was sent to Elkins of West Virginia. Soon after its
receipt he went for a carriage ride in Lincoln Park with New
York's Boss Platt. Sherman came to believe that this ride was
decisive. He was not a vindictive man, and his memoirs are impersonal to the point of dullness. Nonetheless he wrote:

> I believed then, as I believe now, that one of the delegates
> from the State of New York practically controlled the whole
> delegation, and that a corrupt bargain was made on Sunday
> which transfered the great body of the vote of New York to
> General Harrison.

Quay of Pennsylvania was also bargaining. Although he was
pledged to Sherman he had dickered with the Harrison camp
even before the convention was called to order. His price was a
cabinet post and he wanted a promise of it in writing. The price
was high but he had sixty votes to sell. The proposal was sent
to Harrison in Indianapolis. Harrison promptly returned the

letter with NO written across it, and Quay remained loyal to Sherman for five ballots. However, he was anxious to be a king-maker even if he couldn't be a cabinet member and it was ru-mored that Pennsylvania would swing to Harrison at the proper time.

Meantime the Ohio delegates were growing more than a little restive. Blaine's Saturday cable notwithstanding, they were still obsessed with fear of him, and Sherman had stood still for five ballots. Twice in the recent past they had snatched the nomination for the state from nowhere, and there seemed to be a strong undercurrent of sentiment for young William McKinley. In 1880 Sherman had withdrawn and urged un-qualified support for his manager, Garfield. Perhaps—. They wired him that his own cause was hopeless, but that there was a good chance to nominate McKinley.

John Sherman had had enough. He had marched up the hill three times and had marched down twice. This time they would have to pull him down. LET MY NAME STAND. I PREFER DEFEAT TO RETREAT, he wired Mark Hanna.

During the small pre-dawn hours Monday, Harrison repre-sentatives got together with the New York leaders. Their man had been getting most of the New York votes but they wanted them all. It would indicate which way the wind was blowing. No immediate decision was announced, but later in the morn-ing, two hours before the convention was to be called to order, Platt called a caucus of the whole delegation. Knots of anxious men waited outside. It didn't take long. New York came out pledged to Harrison. Before the session convened, the news had spread. It was also reported that Allison of Iowa, who had been getting seventy-five to a hundred votes, was ready to with-draw in favor of Harrison.

There was no break on the sixth ballot. Sherman picked up twenty votes, Harrison eighteen. But on the seventh roll call the tide began to flow. It wasn't spectacular—Sherman down thirteen, Harrison up forty-seven—but it was strong enough to convince delegates who wanted to float to shore with the winner. On the eighth roll call Quay delivered Pennsylvania to Harrison, and Allison withdrew in his favor. He was nominated with 544 votes.

At the end of the roll call an incident occurred that somehow epitomizes the fate of John Sherman in quest of the presidential nomination. The result had scarcely been announced before Foraker was on his feet. "Ohio came here all Sherman men. They are now all Harrison men," he shouted. The King is dead; long live the King. It always went that way. No one seemed to put his whole heart into a fight for Sherman, or care very much if he lost. His warriors always showed indecent haste in deserting to another leader.

He took defeat quietly, as he always did. A newspaper quoted him as saying that it brought him a feeling of freedom so strong that he was glad he did not get the nomination. If he did say it, it was, of course, not true. But he might have momentarily believed that it was. It must have been a strain to be a candidate for the presidential nomination for ten years.

With Blaine eliminated, the candidates for the Republican nomination in 1888 were a colorless lot. Gresham was probably the most able, but the railroad and steel interests opposed him, and the delegates from his own Indiana were for Harrison. Of the remainder Sherman was, on the record, the best man. His long service in Congress had brought a knowledge of national affairs greater than that of Harrison, who was undistinguished as a Senator. As Secretary of the Treasury he had proved himself an able administrator. If, in 1888, he was not a distinguished statesman, his party had none. (Neither did the Democrats.)

As the right man, defining right man as the one most likely to win, Sherman was as strong as his party. He was too orthodox to be stronger. He would not lead the Republicans to victory, nor on the other hand would he lead them to defeat as the more brilliant and personally attractive Blaine had done. He would march firmly along in the front rank to whatever fate held in store for the party. He was not loved but his name was far better known to the rank and file of the voters than that of Harrison, and he was liked better than Harrison by his colleagues in the Senate.

But Harrison was nominated. Sherman's trouble was that although he was better than Harrison his margin was not great enough to compel recognition. He would attract no Democratic or independent votes; he would not move lethargic Republicans to the polls. He would win in November only if the normal Republican vote sufficed. As much could be said for Harrison. This left the convention bosses free to maneuver for personal or local advantage without worrying about the effect of their activities on the November election. They took full advantage of their freedom. No nomination has depended more on petty intrigue.

The choice was made in hotel rooms, in a carriage in Lincoln Park, in Scotland. And Sherman had no representation at the bargaining counters. Quay of Pennsylvania had tried to sell him out before the convention opened, and did it on Sunday morning; Foraker was more interested in getting something for himself than in helping Sherman. Only Mark Hanna really tried, and he, on the threshold of a political career that was to make him the nearest thing to a national boss the Republicans ever had, was not yet accepted by the powerful inner circles of either politics or finance.

Even so Sherman might have been chosen had the powerful business interests that were now a decisive force in the Republican party wanted him. But they did not. They could have accepted him with a good grace born of confidence that he would not injure them, but they preferred Harrison. John Sherman was a professional politician who recognized business as the most important single element among the congeries of interests that constituted the Republican party, but he had a politician's eye on the remaining elements. Benjamin Harrison was a corporation lawyer turned politician. He was less for business than of business. So, TAKE TRUMP, Carnegie had cabled. It was the master's voice—not just Andrew Carnegie's but that of financial industrialism. The convention took Trump. And John Sherman, who had helped organize the Republican party, gone with it through the youthful days of crusading zeal, the dark days of war, the bitter days of reconstruction, the sordid days of scandal, and the fat days of plenty, remained unchosen.

He returned to the Senate and served there until 1897, when in order to make room for Mark Hanna in that body McKinley appointed him Secretary of State. Then, in 1898, past all ambition, he revolted. Disapproving of the war with Spain, he resigned. At last he was done with politics. Two years later he died.

In 1889 General Sherman wrote his brother: ". . . To be a president for four years is not much of an honor, but to have been senator continuously from 1861–1892—less the four years as Secretary of the Treasury—is an honor. Webster and Clay are better known to the world than Polk or Pierce." Consoling words, but they probably furnished little balm to John Sherman who had not aspired to be a Webster or a Clay. He had wanted to be President. However, although in 1888 he was probably about as good and right a man as his party had to offer, he was passed over, and remains today even less known to fame than Polk or Pierce. Perhaps that better than anything else explains his failure to be nominated to the Presidency. Forty years in the Senate and cabinet, and he remains obscure. Although something more than a Pierce, he was much less than a Webster or Clay. No one would ever say of him as a foreign diplomat said of Adlai Stevenson, "He was the best President America never had." But he would not have been the worst. He would probably have been better, although maybe not very much better, than Benjamin Harrison.

The Democrats

1912

WHEN *the Democratic National Convention met in June,*
1912, the party had lost the four preceding presidential elec-
tions by fat popular majorities ranging from a half to two and
a half million votes. Nevertheless, there was a spirit of optimism
among the delegates. Two weeks before, when the Republican
old guard, in control of the party organization, had rammed
through the renomination of President William Howard Taft,
the G.O.P. had split wide open. Outraged progressives then an-
nounced their determination to take steps which would lead to
the birth of a new party. They said, and no one doubted, that
their candidate would be Theodore Roosevelt, the most popular
American of the day. The Democrats did not discount Roose-
velt's strength, but they felt sure Taft would still get a large
share of the Republican vote. To win, the Democrats had only

to hold their normal vote. This they could do with the right man.

Candidates were not lacking. The favorites of the conservatives were Judge Harmon of Ohio and Senator Underwood of Alabama. Harmon was able, respectable and relatively unknown. He had the support of Ohio and the eastern "gold" Democrats. The latter included the New York delegation, which, according to William Jennings Bryan, meant Wall Street and Tammany Hall. Oscar Underwood, a Southern states' rights Jeffersonian, was also able and respected. Behind him were a solid bloc of Southern delegates, who if they could not nominate their candidate might well hold the balance of power. The favorite of party liberals was Governor Woodrow Wilson of New Jersey, who had entered active politics only two years before. In the middle was Champ Clark of Missouri, Speaker of the House of Representatives. Finally there were the favorite sons and dark horses, patiently waiting, hoping for a deadlock, and having a good chance of getting one.

When the convention was called to order Champ Clark held a comfortable lead in pledged delegates. Woodrow Wilson was a fairly well placed second with known second-choice strength. Neither was close to the two-thirds vote that Democratic party rules required for nomination. Harmon and Underwood together could not muster even a majority and were without substantial secondary strength.

There were also a number of uninstructed, uncommitted and undecided delegations. Most of these were controlled by bosses, the most important of whom were Tom Taggart of Indiana and Roger Sullivan of Illinois.

Finally there was William Jennings Bryan. Bryan had been the party's candidate three times and had lost three times, thus tying the record of Henry Clay as the most beaten man in the history of American major party presidential politics. But though oft-beaten, Bryan was still powerful and still ambitious. He said before, during and after the convention that he was not a candidate. Hardly anyone believed him. Other candidates,

Democratic politicians, Republican and Democratic editors and political correspondents joined in saying that he was not only a candidate but was employing every stratagem he could summon to first kill off the conservatives, Harmon and Underwood, and then bring about a deadlock between Clark and Wilson. In its extremity the convention must then turn to the "Peerless Leader," the "Great Commoner"—to William Jennings Bryan.

These were the forces that maneuvered for over forty roll calls as Champ Clark and Woodrow Wilson battled for the nomination—and as Bryan, for the last time, dominated the Democratic scene.

Clark vs. Wilson

What is it that a nominating convention wants in the man it is to present to the country for its suffrages? A man who will be and who will seem to the country in some sort an embodiment of the character and purpose it wishes its government to have,— a man who understands his own day and the needs of the country, and who has the personality and the initiative to enforce his views both upon the people and upon Congress.
—Woodrow Wilson, *Constitutional Government*

I doan' keer if he is a houn',
You gotta quit kickin' my dawg aroun'.
—Champ Clark Campaign Song

It was hot in Baltimore on June 28, 1912. In the hall where the Democratic National Convention was balloting for a presidential candidate it was stifling. The tenth roll call was under way. Since the first one Champ Clark of Missouri, Speaker of the House of Representatives, had led Governor Woodrow Wilson of New Jersey by over a hundred votes. Ohio's Harmon was running third, and Oscar Underwood of Alabama with a solid core of Southern votes was fourth. There had been no significant trends since the beginning. Delegates were literally sweating it out when Tammany Hall's boss, Charles Murphy, arose to cast New York's ninety votes. They had been going to Harmon, constituting the bulk of his strength. Now Murphy, accustomed to power and maneuver, switched them to Champ Clark. It was as though a thunderstorm had exploded on a somnolent summer afternoon. The noise was deafening as Clark's Missouri delegation seized New York's banner and started to parade around the hall. Clark's daughter was near the platform; she was hoisted to strong shoulders where she swayed happily as she waved an American flag. The demonstration lasted an hour and a half as banner after banner was swept into the triumphal march. When William Jennings Bryan croaked grimly that the party's candidate must not be besmirched with Tammany's support he was scarcely heard. Wilson men sat glum and silent.

When order was finally restored and the tenth roll call completed, Clark had 556 votes. With the venerable Democratic two-thirds rule in effect it was not enough, but it was eleven over half and not since 1844 had a candidate who succeeded in reaching a majority failed to win. If a pattern unbroken for sixty-eight years was to be repeated, Champ Clark would be the Democratic candidate.

There is a superficial resemblance between James Beauchamp Clark's career and Abraham Lincoln's. Born in Kentucky of poor parents and orphaned at three by his mother's death, Clark grew up a barefoot boy, self-reliant and largely self-guided. Like Lincoln he had a voracious appetite for facts and knowledge and read whatever he could get his hands on; like Lincoln he was an earthy raconteur, and appealed to the voters as one of their own kind—as plain as dirt, a common sort of fellow. And here the resemblance ended. Clark really was such a fellow; Lincoln wasn't.

As a boy he worked as a farm hand, and attended local schools when he could. At sixteen he got a job teaching but soon quit to go to college at Kentucky University. After two years he was expelled for a fight with a fellow student whom he hit over the head with a board and shot at with a broken pistol. So he went back to teaching until he had enough money to try college again, this time Bethany in West Virginia. He graduated *cum laude,* and accepted a $1,400 a year position as president of Marshall College. In those days college administrators weren't paid very much, so young men took such jobs, served briefly and went on to more useful jobs as teachers, or abandoned an academic career for lusher fields. Clark abandoned it after a year to go to Cincinnati and study law.

After law school he went west to Wichita, Kansas, to seek his fortune, but fortune eluded him and he returned east as far as Missouri. It was during this period of changing residence that he also changed his name. First he chopped off the James and tried Beauchamp, and later when his friends called him Bo or Champ he resolved to solve the problem by adopting the latter. Thereafter he called himself, and signed his name, Champ. He liked it and believed a short name to be an asset to a man in public life.

After a brief stay in Kansas City he accepted a postion as superintendent of schools at Louisiana, Missouri, a lazy sun-baked town on the Mississippi. He soon abandoned the school-master's career—this time forever—for law, and, after he was elected district attorney, for politics. In 1880 he was chosen as one of Missouri's Democratic presidential electors pledged to General Hancock. The same year he moved to Bowling Green, a town in Pike County, Missouri, about ten miles southwest of Louisiana. The surrounding country was rich, with rolling hills that descended to the valley floor. This was to be Clark's home for the rest of his life. A year after he moved to Bowling Green he married Genevieve Bennett. At the age of thirty-one he had settled down.

In 1885 he was elected prosecuting attorney for Pike County, and in 1889 to the Missouri legislature. In the legislature he was associated with two bills that were to be the foundation stones for his later claim to recognition as a fighting liberal. As chairman of the House Jurisprudence Committee he reported, although he had not written, a bill against monopolies doing business in Missouri. The bill passed and was one of the early state antitrust laws in America. Later, he introduced a bill providing for the Australian ballot. The secret ballot was designed not only as a blow against bribery and other forms of corruption at the polls, but also to protect employees against reprisal if they voted contrary to the wishes of their employers. Thus Clark in his first legislative session aligned himself with the opponents of political bossism and plutocracy. True, this was in Missouri where the voice of gold was softer than that of silver and a touch of radicalism was a political asset. Nonetheless, the record was liberal, and in later days when reform was everywhere in the air Champ Clark never let the world forget it.

In 1893 Clark was elected to the United States House of Representatives. He was forty-three years old. Save for two years he was to serve in Congress the rest of his life.

Winston Churchill once declared proudly that he was a House of Commons man. Champ Clark was a House of Representatives man. He liked the House from the very first. There is a Jacksonian flavor in his faith in its power to mold the common man into a Democratic statesman: ". . . I say there is no such training-school for intellectual development anywhere else on earth as the House of Representatives. A man whose mind does not expand there is an incorrigible fool." A true House of Representative man must be a party man. He must believe in the party system and the superior virtues of his own party. He must strive to maintain his party's unity, and if that prove impossible to bind the wounds inflicted during factional clashes. He must protect the party against the heresy of nonpartisanship, or, worse, bipartisanship. He must strive for office for party leaders and jobs for the party troops. Above all he must be regular. In all these respects Champ Clark was a House of Representatives man.

In Congress he drove wedges of disharmony into the bleeding flesh of Republicans and poured healing oils into self-inflicted Democratic wounds. But not quite always. Being human, he had lapses. No Republican mugwump attacked a Stalwart in more hyperbolic terms than those flung at Grover Cleveland by Clark: "There are but two men in all the hoary registers of time that Cleveland's name ought to be associated with —Judas Iscariot and Benedict Arnold. Shades of Arnold, forgive the profanation! Upon reflection I think I ought to beg the pardon of Judas Iscariot, because after his treason he did have the grace to go out and hang himself." He justified the heresy of attacking the leader of his party by declaring that Cleveland was not a Democrat at all but a "tool of the pluto-crats" who had "stolen the livery of heaven [that is, of course, of Democrats] to serve the devil in." Nevertheless, it is not the voice of a House of Representatives man.

When Champ Clark went to Congress in 1893 he had shaved a beard first raised in Wichita days, but retained handlebar mustaches. The mustaches and his hair were reddish yellow. He was over six feet tall and weighed more than two hundred pounds. He was a friendly extroverted man who when out of the political arena spoke warmly, even of Republicans. He had a temper and could nurse a grievance, but most of the time his voice was genuinely warm, his manner genial. This friendliness and his desire for conciliation were his greatest political assets. They brought him the Speakership of the House, and from this vantage point he could aspire to the Presidency.

His principles were those of a good Western Democrat. That is to say that he was not unaffected by the winds of Populism that were blowing from the Western prairies, where farmers denounced the monetary imbalance that drove them deeper into debt and poverty while the bankers and capitalists of the East grew rich. Clark was proud to dine with the eccentric Kansas Populist leader, "Sockless" Jerry Simpson, and he was even prouder to receive a letter from and eat dinner with Henry George, author of *Progress and Poverty*. Throughout his long political career he remained faithful to the principles he held in the beginning. He opposed protective tariffs, monopolies and railroad abuses, all targets of Western radicalism. But in his early congressional career free silver was the burning issue, and he fervently supported it. A speech on the subject not only expresses his faith, but also illustrates his oratorical style: "My brethren, this magnificent silver-white steed stands pawing impatiently at our gates. Let us vault into the saddle and ride him

into the realm of unfailing prosperity, amid the grateful bene-
dictions of a grateful people."

His devotion to silver brought him into close association
with a fellow congressman, William Jennings Bryan of Nebraska. On the eve of the 1912 convention he was to say, perhaps hopefully, that the friendship with Bryan had never been
broken.

In 1894 he was unexpectedly beaten for re-election. During
the next two years (for the most part a period of depression)
he practiced law, but his chief source of income was the chautauqua circuit. He was to continue chautauqua lecturing until
the weight of his duties as Speaker of the House forced him to
give it up. Early lectures were mostly nonpolitical: "Richer
Than Golconda," dealing with the literature of the Bible, was
a favorite with audiences. Others dealt with the lives of great
Americans. After his return to Congress in 1897, his lectures
became increasingly political in tone. As time went by he found
that Congress and chautauqua were mutually beneficial. He
traveled from coast to coast, and people all over America
listened to him, while his activities in the House served as publicity for his lectures. On the chautauqua circuit he was in good
company, too. Senators La Follette, Cummins, Tillman, Taylor
and Borah were lecturing when he was, and others followed
him. These included the most popular of them all, William
Jennings Bryan.

In the party convention of 1896 Clark supported "Silver
Dick" Bland for the Democratic presidential nomination. But
when Bryan stampeded the delegates with his carefully calculated Cross of Gold speech and was chosen, Clark campaigned
for him wholeheartedly. He was to work for Bryan's election
again in both 1900 and 1908. During this period he followed
the party in its antiimperialism, opposing the annexation of
Hawaii and United States occupation policies in the Philippines. His one lapse into jingoism was when in supporting a
reciprocal trade treaty with Canada he said he was for it because
he hoped to see the day when the American flag flew over every

foot of British territory in North America. It was the sort of British lion tail-twisting for political effect that had gone on all over the country, especially in the decade of the nineties, but it was to be used against him in 1912 when the United States and Great Britain were on more friendly terms.

By 1904, a veteran of the House, he made his bid for the minority leadership. He was defeated, a setback which he later regarded as fortunate, "because at the time the Democrats were so thoroughly factionalized that it may well be doubted whether any man could have led them in four Congresses without making enemies enough to defeat him for Speaker." This mature judgment is a revealing commentary on the Democratic party under the leadership of William Jennings Bryan. From 1876 to 1896 the party had successfully performed the function of an American major political party in harmonizing through compromise the congeries of interests that constitute the whole. Consequently, while Republican Stalwart, Half-breed and mugwump feuded, the Democrats offered a united front, and in doing so turned in a good, if frustrating, record of popular majorities in presidential elections. They lost the Presidency in 1876 and 1888 despite a larger popular vote than that of the Republicans. During the same period they were either a strong minority or a majority party in Congress.

Bryan changed this. He had help from Mark Hanna who reorganized the Republican party on a foundation of solid industrial support, from Theodore Roosevelt who stole much of his thunder, from Grover Cleveland who was as stubborn as he was, and from municipal scandals that, though not confined to Democratic-bossed machines, became identified in the minds of the public with Tammany Hall. But he could have done quite well all by himself.

William Jennings Bryan was a man with a Messianic sense of mission. Occasionally he stomached support from the forces of evil, but he would make no concessions to them in opposition. Silver, temperance, fundamental Protestantism, anti-imperialism—whatever the cause, when it became Bryan's it represented truth, and even divinely revealed truth, as opposed to error spawned in hell. It was the devil on one side and Bryan on the other. Democrats must choose their side. Many of them must, on occasion, have shared the English Tory leader Disraeli's sentiments when he declared that he didn't really mind when Gladstone, the Liberal leader, had an ace up his sleeve, but he resented his claim that God had put it there. Bryan's sleeves were full of God-sent aces. It was not that he was insincere, but his sincerity only made his claim to leadership, and his determination to attain his personal objectives, the more intolerant. He was convinced that he alone was destined to bear the burden of command of the virtuous. To reject his leadership was, in his eyes, to reject virtue. And such was his vigor, his eloquence, his fervor, that he carried millions of men and women with him. But many revolted.

Under such leadership the factionalization of the Democratic party that Clark spoke of was inevitable. Although in 1896 Bryan waged a spectacular campaign, arousing the country into an emotional frenzy unequaled since the slavery controversy, he was beaten. He was beaten even worse in 1900 and 1908. And the Democrats not only lost successive presidential elections but also failed to capture control of either branch of Congress. It was the longest period of minority status in every branch of the national government in the party's history.

Perhaps in order to compensate him for his defeat for minority leadership, or more likely because it was held at St. Louis, in his home state, Clark was selected as permanent chairman of the 1904 Democratic National Convention. It was a hectic session—two hundred city policemen were called in to keep order and fifty spectators were thrown out of the convention hall. The delegates themselves were orderly, and Clark ruled so firmly that no one whom he suspected of designs to disrupt party harmony was permitted to speak. He believed that his convention performance contributed to his subsequent election as House minority leader.

Whatever the reasons, Clark was elected Democratic leader

of the House in 1907. During his tenure as minority leader he devoted himself to establishing party harmony, and was so successful in 1910 that he was unanimously nominated by the Democratic caucus for his first term in the Speakership. He did not, however, devote himself entirely to reuniting the factionalized Democrats; he was equally fervent in promoting discord among Republicans.

The Republican schism during the nineteenth century was not because of deep disagreement over public policy, but because of the intraparty fight between Stalwarts and reformers bent on stamping out corruption. But the rebels of the early years of the twentieth century were of a different breed. They called themselves not reformers but insurgents, and their revolt was against the party's stand on issues as well as its leaders. Essentially they agreed with Bryan that financial industrialism (Wall Street) dominated American government and must be shorn of its influence. And they understood the forces that they were opposing a good deal better than the Great Commoner did. They were against the railroads, trusts and other "interests" that they believed controlled the Republican party. They were for tariff reform, and more government regulation of business, and direct primaries. Their strength centered in the small cities and towns of the Middle West. They were tougher than the mugwumps, far better politicians, and their cause had greater popular appeal. However, although they made progress in their states, with William McKinley President, Aldrich in the Senate, "Boss" Cannon ruling the House and Mark Hanna keeping a firm reign on the whole team, they could do little in Washington. On the other hand, since they could sway tens of thousands of voters the party conservative bosses could not entirely ignore them, and the national party convention of 1900 threw them a bone in the person of Theodore Roosevelt as vice-presidential running mate for President McKinley. Roosevelt was not numbered among the insurgents, but he was progressive and a reformer, and as such was acceptable to them. Then McKinley was assassinated.

Mark Hanna mused ruefully on his way to the dead McKinley's funeral that the "wild man," or "damned cowboy," for those were his epithets for Roosevelt, was going to be President.

The "damned cowboy" took over with boiling enthusiasm and a genius for politics. The progressive era had dawned. The old guard submitted to the inevitable, and did no more than break the force of the storms blowing out of the White House. But they did not surrender. They were waiting. Hanna, who was never quite one of them in spirit, died, but the vigil continued through Roosevelt's first and second administrations. It continued through the national convention of 1908 which dutifully accepted Roosevelt's hand-picked heir, William Howard Taft. Then, with Taft elected President, Roosevelt went big-game hunting in Africa where he got a good bag. But the old guard got an even better one in America. It bagged Taft. The Republican insurgents were once more stirred to revolt.

The open break came over the tariff. The Republican platform had pledged revision and, though it did not say so, it was generally understood to mean revision downward, and a bill lowering duties was passed in the House. But the Senate mutilated and reconstructed it so that the end product was higher rather than lower duties. Aldrich, high priest of protection, justified it cynically. The platform, he said, had promised revision. There was revision. Taft, though disapproving, when forced to choose between old guard and insurgents, chose the former and thereby became their captive. He even said the tariff was the best the party had ever supported. This marked the degree of his subservience to his captors.

Clark, as ranking minority member of the House Ways and Means Committee, had taken a prominent part in writing the original tariff bill. When the Senate version was returned to the House he led the Democrats in a blistering attack on it, but in spite of his efforts the measure, guided by the iron hand of Speaker Joseph Cannon, passed. In Clark's opinion the defeat was not without compensation, as it split the Republican party wide open and gave the Democrats a campaign issue. But, important as the tariff fight was, he believed that his part in the House revolt against Cannon was of even greater value in advancing his fortunes and those of the Democratic party. He wrote:

> If we had not made the rules fight in the House, a Democratic Senate, House and President would not have been elected in 1912. . . . Because I led the fight which overthrew the Republican House machine, split the Republican party in twain, and made national Democratic success possible is the reason why the story is entitled to be set forth. . . . It is also the principal reason why I should have received the Democratic presidential nomination at the Baltimore convention in 1912.

There are two versions of the revolt against "Cannonism." One is that it was primarily the work of insurgent Republicans led by George Norris of Nebraska. It hardly acknowledges that the Democrats were there. The other features the Democrats, and Champ Clark is its hero. Since it was the Democrats who furnished most of the votes that broke Cannon, this version, as Clark insisted, "is entitled to be set forth."

Joseph ("Uncle Joe") Cannon did not invent Cannonism; Reed of Maine had been known as "Czar" before him. But he wielded the powers of the Speaker more crudely and brutally than any of his predecessors, and like other monarchs whose thrones were tottering he was unwilling to acknowledge that times had changed. He packed House committees with creatures subservient to or agreeing with him, and dictated their decisions. He was not an absolute monarch but one of a presidium of old guard leaders who determined the party line and transmitted party orders. And in his way he, too, was a House of Representatives man. He would grant to Democrats the privileges due a minority. They were the acknowledged opposition, and as such were permitted to play their role before being outvoted. But insurgents within the party were just that—traitors to be squashed. The trouble was the rebels wouldn't squash. And Champ Clark joyously threw his Democratic battalion into the brawl. But he claimed that his role was far more important than merely to furnish troops. According to his version the fight was Democratic in origin, having been planned by himself and Albert Burleson (later Wilson's Postmaster General) during the special session of Congress called to deal with tariff reform. Burleson was to work on Republican malcontents while Clark rallied the Democrats.

Whoever was responsible, the revolt succeeded. Cannon remained as Speaker, but lost his power to appoint the majority members of House committees. In his own words, he was "a little shot up." It was said that the pathos of this admission moved fellow members, including Clark, to tears.

The reduction of the power of the Speaker was the beginning of a new day for the House of Representatives, and, in Champ Clark's opinion, for Clark. It demonstrated his qualities as a leader and split the Republicans beyond mending. He probably overestimated its importance in both instances. The bloody congressional fight did not bring him general recognition as a national Democratic leader, and Theodore Roosevelt, who was about to land in America, was, with the assistance of the old guard, capable of splitting the Republican party without the aid of Democrats.

The Democrats, however, did score impressive gains in the election of 1910. They won their first majority in the House in eighteen years, increased their membership in the Senate and elected governors in states that had been held as safely Republican. Clark's admirers claimed on his behalf major credit. He did not dissent.

In 1911 he was elected Speaker of the House, and thus became the ranking Democratic official in the national government. For a House of Representatives man it was the ultimate goal, and Clark was quoted as saying that he would rather be Speaker than President. But he didn't act as though he meant it. Instead he started out to compile a record for the House that would make him President, and he personally undertook to publicize that record. In an article in the *North American Review* he wrote that the Democratic House had revised the rules, passed a bill to admit New Mexico and Arizona to statehood, another requiring publication of campaign funds before elections, and made starts toward economizing on public expenditures and reducing the tariff. His evaluation tends toward extravagance, and is not without an undertone of self-congratulation.

> The Democratic House has, during the extraordinary session of Congress, made a record so excellent as to surprise its friends and dumfound its enemies. Its superb discipline [who but Champ Clark was the disciplinarian?], its industry . . . its unanimity on all great questions [Champ Clark had established it], seem to be exceedingly pleasing to the masses of our people. For years we had been sneered at as the party of mere negation, as being absolutely without the faculty of constructive statesmanship. The House [with Clark as the master builder] has taken away from the party that great reproach, and in four months has passed more constructive legislation than any House has passed in the same length of time in two decades. . . .

The article was published in September; a few weeks later Clark for President headquarters were opened in St. Louis.

He was sixty-one years old, a tall heavy man. The fierce handlebar mustaches he had worn when he entered Congress were gone; he was clean-shaven. His thin grayish white hair was parted in the middle; his eyes under heavy bushy brows were alert. The general impression was that of a solid homespun politician and he dressed the part: black alpaca suit, with long frock coat with satin lapels, white shirt, gates-ajar collar, a black tie with a large loose knot. A spectator looking at him as he stood at the Speaker's desk was reminded of Henry Clay. Clark would probably have been pleased at the comparison. It was the image of a statesman of the people.

Clark was a homespun statesman of a sort, but not so much as the image he more or less deliberately projected. Twenty years in Congress, half of it spent as his party's leader, had given him experience in public affairs and skill in managing

men. He was widely read and knew a lot about many things—
politics, history, politicians, literature, the Bible, America and
Americans. He had fought monopoly, railroad abuses, government "by court injunction," Cannonism, high protective
tariffs, imperialism, the importation of immigrant contract
labor. He had supported conservation, pure food laws, the regulation of the hours of labor, the direct election of Senators, the
direct primary, the initiative and referendum. It was a good
record. And it was a party record. He was a tried and dependable Democrat; politicians could understand and work with
him. Democratic voters could vote for him without thinking
too much about what they were voting for. Champ Clark and
the donkey in the circle at the top of the column were synony-
mous. All this made him a strong candidate at a time when long
years out of office had left the Democrats with no outstanding
leader save the thrice-defeated, somewhat shopworn—though
still potent—Bryan. Nonetheless, when Clark headquarters
were opened in St. Louis he was not the favorite for the nomination. Woodrow Wilson was the favorite.

Wilson, six years younger than Clark, was born in Staunton,
Virginia. He grew up in the South during the Civil War and
reconstruction. He was educated at Davidson College, Princeton, the University of Virginia law school and, after a brief
fling at the practice of law in Atlanta, Georgia, at Johns Hopkins, where he received a Ph.D. He taught at Bryn Mawr, Wes-
leyan University and Princeton. In 1902, ten years after Champ
Clark was first elected to Congress, he was made president of
Princeton.

As a university president he was able, energetic and controversial. His interest was primarily in the students, his faculty
and education. He established a preceptor system of study, attracted able young scholars to the university and attempted to
change undergraduate social institutions. He was also a productive scholar, highly articulate as both a writer and speaker, so
that he came to be recognized as a conservative Democratic intellectual, opposed to the shallow flamboyant liberalism of

Bryan, who, he wrote in 1907, would aid his party most by being knocked into a cocked hat. Besides Bryan and Clark, Wilson was opposed to high protective tariffs, restrictive practices on the part of labor unions, and government regulation.

In 1906 George Harvey, of *Harper's Weekly* and close to Wall Street and big business, launched a Wilson for President movement. It was premature but in 1910 Harvey got his candidate on the road by convincing New Jersey Democratic boss James Smith, Jr., that it would be smart politics to nominate him for governor. The time was ripe. The New Jersey Democratic organization was in trouble with a progressive reform element within the party, and could not hope to win with a machine candidate. Wilson might stem the revolt and constitute a front behind which the organization could continue to function. Stronger than his party, he might carry a Democratic legislature into office on his coattails—a legislature that would elect Smith to the United States Senate. Beyond these immediate dividends Smith was dreaming a little. Both he and Harvey saw themselves as President makers, manipulating power through their influence with the brilliant and eloquent but politically inexperienced professor.

Wilson *was* politically inexperienced. Moreover, in 1910 he seems to have been even less aware than Champ Clark of the new forces and problems that faced America. But he learned fast. Elected governor, he broke with the New Jersey Democratic machine, refused to support Smith for Senator and, by rallying support and using patronage, took over the state organization. He then pushed through a legislative program as enlightened as any of those enacted by insurgent Republicans in the prairie states. The New Freedom was marching. And although he was new to the practice of politics Wilson was historian enough to know that identification with Wall Street and big business might well be lethal to a Democratic politician in search of a national career. He broke with George Harvey, his original sponsor and the first architect of his political fortunes. Having thrown out Smith and Harvey, he gathered around him a group of political amateurs long on vision and short on knowledge of how to win the support of state and local bosses.

During the summer and fall of 1911, Wilson spoke throughout the country. He was somewhat vague as to program but he talked eloquently and without bombast about government of the people and the evils of special privilege. He was austere; he lacked "folksiness" and warmth; he was still too much the professor—the old-fashioned sort who knew and was not afraid of truth based on values. He was accustomed to instruct and enlighten and savored the advantage of prestige derived from the professorial rostrum. He tended to get his learning and light from books rather than men. He was not skilled in human relations. He would not indulge in reciprocal back scratching and his enemies said he was an ingrate. He discarded selfless supporters as well as selfish ones. And yet he was a leader. Alone too often, too far out in front, but yet a leader. He wrote that a nominating convention wanted for its candidate "a man who will be and who will seem to the country in some sort an embodiment of the character and purpose it wishes its government to have." He believed himself to be that sort of man, and although there is no evidence that the nation at large agreed, Wilson clubs sprang up throughout the country, and if an embittered George Harvey would not permit his name to be printed in his magazine, and Wall Street and political bosses alike distrusted him, it didn't seem to matter much in early 1911. There was no significant opposition. That was before Champ Clark opened headquarters in St. Louis.

> I doan' keer if he *is* a houn',
> You gotta quit kickin' *my* dawg aroun'.

Surely, nothing could have seemed more incongruous to Woodrow Wilson than the intrusion of the "houn' dawg" into democratic electoral decision. The slogan had neither political undertones nor overtones. Nonetheless, William Gibbs McAdoo, who rallied the Wilson forces when his cause was at its lowest ebb, paid tribute to the power of the "houn' dawg" image:

> . . . This strenuous objection to the kicking of hound dogs was shouted, screamed, whispered and catcalled until the air quivered with its echoes. It was silly and meaningless, of course, but if you think it was ineffective you would change your mind if you ever watched a political convention. The Clark men seemed to be comforted by saying it over and over, as the old lady in the story was by the word "Mesopotamia." They shouted it in chorus; they shouted it to strangers who shouted it back. We had nothing in the way of a battle-cry that was equal to the "houn' dawg" in noise.

So perhaps it did mean something to the delegates who shouted it—just as Mesopotamia may have had some meaning to the old lady. Maybe it meant the approaching dawn of glory with Champ Clark in the White House, or maybe it was the symbol of something familiar and comforting as opposed to the Princeton professor with his high-flying ideals and high-sounding phrases. It was as pungent, but less dangerous, than "back to normalcy." Whatever it meant, it was more than convention noise and hysteria. For months before the convention Clark was receiving toy houn' dawgs of every variety, from people everywhere. A visitor found his Washington office adorned with them.

Not that Clark was, himself, leading the chorus. He was busy running the House and claiming credit for everything that was done there. This was his method of campaigning. He was basing his case on his record as a party leader. He envisaged no new freedom, new deal, or new frontier; he was merely a Democrat who had espoused Democratic principles for twenty years, and could lead the Democrats to victory. Since national conventions are largely composed of politicians hungry for party victory with its accruing benefits, this appeal was a strong one.

Clark also appealed for support on the ground that he had established harmony in the Democratic ranks; and there was, in fact, general harmony in the party. To be sure, it had its progressives and its conservatives, but while rival Republican factions were battling to the death Democrats could not always distinguish between progressive friend and conservative foe, or vice versa. Frank Kent, political correspondent and historian, describes the situation:

> There was little talk about concrete ideas or issues in the Democratic pre-convention canvass. . . . It was not so much a matter of ideas as it was a matter of the crowd you trained with and the tag placed on you by the papers. Accused of being a reactionary by *The Baltimore Sun* the late John Walter Smith, then senator from Maryland, exasperatedly exclaimed: "Hell what do they want me to do to qualify as a progressive? I have thrown away the long drawers I have been used to all my life and have taken to wearing these little short running pants. What more can a man do? I don't know what they mean."

Whatever their meaning, tags were attached. Wilson was a progressive; Judson Harmon and Oscar Underwood were conservatives; Clark tried for the middle ground, a liberal, standing on the liberal principles of the Democratic party—the harmony candidate. He submitted his case in campaign literature and through friendly congressmen and ex-congressmen to state, county and city organizations all over the country. It was couched in terms they could understand and be comfortable with. He did not call them to Armageddon or admonish them to prepare for a strange new dawn; he just urged them to get out and support a seasoned Democrat, one who was tested and whom they all knew. Maybe there was sense to the "houn' dawg," after all; maybe Champ Clark was the houn' dog, faithful, familiar and dependable.

Clark got the support of the editor of William Randolph Hearst's New York *American*, who declared that the Missourian was "fearless, aggressive, undaunted and clear." Actually Hearst himself was not as enthusiastic as all that. He did undoubtedly prefer Clark to his avowed rivals, but he had ambitions of his own. He wrote to the editor of *Pearson's Magazine*:

> I have declared a preference for the man [Champ Clark] who
> I believe represents [my policies] best, and I shall labor to secure
> the presidential nomination for him. *If at any time, or for any*
> *reason, he should retire,* and the selection of a candidate to
> represent true Democracy and genuine progressive principles
> should lie between an avowed reactionary and a pretended pro-
> gressive, *I might become a candidate.*

But regardless of his motives Hearst's support was unqualified, and Clark's gratitude was equally unrestrained: "William Randolph Hearst, the greatest newspaper publisher the
world ever saw." "Hearst is an iconoclast with the heart of a
poet and the spirit of a crusader." "No great reform has been
accomplished . . . in a quarter of a century, without the powerful and aggressive aid of his newspapers and magazines."

Hearst's support helped in some areas, notably Illinois and
California, but it hurt in others. Clark's opponents seized upon
it as proof that if elected President he would be controlled by
Hearst. A cartoon of the day shows the White House on a hill
in the distance, with a very crooked path leading up to it. In
the foreground one of the primate Edison-type gramophones
with a megaphone speaker is playing. It is labeled HEARST.
Sitting next to it with ear inclined to hear every word is a bony
old houn' dawg.

Aside from Hearst, the metropolitan press was generally
against Clark, charging that he lacked stature and was little
more than a political hack who in seventeen years had risen
to the Speakership of the House through no merit greater than
that of being re-elected from Pike County, Missouri. Intemperate speeches were recalled—the Cleveland Judas Iscariot
outburst, an attack on civil service reform, the desire to see
British North America under the American flag. His critics said
they proved him irresponsible. It was charged that he was
financed by the liquor interests. The New York *World* said his
nomination would be party suicide.

More troublesome than newspaper opposition was the attitude of William Jennings Bryan. Clark believed that he merited Bryan's support on the grounds of both principle and gratitude. But Bryan was coy. He admitted that Clark was a good man but added that Wilson was too. And if Wilson's conversion to liberalism was so recent as to render it suspect, Clark was too much inclined to compromise. It was the latter complaint that marked the real issue between Clark and Bryan. Clark was for party harmony even at the price of compromise; Bryan saw only black and white and was dedicated to rule or ruin. Those who disagreed with him were not good Democrats, or good men.

The difference over a tariff on wool that arose between them during the pre-convention campaign is illuminating. Bryan wanted free wool. So did Clark, but he was willing to accept a low duty demanded by a majority of the House Democrats. Bryan admonished him: "If free wool is right . . . lead the fight for it . . . the right wins in the end . . . one can better afford to be defeated for the right than to win on the wrong side." But Clark did not see a tariff on wool as an issue between right and wrong. It was Schedule K of the tariff bill, an economic and political problem to be settled as such. He explained his position years later:

> The majority of the House Democrats favored a low tariff. Colonel Bryan did not want it and worked himself into a passion over it. He became offended at me because I would not help him split the party on the infinitesimal difference between a small tariff on wool and no tariff on wool. *As I had gotten the Democrats together for the first time in twenty years . . .* I did not propose to help divide them again and set out on another long spell of wandering in the wilderness.

Actually Bryan was probably motivated as much by ambition as by principle—he had a genius for equating the two—and although he was not a declared candidate, every move he made indicates that he planned to play Clark and Wilson against one another to create a deadlock and turn the convention to him, the proved leader. He was the middle man on a seesaw throwing his weight on the lighter side, keeping both candidates up in the air. In the late winter of 1911 he seemed to favor Clark, but as Clark grew stronger he leaned toward Wilson. Finally he declared both acceptable, and that he would campaign in a given state for the one who had the best chance to win over a conservative. In his own Nebraska he advocated a split delegation. Clark had no choice but to accept this declaration of neutrality but he did not like it, and at the end of the campaign he did not believe in it, suspecting Bryan was after the nomination for himself.

Despite difficulties Clark's campaign flourished, and in May he forged out of the field and into the lead. State after state convention instructed for him and, more gratifying, he defeated Wilson in the recently adopted presidential primaries in Massachusetts, California, Nebraska, Iowa—and in Illinois where his greatest popular triumph brought him 213,483 votes to Wilson's 75,527. When the news reached Washington, Democratic congressmen applauded him as the next President. By May 18, the Portland *Oregonian* reported that Wilson's strength had passed its peak while that of Clark was increasing.

Wilson was not without victories. He won the Texas and New Jersey primaries, and all or a majority of the delegates instructed by Minnesota, Wisconsin and Pennsylvania party conventions. But by June, when results from all primaries and conventions were in, Clark had 436 pledged delegates to Wilson's 248. The remaining 410 were pledged to minor candidates or uncommitted. With a lead over Wilson of almost two hundred delegates and a total primary majority over Wilson of more than 300,000, Clark could justly, although not necessarily truly, claim to be the choice of the people as well as that of the politicians. Wilson, discouraged, consoled himself with the conviction that his weakness lay in his virtue, and pretended that he didn't really care very much anyway.

Although comfortably ahead, Clark was still a long way from the two-thirds necessary to nominate, and none of his opponents were ready to give up. Besides, there was still Bryan.

Clark wrote in his Memoirs that as early as January 8th, at the Jackson Day banquet in Washington: ". . . [Bryan] treated me with scant courtesy, and he and Governor Wilson lathered each other up with such fulsome eulogies, that it was clear that Bryan was for Wilson as his second choice—Bryan, of course, being Bryan's first choice." Clark was prejudiced but his views on the matter were shared by observers who were not. Commenting on Bryan's suspected strategy of deadlocking the convention and grabbing the prize for himself the Republican Columbus (Ohio) *Journal* wrote:

> That two-thirds rule will make it exceedingly difficult to name Clark, Wilson or Harmon; but a groundswell for Bryan is liable at any moment, and the two-thirds rule will be washed out by the rushing of many waters.

The Glens Falls (New York) *Times,* also Republican, agreed:

> . . . Most people, aside from those who do not want to believe it possible, anticipate a deadlock at Baltimore, to be ended by the casting of Mr. Bryan's hat into the ring and a tumult of acclamation like that in the memorable Convention of 1896.

The Montgomery, Alabama, *Advertiser*:

> Mr. Bryan's purpose is clear. He would muddy the waters and snatch the nomination for himself.

Cheyenne, Wyoming, *Tribune*:

> [Bryan] anticipates there will be a deadlock, none of the candidates being able to secure the necessary two-thirds. The "boy orator of the Platte" then will get the floor, make cross and crown speech, and stampede the Convention.

On the eve of the convention Bryan-Clark relations were further worsened by a conflict over the appointment of a temporary chairman. The Clark choice was Ollie James of Kentucky and on this occasion Bryan agreed with him. Wilson was for Judge O'Gorman of New York. The matter came before the National Committee where neither side had enough votes to elect its candidate. The committee compromised on Alton B. Parker, the party's 1904 presidential candidate. Clark accepted the compromise but Bryan, then in Chicago attending the Republican National Convention as a correspondent, protested. He sent letters to all the candidates for the nomination asking them to join him in a fight against Parker. Wilson's reply promised nothing but agreed on the necessity of a progressive as temporary chairman; Clark said that he agreed with the National Committee that the most important aim should be to prevent discord, and urged that everyone unite in promoting harmony. Bryan rejected the plea. He had reasons that seemed to him sufficient. In Chicago he had just witnessed the bolt of the Republican insurgents after the regulars had shoved through the renomination of Taft. The rebels had held a rump meeting and announced the birth of the Progressive party. It was almost certain that the Progressive candidate would be the redoubtable vote getter Theodore Roosevelt. With the Republicans thus split, the Democrats would surely win if they could avoid a suicidal error. In Bryan's opinion to submit to even a suspicion of Wall Street influence would be such an error. It would throw the Democratic progressive vote and the election to Roosevelt. He announced that neither Underwood nor Harmon was acceptable as a presidential candidate, and that Parker, a Cleveland "gold" Democrat, must not be temporary chairman of the convention. To enforce his ultimatum he was prepared to plunge the party into a factional fight.

On Friday afternoon, June 25th, Cardinal Gibbons delivered the invocation and the 1912 Democratic National Convention was under way. "It was one of the most dramatic and thrilling conventions in the history of the party," wrote Frank R. Kent. "The fight for the nomination was a tremendous and bitter one, in which feeling was aroused to fever pitch, and at times the whole gathering seemed on the verge of a riot."

The excitement and the bitterness were not long in coming.

On Wednesday morning the name of Judge Parker for temporary chairman was presented. Bryan, in his role of delegate
from Nebraska, took the floor to protest. The convention
greeted him uproariously—cheers, hisses, applause, curses, all
loud and from the heart. He was an old campaigner, skilled at
arousing emotion—and thriving on it. He stood on the platform, the eye of the tempest, fanning himself with a palm-leaf
fan, until the crowd was still, or at least as still as such a crowd
can be.

Witnesses reported that he made one of the best speeches of
his career. He closed it by nominating Senator Kern of Indiana
for the temporary chairmanship. Kern took Bryan's place on
the platform. He had been Judge Parker's running mate in the
presidential campaign eight years before. He now appealed to
Parker to withdraw. The galleries—pro-Wilson—cheered; delegates applauded or jeered. Parker was silent. So Kern withdrew his own name and nominated Bryan. The battle lines
could not have been more clearly drawn. The vote was taken
in an atmosphere of angry excitement. The result was Parker
576, Bryan 508. Bryan had lost but no one had won. Dissension engulfed the convention.

Wilson delegates had supported Bryan; those of Harmon
and Underwood backed Parker. Clark men divided but their
leaders saw to it that enough of them voted for Parker to insure
his election. Bryan interpreted this as evidence that Clark was
courting Wall Street and Tammany Hall, and although there
was no open break—as a delegate from Nebraska he was instructed to vote for Clark—the tension between the camps increased. Clark managers tried to make peace by offering to support Bryan for permanent chairman of the convention. He
rejected the olive branch. "Those who owned the ship should
furnish the crew," he told them.

But he was not through with the owners of the ship. On
Thursday he led another and more violent mutiny by submit-
ting a resolution to the convention that read:

. . . We hereby declare ourselves opposed to the nomination of any candidate for President who is the representative of or under obligation to J. Pierpont Morgan, Thomas F. Ryan, August Belmont, or any other member of the privilege-hunting and favor-seeking class. . . . That we demand the withdrawal from this convention of any delegate or delegates constituting or representing the above-named interests.

The resolution was in effect a demand that the convention go on record as opposing Harmon and Underwood—both serious if secondary candidates—before their names had even been placed before the delegates. The closing sentence read Thomas Fortune Ryan and August Belmont, duly accredited delegates, out of the convention, and presumably out of the Democratic party. Logically it would also expel Murphy and his whole New York delegation. Bryan withdrew the last sentence as the voting began, but it is doubtful if most of the delegates heard him. The convention was in a worse uproar than it had been on Tuesday. As the roll was called, fist fights broke out all over the place. Bryan wrote:

I do not think there were ever so many people in one hall, wildly excited and swearing at one another without someone being hurt. I heard afterwards of delegates who were loudly expressing the hope that somebody would take me out and hang me. One delegate, whom I afterward aided to a high position, stated that he would give twenty-five thousand dollars to anybody who would kill me.

Bryan waited. He knew what he was doing; he knew with the deadly certitude of the righteous that his cause was just. And though intellectual subtleties might escape him, no one was his superior in rough and tumble battle where black was black and white was white. Nor in his long career did anyone ever question his courage. The roll call was tumultuous. "A state would be called; its chairman would announce its full vote, 'aye.' Then half the delegation would jump to their feet and demand a poll, shaking their fists and shouting in violent language." When it became evident that the resolution would carry, even the New York delegates, attempting to make the whole thing appear ridiculous, switched their votes from no to aye. After that the ayes were virtually unanimous.

When it was over, delegates, especially those who were for Clark, whistled in the dark, pretending that the incident was meaningless, that it was merely another Bryan exhibition, and that it changed nothing. This was not true. Bryan had advertised in newspaper headlines across the nation that the issue before the Democratic National Convention was that of God or Mammon; that it must choose between the people and Wall Street. He had succeeded in killing the slender hopes of Harmon, and probably those of Underwood as well. He had made it dangerous for any candidate to court Boss Murphy. And, although it certainly had not been his intention and he probably did not realize it, he had made his own nomination virtually impossible. Men who cursed him on Thursday were not likely to vote for him later in the week, or the week after. It was his last great political performance, and one of his most fruitful ones. Some observers believed that it determined the convention's eventual nominee—although by embittering the opposing factions it may have postponed the decision.

So William Jennings Bryan made his exit from the stage as a major Democratic leader as he had come upon it—on the wings of passionate oratory that evoked a passionate response. He was not constructive, he didn't stand for very much, he was not so much for virtue as against sin. But he served a purpose. He was the fire that consumes a city so that a new and better one can rise from its ashes.

Not until Thursday night, after almost two days of fierce fighting, did the convention turn to the job of nominating candidates. James Reed of Missouri submitted Clark's name. He praised him as the Lion of Democracy, a veteran of twenty-five years' experience, and by far from subtle inference he attacked Wilson: "Give me no political dilettante who comes into camp when honors are most ripe to pluck. I want no half fledge chanticleer who is only just beginning to acquire a Democratic crow." A demonstration lasting over an hour followed Reed's speech.

Judge John W. Wescott put Woodrow Wilson into nomination. His speech was less flamboyant than Reed's. He spoke of the schoolmaster, the Princeton philosopher. The demonstration that followed lasted longer than Clark's. Harmon, Underwood and favorite sons, including Tom Marshall of Indiana, were also nominated.

By the time all nominating speeches had been made it was seven Friday morning. The convention had been in session all night. But it did not adjourn. The first ballot was taken. Clark got 440½ votes; Wilson, 324; Harmon, 148; Underwood 117½; 56, including one for Bryan, were scattered and two did not vote. It was about as expected and it continued that way through nine roll calls. Then, on the tenth ballot, came the switch of New York's ninety votes from Harmon to Clark and the boisterous Clark demonstration.

Clark got the news in Washington. He was so sure he would win that he told a colleague he would be nominated on the next ballot. He wrote, but did not dispatch, a telegram to the convention accepting the nomination. In Baltimore Wilson's manager, William McCombs, was ready to quit. He telephoned Wilson for permission to release his delegates so they could climb on the bandwagon in time to salvage some influence with the new administration. Wilson consented and was even preparing to send congratulations to his rival when William Gibbs McAdoo, rushing into the breach, made another call from Baltimore and persuaded him to hold fast.

There was justification for McAdoo's action. When the tenth ballot was analyzed the result was not entirely reassuring for Clark. Wilson had weathered the storm with a loss of only two votes; Underwood had held his solid block of Southern delegates; Tom Taggart, Indiana's boss, had kept his delegation in line for Marshall. Clark had picked up only twenty-two votes, in addition to New York's ninety. The convention had not been stampeded.

And the break Clark had so confidently anticipated on the eleventh ballot did not materialize. Instead he lost a few votes while Wilson gained some. This trend, although not decisive, continued throughout the day. Clark did not regain his 556-vote peak. Bryan contributed to the move to stop Clark. On the fourteenth ballot he switched his vote to Wilson, explaining he could not vote for Clark while New York did. At this point, however, the Underwood delegates rather than Bryan probably held the key to the nomination. Had they cast their votes for Clark it would almost certainly have furnished the momentum to carry him over. But they were playing for a deadlock between the leaders and held firm. The roll calls dragged on. When the convention finally adjourned for the day, Harmon was out of the race, Underwood was firm, Wilson was creeping forward and Clark was unable to move. It looked as much like a deadlock as anything else.

Notwithstanding their disappointment, the Clark forces were still confident and still fighting. On Saturday they brought to the convention floor a large banner on which was printed a sentence Bryan had used in praising Clark two years before. They dispatched a telegram to Wilson reminding him that he was on record as favoring nomination by a simple majority; as a man of principle, he should withdraw in favor of Clark. Clark himself rushed to Baltimore. After conferring with Hearst and other supporters, he issued a statement declaring that Bryan's charge that he was compliant toward Wall Street was outrageous and false and demanding proof or retraction. Bryan responded lamely that he had not criticized Clark for doing anything wrong, but because he had failed to act. If this meant anything, it appeared to mean that Clark should refuse the votes of New York delegates, something Bryan himself had never done. The Clark leaders rejected his explanation and openly accused Bryan of trying to grab the nomination for himself.

As the balloting ground on, the drift against Clark continued. When the convention adjourned until Monday he had lost Massachusetts and Kansas, and was down to 463½ votes, almost a hundred below his crest of 556, while Wilson had crawled up to 407½. It appeared that Clark was stopped. He was by no means ready to admit it and angrily declared he would prevent Wilson's nomination if it meant staying in Baltimore all summer.

Meantime the delegates were hearing from the country. In an era before public relation firms had learned to manufacture public opinion in virtually any form or quantity a client is willing to pay for, telegrams were pouring into Baltimore. Telegraph agents estimated the total during the convention at 110,000, and many of them had more than one signature. Never before had a national political convention been so deluged. Most of them were pro-Wilson. This was in part the work of Wilson clubs, but to a much greater degree it was in consequence of the issues raised by Bryan. He himself received over a thousand wires.

The telegrams weakened Clark, especially his claim that the primaries had proved he had greater popular support than Wilson. The convention delegates were seasoned politicians who had already learned that although it cost more in money and work they could name the candidate in primary elections as surely as they could in state conventions. So Clark's primary victories could be attributed to politicians, but the storm of telegrams blowing chiefly from farm market towns all over the country was the voice of rural America raised in protest against Babylon. And Bryan had identified Clark with Babylon.

His inability to move forward, the protest from the grass roots, Wilson's gains, caused restlessness among Clark supporters. On Sunday evening delegates from border states stretching from Delaware to the Mississippi River who had been voting for Clark met and informally agreed to shift to Wilson if it appeared he might be nominated. For the time being it was not a bolt, but it was ominous.

And despite Wilson's warning that he would not feel committed by deals made in his name, his managers made deals. Tom Taggart was promised the Vice-Presidency for Indiana's governor, Thomas Marshall, in exchange for the state's twenty-nine votes; Underwood leaders were promised wholesale Underwood support if they would stand firm against Clark, in case Wilson ultimately failed to reach the necessary two-thirds.

There was not much Clark could do. Suggestions of a Clark-Underwood ticket were made, but Underwood did not want to be Vice-President and his managers preferred their arrangement with the Wilson leaders; Taggart had decided which way the cat was going to jump and had jumped ahead of it; there was no other substantial block of unattached votes.

On the second ballot cast on Monday morning Taggart switched Indiana's votes from Marshall to Wilson. Iowa, Vermont, Wyoming and Michigan deserted Clark for his rival. On the thirtieth ballot the count was Wilson, 460; Clark, 455.

At Sea Girt, New Jersey, where Wilson was sitting out the convention, newspaper reporters asked him for a statement. He was too canny to crow. "You might say that Governor Wilson received the news that Champ Clark had dropped to second place in a riot of silence," he told them.

In Baltimore, Clark was being told by his convention managers that Bryan had made his selection impossible, and was now maneuvering to snatch the prize from Wilson. To prevent this catastrophe Clark was urged to consent to the release of his delegates at the expedient moment. He consented but continued to hope. On Tuesday he suggested that he himself visit the convention in an effort to turn the ebbing tide. His managers dissuaded him, but he remained in Baltimore.

By Monday night Clark was out but Wilson was not yet in. He had been climbing steadily but to reach the necessary two-thirds vote he needed either wholesale Clark votes or those of Underwood. Otherwise the stalemate foreseen by pre-convention prophets might develop. Something was needed to break the jam. Wilson's manager, McCombs, visited Roger Sullivan, chairman of the Illinois delegation.

Roger Sullivan was not in the great tradition of American city bosses. He was not well known nor long remembered. But he had his hour. In 1912 he was fighting for control of the Cook County (Chicago) organization and was anxious for federal patronage. His rival in Chicago was allied with Hearst, and such was Hearst's influence with Clark that Clark had ignored Sullivan when he rushed to Baltimore to confer with his supporters. As a consequence Roger, who in compliance with the Illinois primary verdict had been casting the state's votes for Clark, was in a receptive mood when he greeted McCombs. "Sit steady, boy," he is reported to have said when Wilson's manager cried out in anguish that he must have Illinois votes. Such are the great moments of history.

On the first ballot taken on Tuesday, the forty-third of the convention, Sullivan cast Illinois' fifty-eight votes for Wilson. This was by no means enough for the nomination, but as Taggart's delivery of Indiana had done before, it dynamited the log jam—this time decisively. Virginia and West Virginia followed Illinois on the forty-third roll call, others followed on the forty-fourth, and after the forty-fifth Underwood's name was withdrawn. Senator Stone then formally released Clark delegates, and on the forty-sixth ballot Woodrow Wilson was nominated.

Clark was too disappointed to accept defeat gracefully. His bitterness boiled over in a public statement in which he declared: "I lost the nomination solely through the vile and malicious slanders of Colonel William Jennings Bryan, of Nebraska." Years later, after the dust of battle had settled, he repeated and amplified the charge.

> Bryan was dishonest in his contention that he changed his vote because New York was voting for me. The principal reason he changed his vote, thereby flagrantly violating his instructions and thereby proving that all his prating about "the people's

rule" was hypocrisy, was that he wanted to create a deadlock and grab off the nomination for himself. He had no more idea of nominating Governor Wilson for President than he had of nominating him as Ahkoond of Swat.

Nevertheless Clark campaigned for Wilson and Marshall. After the election he returned to the House, where as Speaker he formally led the Democrats in the enactment of the Wilsonian legislative program. He rebelled against the Selective Service Act, but joined the rest of the Congress in supporting the President in the war. In his final verdict on Woodrow Wilson he does not commit himself: ". . . The consensus of world opinion is that he has been, and is, a great President."

The convention nominated the best man. Woodrow Wilson lacked Champ Clark's easy gift of getting along with people, of accommodation, of leading only as far as others were willing to follow. He was intellectually arrogant. He quarreled with and discarded devoted friends and refused to compromise with opponents. He failed in his greatest cause, the League of Nations. Yet he was, as Clark admitted the world held him to be, a great President—the greatest America had had since Lincoln, and his vision, though burdened with the curse of Cassandra's, was greater than Lincoln's.

Champ Clark was not a great man. If Wilson lacked the common touch, Clark lacked vision. He was America's average man, a fellow "just like you and me." He wanted what the average man in a small town in Kentucky or Kansas or Missouri wanted. He saw as far as they saw and not much further. He dressed and spoke like such a man's image of a politician. He didn't frighten people with unfamiliar ideas, or ask more of them than they could casually give. He distrusted monopoly and the cross of gold, but he respected material success. He was proud that he had lunched with "Sockless" Jerry Simpson and dined with Henry George, but he did not join the Populists or advocate the single tax. His total record is more liberal than Wilson's,

before 1911, but in all his years in Congress he was not identified with a single great cause.

He was old-fashioned. He remembered that as a boy he had
heard the guns of the Civil War. He was of a fading age—the
chautauqua circuit, flowery oratory, the frock coat with velvet
lapels. He belonged in the company of Garfield, Sherman, Harrison, Cleveland, and he was their equal in stature. With Woodrow Wilson and Theodore Roosevelt he was out of his class. He
was a House of Representatives man who knew the business of
the House; he was not a leader into the dawn of a new society.

The convention also nominated the right man. Not because
it recognized Wilson's greatness—there is no evidence that this
or any other American national party convention ever recognized greatness in a first-term candidate—but because after a
long, hot, angry week Wilson emerged as the candidate most
likely to succeed. With the Republicans split, the Democrats
were *almost* sure they would win, but not *completely* sure, and
they could not afford to take a chance. They needed and took
their strongest candidate.

Bryan may have prevented Clark's nomination. Clark
thought so; Frank Kent thought so; Carter Glass and Newton
D. Baker, Wilson men, thought so. Wilson himself must have
thought so when he appointed Bryan, whom he neither respected nor liked, and who had no qualifications for the job, as
Secretary of State. But if Bryan stopped Clark he did not nominate Wilson. He bolted his delegation on the fourteenth ballot,
and suggested that others might wish to join him. Few did. Balloting continued for over thirty more roll calls before Wilson
was nominated.

Bryan believed and tried to convince others that Clark beat
himself by accepting New York's support. This is highly improbable. The delegates did vote for the anti-Wall Street resolution, but they were practical politicians who would not reject
a man for accepting all the votes that came his way. (When New
York voted for Wilson on the last roll call no Wilson leader protested.) Clark needed New York in order to reach the majority

that he and his managers believed would carry him the rest of the way to the nomination. Events proved them wrong, but history was on their side.

It has been suggested that Wilson was nominated by the party bosses. Of course he was. Every candidate ever nominated by a major party has been nominated by that party's bosses. National conventions are composed of party bosses, big bosses and little bosses. More specifically it has been argued that Taggart on Monday and Sullivan on Tuesday furnished the momentum Wilson so sorely needed, and that the Underwood managers (bosses) held the balance of power during most of the roll calls, and finally that the Clark leaders controlled a hard core of votes with which they might have been able to stop Wilson if they were determined to do so. All this may be true, but the question *why* remains. Why did they, in the end, take Wilson? Not because of his greatness, which was not recognized, but because of his availability. His record as governor made him acceptable to party liberals; his beliefs, as expressed in his writings and public addresses, reassured conservatives. He was a segregationist on racial issues, he opposed woman's suffrage, he believed in states' rights in regard to such matters as prohibition. So he faced both ways, and his barnstorming throughout the country in quest of the nomination had proved him able to meet Theodore Roosevelt on the hustings.

In the end, then, the bosses took the man they thought most likely to win. Events proved them right. Taft and Roosevelt split the Republican vote while Wilson held most of the Democrats and won by a comfortable popular plurality and a large electoral college majority. The party convention system had worked. It had nominated the best and right man.

There is a postscript. In 1936 the Democratic National Convention repealed the two-thirds rule and substituted one providing for the nomination by a simple majority. The leader of the successful fight for repeal was Senator Bennett Clark of Missouri. Had this occurred twenty-four years earlier his father probably would have been President of the United States.

The Republicans

1920

THE Republicans were complacent in 1920. They felt certain that in the November election they would recapture the Presidency. Woodrow Wilson had defeated them in 1912 and again in 1916, but statistically his feat was not discouraging. Basically the electorate was still Republican as it had been since the Civil War. Since 1860 only two Democrats, Grover Cleveland and Woodrow Wilson, had won the Presidency. The country could be counted upon to return to the pattern of the past. But that was not all. There were signs that the American people were tired of idealism and calls for sacrifice, that they were ready to forego, for a while, wrestling with the problems of the twentieth century. They wanted to relax. Moreover, Wilson, stricken by illness, was unable to lead his party, but still pre-empted leadership. The Democrats were on a ship with a damaged rudder.

The Republicans were as confident as they were complacent

when they gathered for their national convention. Any man would be the right man so there was no need to find the best man. That is the key to understanding what happened. It is the only time since ante-bellum days that a party deliberately nominated a candidate for his weakness rather than his strength. It was not necessary. Good men were available.

There was Governor Frank Lowden of Illinois. Lowden presented himself as a conservative acceptable to liberals. Like Janus he looked both ways and appeared capable of drawing support from both directions. He had other advantages. He had served in Congress and as governor of Illinois. Theodore Roosevelt had recognized him as one who could help pull the wings of the party together. In the pre-convention campaign while his rivals attacked one another he remained aloof. He was the ideal compromise candidate—or so it appeared.

But there was also Senator Warren Harding, who was beginning to dream of being more than Ohio's favorite son. Harding looked more like a President than any chief executive since George Washington. He was affable; he wistfully if ineffectually wanted to do the right thing. He was a member of the Senate old guard with a place in the rear rank. He was determinedly mediocre. Few men so content to follow have been thrust into a position of leadership. He was badly beaten in every primary he entered except that of his own Ohio. But he was around, any man was the right man, and Harry Daugherty, his manager, was "making sweet music for Harding," in hopeful anticipation of the moment when party bosses met in a smoke-filled room to pick a President of the United States.

Lowden vs. Harding

He is the leading candidate this year because the turn of the
calendar brings the campaign at a time when old situations are
still controlling and newer alignments are not quite formed.
The logic of Lowden is excellent on the premise that the public
mood is a true reflection of what the next President must face.
—WALTER LIPPMANN, The Logic of Lowden

HORATIO ALGER could have used Frank O. Lowden as the
hero of one of his American-boy success stories, and Frederick
Jackson Turner could have pointed to him as the embodiment
of his scholarly and romantic thesis concerning the influence of
the frontier on American history and the American character. Of course, bromides to the contrary, fact more often than
not lags behind fiction and Alger would have had to forego
the ultimate title, *From Smithy to White House,* for something
a little more modest. *From Sunrise to Sinnissippi* probably
wouldn't have occurred to Alger, but *From Prairie Schooner to
Pullman* might have, and it would have done quite well.

Lowden was born on January 26, 1861, on a farm near Sunrise, Minnesota, where his father had a blacksmith shop. Lo-
renzo Lowden helped build a schoolhouse in Sunrise so that his
children might have a proper education, and according to a
campaign biography written in 1920, young Frank trudged the
two miles from farm to school "carrying a book close to his face"
and interrupting his studies only long enough to "trounce the
boys who distracted his attention from his reading."

His family moved to Iowa when he was only seven. It must
have been an exciting journey for the boy. Barefoot, of course,

and clad in overalls or jeans, he walked as far as St. Paul behind a prairie schooner drawn by oxen. At St. Paul, the family took a steamboat to Dubuque, Iowa, and went from there overland to Point Pleasant in Hardin County where they built a cabin home and turned to farming. Thus it was all there: village smithy, ox-drawn prairie schooner, diligent barefoot boy, cabin home. Actually it was the story of thousands of American boys of the period, but few of them aspired to the White House and only a handful came within clutching distance of the dream.

At Point Pleasant, Frank helped on the farm and continued to go to school. When he was fifteen years old he changed his status from pupil to teacher in order to earn enough money to go to college. It took five years but he entered the University of Iowa at the age of twenty and graduated as valedictorian of his class. From Iowa he went to Chicago and a job as a law clerk at eight dollars a week. He enrolled at Union College of Law (later Northwestern University). He finished the two-year law course in a year, winning first prizes in oratory and scholarship, and again graduated as valedictorian. He was admitted to the bar in 1887. He was twenty-six years old.

He was so successful in his law practice that he soon gained not only professional but also social recognition. When he met Florence Pullman, daughter of the railroad car magnate, he was well established as a corporation lawyer fully able to care for a wife and family. He could not be accused of being a fortune hunter, but when he married Miss Pullman in 1896 it did ally him with one of America's great fortunes. This had many advantages but identification with the Pullman fortune hurt him politically. This may account for the barefoot boy theme in his campaign literature.

Frank Lowden became one of Chicago's leading corporation lawyers—he helped organize the National Biscuit and American Radiator companies—and his political career led him almost to the White House, but unlike most of the boys of his time who went from the farm to the city to seek their fortunes, he remained devoted to the country and farming. At one time or another he or his wife owned a plantation in Arkansas, land in Michigan and Idaho, and a ranch in Texas. After 1904 their home was a farm on the beautiful Rock River in northern Illinois. They named the estate Sinnissippi and Lowden was sometimes called—and liked it—the Squire of Sinnissippi. However, his life there was more like that of a British nobleman than a mere country squire. Nor was this eccentric. At the turn of the century many wealthy Americans were aping and even marrying into the English nobility.

Sinnissippi was a great estate—a show place known for miles around in a region where the Rock River traverses a picturesque valley through wooded bluffs and verdant farmlands near Oregon, the seat of Ogle County. On certain days each week, the entrance gates of Sinnissippi were thrown open to visitors of the countryside. They approached the mansion along tawny graveled drives. In every direction there were attractive vistas of gardens, green fields, and forest; there were oaks, towering elms, nut trees, evergreens and well-landscaped shrubbery. The cluster of gleaming white farm buildings was a marvel of neatness and opulence. In the horse barn were luxurious box stalls and a room filled with polished harness; nearby, a carriage shed housed sparkling vehicles. The dairy barn, almost antiseptically clean, was equipped with electric lights and the latest in milking apparatus. Beyond, the land sloped downward to the muddy brown river. Acquired progressively by purchase through the years, Sinnissippi stretched out over four thousand acres after World War I. Within its white-wooden and wire fences it enclosed primitive wilderness land (part of which was later a gift to the Boy Scouts as Camp Lowden) known locally as "Lost Nation," an area that extended for miles along the left bank of Rock River. It sheltered deer, foxes, raccoons, and other wildlife. Then too, there was the large planting of half a million conifers which reflected Lowden's interest in forestry. The light soil of the arable fields was planted with new strains of crops and constantly fertilized. The pastures and meadowland, the orchards and vegetable gardens served well the Sinnissippi community of seventy-five or so people.

The large Tudor brick house at Sinnissippi had twenty rooms including a luxurious walnut-paneled library containing several thousand carefully catalogued volumes. Lowden's taste in literature was catholic, embracing Walter Scott, Thackeray, the British romantics, history, biography and treatises on scientific agriculture. He was especially interested in Lincoln and early Illinois history. Besides Lincoln, Alexander Hamilton was his American hero. Apparently he found no incongruity in enshrining Lincoln and Hamilton together. Maybe there was none. Perhaps he admired Lincoln for what he was and Hamilton for the principles he advocated.

The master and mistress of Sinnissippi did not neglect the surrounding countryside. Lowden led in the promotion of good roads in Ogle County and joined his neighbors in shoveling rocks on a community road project. He supported the farmers' institute, paid for premiums to be awarded farm boys and girls for their stock and crop exhibits at fairs, and sent neighboring young people to the University of Illinois for short courses in agriculture. Mrs. Lowden developed a ten-acre tract where underprivileged children could come for a summer vacation, or to recuperate from illness. So life at Sinnissippi was full, useful and gracious, and, in addition, its lord was proud of the fact that the farm was a going concern that paid its way.

Lowden first became active in politics in 1896 when he campaigned for William McKinley. After his election, McKinley sought to appoint him Assistant Postmaster General. He was unwilling to abandon his law practice and rejected the offer, but he served as a delegate to the 1900 Republican National Convention and again stumped for McKinley. In 1903 he made his first bid for elective office, presenting himself to the Republican state convention as a candidate for the party's nomination for governor. This precipitated one of Illinois' most famous political fights. After leading for the greater part of the time through seventy-eight ballots Lowden lost to Charles S. Deneen on the seventy-ninth. He accepted defeat without rancor and campaigned for Deneen. In 1904 he was appointed Republican National Committeeman for Illinois, a position he held until 1912.

Two years after moving to Ogle County he was elected to Congress. Given an interest in politics, this was in character. It followed the Hamiltonian tradition of government by men of wealth and education, and the older English one of the obligation of the governing class. Moreover the prize was within easy reach. The thirteenth Illinois congressional district was easy to satisfy, providing the candidate was a Republican and conservative. The squire of Sinnissippi qualified on both counts. He was twice re-elected and served in Congress until 1912. As a rule five years is too short a time to make an impression in the United States House of Representatives, and Lowden made none of consequence. He supported the Republican administrations' programs which in general followed the line of Theodore Roosevelt's eclectic progressivism. This was true in Taft's term as well as Roosevelt's despite Taft's popular reputation as a reactionary. Although a member of the Foreign Affairs Committee, Lowden apparently had little interest in it, and was not particularly well informed on world politics. He was a legitimate son of the Midwest, breeding grounds of isolationism.

He declined to run for Congress for a third full term, giving health as a reason. But in good health or bad he could not stay out of politics, and after 1904, although he retained corporation directorates and kept a knowing eye on the management of his land, his career was politics. For a quarter of a century he was an almost perennial delegate to the Republican National Conventions; for years he was Republican National Committeeman for Illinois; he ran for Congress three times and for governor twice. He spared no effort to win the presidential nomination in 1920, and was not without hope for it in 1928. He was tenacious rather than pugnacious; he accepted defeat quietly. But having once resolved upon a public career, he did not put aside ambition for over twenty-five years, and behind the façade of the wealthy squire who held himself ready if called upon to devote himself to public service was the talented and ambitious boy and young man who had won all the prizes and scholarships at two universities and risen to position and wealth before he was forty. He coveted political power and public office, and he always went for the top. In politics that was the Presidency of the United States.

In 1912, the year he declined to run for Congress, Lowden was again a delegate to the Republican National Convention. He stuck with Taft and the old guard throughout the fight that culminated in the bolt of the insurgents and the Roosevelt Bull Moose ticket. Eight years later when the old guard was again tight in the saddle of party control, he was not tainted with treason. In 1916 he again ran for governor of Illinois. This time he won the Republican nomination and beat his Democratic opponent by 150,000 votes. Theodore Roosevelt—who had put aside his hatred for the old guard to concentrate on hating Wilson—wired congratulations. "We want leadership! What I most desire is that you shall help bring the Republicans far enough forward to enable us to hold the Progressives far enough back to keep a substantial alignment." This was, in fact, a description of Lowden's own aim. Both Republicans and Democrats had supported him in the recent election, and his policy was to turn the alliance into a fusion of the two. Although basically conservative he recognized the forces that were transforming society, and the need of new policies, even if based on old principles, to meet new problems.

When Lowden took office in January, 1917, an observer wrote: "He will challenge the interest of the entire nation." This did not come to pass. Lowden lacked the color to attract popular attention. Nonetheless his achievements were substantial. His most lasting and valuable contribution as governor was the reorganization of the state government. When he took office there were one hundred and twenty-five state agencies and bureaus. These were centralized into nine departments. The twenty-five-man Board of Equalization was replaced by a three-man tax commission. A new budget system was established. For a generation students of state government were to speak of the "Illinois plan" as a model. Lowden could also point with pride to his financial administration. The state tax rate fell; cash in the treasury rose from $500 in 1917 to $13,000,000 in 1919. This may not have been entirely due to the governor, but the Nonpartisan Legislative Voter's League of Illinois said that he had done much to create an atmosphere of efficiency in Illinois.

Lowden, however, was not among those who considered business efficiency the panacea for all political and government problems. He supported blue-sky laws for the protection of the public against stock promoters, an act to permit dairymen and farmers to enter into collective marketing agreements, and for the development of vocational education.

Although he was a multimillionaire, a corporation lawyer, and identified with a name hated by labor since the notorious Pullman strike, Lowden achieved satisfactory relations with labor. He was neither pro-labor nor a labor baiter. The president of the Illinois Federation of Labor wrote: "He has not always given us what we wanted, but he has always given us a hearing and said what he would do and what he would not do. We could always find out where he was."

Naturally he did not neglect business. Aside from governmental reorganization and tax reduction, he supported the development of water and road use, and plans were completed for the last link of the Lake to Gulf waterway. He also pleased the business community by denouncing socialists as obstructors of government and bolshevists as destroyers of the home and the church. When Mayor Thompson of Chicago refused to act, he sent state troops to Chicago to prevent a meeting of the People's Council of America for Democracy, a group which he regarded as pro-German.

On the eve of the 1920 National Republican Convention, and

as his term as governor was drawing to a close, Walter Lippmann, weighing him as a presidential candidate, summed up his political career:

> His political associations from the Republican Convention of 1900 through the gubernatorial contest of 1904 when he was defeated for the nomination, through three terms in Congress, through the convention of 1912, to his election as Governor in 1916 is [*sic,* are] without evidence of independence of the dark forces of American politics. Lowden went to the top through the usual channels, a rich man and a favored man accepting the standards of his time.
>
> The change came after his election as Governor. Lowden braced up. Lowden reformed. Lowden made himself one of the very best state governors in America. Again and again I was told in Chicago by friends and opponents that they had expected nothing and that he had done extremely well.

When Frank Lowden entered the race for the Presidency he was fifty-nine years old, a handsome man, stocky and of medium height. His hair was iron gray, his eyes blue, his mouth broad, firm, forceful, and, said some, stubborn. He was neat and well groomed. One of his favorite photographic poses was to be attired in riding breeches, riding coat and boots, mounted on one of his blooded Arabian horses. This was the image of the country squire; it was not the Frank Lowden seen by the correspondents who came to Springfield in 1920 to interview the presidential aspirant. They saw him as a successful businessman and executive. One correspondent wrote that Lowden "looks far more like a business executive than a politician." The theme recurs over and over again in their reports. This is probably the impression that he wanted to make but it is misleading. Although he sat on company directorates he was not primarily a businessman, and while he was an able corporation lawyer there were a number in Chicago alone as good or better. But as governor he had few equals. And the art of governing a state is that of politics—not business. Moreover, his ambition was for political rather than business eminence. He withdrew from his law practice when he moved to Sinnissippi, but he remained in politics for many years.

Nor did he disdain the lesser arts of politics. He was "a good-natured gentleman," a good "mixer" who used his natural warmth to win political support, and although he lacked the master politician's gift of moving people en masse, he won the liking of most with whom he came into personal contact.

Naturally he did not offer himself to the party as merely a handsome man possessed of a pleasing personality. In early 1920 only Harry Daugherty believed these qualities sufficient to entitle a man to the Presidency of the United States. Lowden had a record, a philosophy of government and, in broad terms, a program.

The record had been made as governor and he was willing to stand on it. It emphasized the business-in-government theme. The country was troubled by high taxes, the cost of living and a growing bureaucracy. Although he repudiated claims to a panacea, Lowden offered what he seemed to believe was one. In a speech he declared, "We're hearing strong preachments about profiteering and extravagance. Yet it is hardly dawning on the public mind that we may be paying excessively for government as well as for sugar, meat or fuel." In an interview he went into greater detail. ". . . There are other problems before us. One is to reduce the high cost of living. Now you cannot do that until you reduce the high cost of government. . . . Why not apply modern business principles to governmental methods?" This was to be the theme of the 1920 Republican platform and campaign, but Lowden was not to be its chief expositor.

In 1920 America was being swept by its first great Red scare. Labor disorders—a part of the general reaction to the relaxation of wartime disciplines—were identified by conservatives as "un-American radicalism." On these issues Lowden was uncompromising. He told a journalist:

"Present conditions in America bring two elemental questions to the fore.

"The first is shall we have law and order?

"The second is shall we have one hundred percent Americanism?

"These questions are intimately related. All good Americans should instantly resist every sign of disloyalty and disorder."

On foreign policy Lowden's views were restricted by his own provincialism and the Republican party record. The war challenged the United States to assume world leadership. Woodrow Wilson had accepted the challenge unreservedly—and, unfortunately, in a political sense unilaterally—but Senate isolationist and old guard found common ground in rejecting the League Covenant unless reservations unacceptable to Wilson were attached. Lowden defended the party record. "Without [the reservations] the League would have become a superstate. It would have overawed and might have overcome the American Republic." But he was not a bitter end isolationist. He joined those who occupied the party center in promising either the League of Nations with reservations or something "better" —noble in phrase if flatulent in content. "When the Republican party is in power," he said, "we shall, I hope, proceed to establish this machinery for adjusting international differences. The Republican party will, I trust, have the wisdom and courage to take up the great work of the Hague Conferences and carry on that work until the wars of the future shall be reduced to a minimum." Here, in addition to taking refuge in more or less glittering generalities, there is a note of uncertainty. "He hopes"; "he trusts." It is not the same voice that rings with such confidence when speaking of reorganizing the federal government on a basis of economy and efficiency.

Given the party orientation and the mood of the nation, Lowden's advantages as a Republican presidential aspirant were substantial. He understood business, he understood government, and although never a master politician he understood politics. He had proved on the hustings that he could get votes and win elections. His record in Congress was one of party regularity during the administrations of both Taft and Roosevelt.

He had not bolted the party in 1912, but Roosevelt had wished him well in 1916 when he was elected governor of Illinois, where he had had the support of both old guard and Progressives. Walter Lippmann summed it up:

> There is a logic to Lowden, once you grant the premises. He comes from the middle of the country, he stands in the middle of the road, in the middle of the party about midway between Wood of New Hampshire and Johnson of California. He has risen from a farm to an estate, from obscurity to moderate fame, perhaps not quite the darling of the gods but surely one of their favorite sons. . . .
>
> The people are tired, tired of noise, tired of politics, tired of inconvenience, tired of greatness, and longing for a place where the world is quiet and where all trouble seems dead leaves, and spent waves riot in doubtful dreams of dreams. . . .
>
> Lowden is the noiseless candidate in this campaign. I have watched his appeal to the voters. He tells them that he will talk only of prosaic things and he does. He assures them that he will not bother them much and he will not.

Lippmann's perception of the mood of the people was extraordinarily keen, and his analysis of Lowden as the candidate most appealing to a people in such a mood is faultless. But he miscalculated either the identity or the quality of those who were, in the end, to choose the candidate. The American people were asking for, and perhaps they needed, a mild sedative; they got knockout drops, which they swallowed meekly and slumbered through living dreams of gold and irresponsibility until they awakened almost ten years later with a well-nigh lethal hangover.

But no matter how well Lowden might fill the role of right man, the race for the nomination, especially after Theodore Roosevelt's death in 1919, was wide open, and there were rivals. The most formidable of these were General Leonard Wood and Senator Hiram Johnson.

Wood won the most votes in both primaries and state conventions, and led in the recently introduced public opinion polls. His varied and colorful career was the American success epic written in large letters. He was assistant surgeon in the command that hunted down the Apache chief Geronimo in the Southwest; he was personal physician to President McKinley; he was a colonel of Theodore Roosevelt's Rough Riders; he was military governor of Santiago, governor of Cuba and of Moro Province in the Philippines. From 1910 to 1914 he was Chief of Staff of the United States Army. He was one of the first to advocate military preparedness after the outbreak of war in Europe in 1914, and established the officers' training program at Plattsburg. When the United States entered the war he was anxious to be sent to Europe, but President Wilson kept him at home. In the eyes of anti-Wilson Republicans this made him a martyr and led a Wyoming rancher to say, "All General Wood represents is a grouch."

He did represent a grouch, and probably got some support from men who wanted above all else to spite Wilson, but he also represented things that were more important. He was a success. His record as an administrator in the Philippines was good. World War I produced no military hero who was to rise to the Presidency by virtue of his war record, but Wood could pose as a man who might have been such a hero, but for a spiteful President.

Wood's claim to Roosevelt's mantle was about half valid. He was the legitimate heir to that Roosevelt who had labeled as muckrakers the journalists who early in the century were exposing corruption in business and politics; he was the heir of the Roosevelt who after 1912 was more intent on beating Wilson than on social reform; he was a personal friend of Roosevelt and was heir to some of his mannerisms; Roosevelt had declared him presidential timber. But all the efforts of his managers could not make him heir to Roosevelt's popularity with the American people. As a matter of fact, he was not very well known to the American electorate early in 1920. His accomplishments had not been in America, or dependent upon popular approval. He had not been an American politician, but a proconsul in Cuba and the Philippines. Draining swamps in Cuba, pacifying Moros in the Philippines, was good for Cubans and maybe for Moros; it didn't excite many American voters.

Hiram Johnson, a native of California, had had by 1920 a long and successful political career. It had included two terms as governor of California, one in the United States Senate and a place as vice-presidential candidate on the Progressive ticket with Roosevelt. As a "reform" candidate he could capitalize on what was left of the insurgent spirit. But this was also a source of weakness. He represented virtue and in 1920 most Americans were weary of virtue, and looked forward to a spasm of indulgence and even a little vice.

On foreign policy, unlike Lowden and Wood, Johnson did not straddle. He was an irreconcilable isolationist. He hated the Japanese, disliked the British and was against the League of Nations with or without reservations. This attracted support as isolationism was increasing, but it was still minority support even among Republicans. Nonetheless, he could not be ignored. He was a seasoned campaigner who carried his fight directly to the people. He had greater political appeal and more political intuition than either of his rivals. It was improbable that he would win the nomination, but he might well hold the balance of power.

There were also minor candidates. Herbert Hoover, a successful mining engineer with a brilliant record as head of the United States relief campaign for Belgium during the war, was talked about and highly praised by the press. Early in 1920 the New York *World* printed a two-and-a-half-column editorial endorsing him for the Presidency, and the Grand Rapids *Herald* cried: "May his specter penetrate to the darkest corners of the closets where kitchen cabinets plot destiny." His boom, however, was mostly in the newspapers. He was not seriously considered by many local or national politicians. In 1920 he was more a world than a national figure, and he didn't seem quite sure which party he belonged to. He entered both Republican and Democratic primaries and on the whole did better with the Democrats. Johnson thrashed him soundly in California. His political sun was rising, but in 1920 it was still a false dawn, and if his candidacy had any significance at all it was as an indication of the inability of any other candidate to set a pace that would discourage outsiders. Thus the Baltimore *Sun* called Hoover the "Great Neutral," and predicted that both parties would engage in a race to capture him. They didn't, but even such a suggestion from a responsible source indicated a situation in which almost anything might happen.

It was this situation which was the basis of the candidacy of Senator Warren Harding of Ohio. Harry Daugherty, his manager (who later complacently accepted credit for prescience and skill in political legerdemain that he did not in fact possess), set up headquarters in two rooms of a Washington hotel and hoped for a deadlock, a dispensation from heaven for his candidate's shortcomings, and the patronage of politicians who might be looking for a weak President. Daugherty was not an honest man but he had moments of candor.

"I won't try to fool you," he told a reporter. "You can see what we've got here, it's only a shoestring. I'll tell you in confidence what's in my mind. All I'm doing is getting in touch with the leaders and delegates who are for Wood and Lowden, being friendly with them. When the convention comes, those two armies will battle each other to a standstill. When both realize that they can't win, when they're tired and hot and sweaty and discouraged both the armies will remember me and this little headquarters. They'll be like soldiers after a battle, who recall a shady spring along a country road where they got a drink as they marched to the front. When they remember me that way maybe both sides will turn to Harding—I don't know—it's just a chance."

It was just a chance, but it was more realistic than the Baltimore *Sun*'s wishful dream that a major political party with almost certain victory ahead would turn to the Great Neutral.

Warren Harding was a successful journalist and publisher —the only representative of the press to be elected President of the United States. He was at one time or another printer's devil, typesetter, pressman, job printer, advertising man, reporter, circulation manager, business manager, editor, publisher. The Marion, Ohio, *Star* prospered under his direction, and he was proud that he had never had a strike.

His ascent of the political ladder was rung by rung: two terms in the Ohio state legislature, lieutenant governor, party nominee for governor, a race which he lost. In 1914, guided by Harry Daugherty, he ran for and was elected to the United States Senate. He was always "regular." He presented Taft's name to the 1912 Republican National Convention, and attacked Roosevelt in the subsequent campaign. But after 1916 when Roosevelt had returned to the fold, he sang his praises: "If Theodore Roosevelt had been President, the *Lusitania* would never have been sunk and we should today be living under the guarantees of peace."

Paradoxically his chances for the nomination lay in his weakness. For men who wanted a President who would at worst refrain from any effort to interfere with them, he was made to order. There were such men, and although they could not know in 1920 how really weak Harding was, they recognized that he suited their purposes and they made capital of their opportunity. Mark Sullivan relates a revealing incident.

One night at a card game in the home of ex-Senator Jonathan Bourne of Oregon, a group of Senators with Harding were awaiting latecomers when Harding "fell into a doze, his head resting on the back of the chair." Bourne asked: "Do you really intend to try to put that man in the White House?" One of the others in an accusing manner replied: "Anyhow, you could talk to him, he would 'go along.' "

Harding himself made a virtue of his belief in accommodation. He said, "Believing as I do in political parties and government through political parties, I had much rather that the party to which I belong should, in its conferences, make a declaration, than to assume a leadership or take an individual position on a question." This is a defensible position for a backbench legislator, but he was a candidate for the Presidency, an office that under the American system of government requires leadership.

Daugherty entered Harding in a few primaries but this was a mere formality designed to lift him out of the favorite-son category. Harding's only chance was a deadlock leading to a "smoke-filled room." Daugherty knew it.

By 1920 the nature of the pre-convention presidential campaign had changed radically. The old tradition requiring hopefuls to assume an attitude of aloofness while they waited for the office to seek them had passed into history. It was given the death blow by the introduction of the presidential primary. By 1920 sixteen states had adopted it, and a major candidate for nomination had to meet its challenge by filing and campaigning in some of them, or suffer certain disadvantages. Among these the loss of delegates was not necessarily the greatest. In some of the primary states the party conventions still chose the delegates to the national convention, and they were not bound by the result of the popular vote. In others where the delegates were elected they were not usually bound for more than a roll call or two. As a result primary victory was of uncertain value, and it was not until 1952 that a case could be made that a major party candidate was nominated because of his primary showing. On the contrary, the record shows that in cases where there was a real contest the candidate who received the most votes in the primaries was defeated more often than not.

This was not because delegates were so blind that they spurned a popular candidate. It was because the mechanism of the presidential primary—if not the theory as well—was at fault. It was not a demonstrably true test of strength. Candidates carefully selected which of the sixteen states they wanted to enter, and naturally chose those in which they were strongest. Or they refrained because to enter would offend a favorite son, or because a state organization wanted to bring an unfettered delegation to the convention. Some stayed out because they didn't have enough money to go in. Finally, the vote in the primaries was generally relatively light and it was possible —though probably not sound—to argue that the voters who stayed home did so because they preferred someone not entered. All this added up to the facts that more votes were to be won through state conventions and negotiations with politicians than in the primaries, and that the primaries did not carry sufficient weight to convince party leaders that they represented a significant popular verdict.

The primaries have other and graver weaknesses. A major American party is a congeries of elements that must be held together at least for the duration of the national campaign. Democratic politics are the politics of adjustment, of glossing over differences, relieving tensions, compromising interests. There was always the danger that the primary might result in candidates, or their supporters, attacking one another so viciously that resultant breaches could not be closed; or of issues being raised or commitments being made in a primary that would damage the party's chances of winning in November. The primary is a civil war preceding by only a few months the great war against the real foe, and it is altogether possible that the most able potential leader may be so gravely wounded in the civil war as to be unavailable for the larger battle.

All this was evident by 1920, but to ignore the primary entirely was a dangerous gamble. In the first place there was a certain number of delegates to be picked up; opponents would proclaim that failure to enter the lists was a confession of weakness; and a candidate could get headlines, meet people, attract national attention. The last was particularly important in 1920 because, with the exception of Herbert Hoover, none of the aspirants for the nomination was exceptionally well known.

Wood and Johnson campaigned extensively in the primaries. Lowden, although he contested fewer states, was not far behind his opponents in activity. During the winter of 1919-1920 he spoke in Chicago, New York, Detroit, Minneapolis, Omaha, Denver, St. Louis, Indianapolis, western New York State, rural

Michigan and South Dakota. But despite the rivals' sound and fury, few substantive issues were debated. Wood and Johnson each proclaimed himself the legitimate heir of Theodore Roosevelt, but Wood's claim was based chiefly on personal friendship rather than principles, and Johnson although expressing his progressivism did not spell it out.

Lowden was content to let his opponents wage their tug of war for the Rooseveltian mantle—which fitted neither—while he advanced his own claim as one qualified to give the country an enlightened business administration. He hoped to be nominated by the conservatives while proving acceptable to progressives. On foreign affairs he was nearer to Wood than to Johnson. He said he did not see how the United States could be injured much by the League of Nations and something of value might come of it. He was willing to join, with reservations. Wood took about the same stand. Johnson was an uncompromising isolationist. All three were opposed to radicalism, which they equated with bolshevism. Wood was quoted by the *New Republic* as saying: "My motto for the Reds is S.O.S.—ship or shoot. I believe we should place them all on a ship of stone, with sails of lead and that their first stopping place should be hell." He protested that this was a quotation borrowed from Dr. John Wesley Hill, and that he had never acknowledged it as expressing his own views, but he did not say that it didn't. It did not matter much, since Communism failed to catch fire as an issue in the 1920 campaign.

If no deep issues developed between the candidates, ill-feeling did. This was chiefly between the Wood and Johnson camps, but Lowden was caught in the backwash in a manner which some observers—and Lowden himself—believed cost him the nomination.

Despite a banquet at the Waldorf-Astoria at which Lowden spoke to American plutocracy, it was Wood who received heavy financial backing from big business, and who spent money on what was for that time an unprecedented scale. As a consequence Senator Borah, Johnson's campaign manager, making a virtue of his own candidate's relative lack of funds, demanded and got a Senate committee appointed to investigate campaign expenditures. The committee, headed by Senator Kenyon of Iowa, was composed of three Republicans—one of whom was for Wood and the others for Wood or Harding—and two Democrats. Thus by accident or by design Wood, the main object of the investigation, was well protected; Lowden was not. This did not disturb Lowden, who felt he had nothing to hide and that Wood was vulnerable.

As anticipated, the committee found that Wood had spent the most money—about one and three-quarters million dollars. Lowden had spent a little over four hundred thousand, of which he and his wife had put up all but about thirty-five thousand. Opponents cried that he was a rich man, but they could not charge he was contracting obligations that might embarrass him if elected President. Wood, however, had spent over four times as much money, much of it contributed by large donors. Yet five thousand dollars stole the headlines from millions.

During the committee hearings the question of why a number of local Missouri politicians were changing from Wood to Lowden was raised. Could it be because of Lowden money? Louis Emmerson, one of Lowden's managers, was called upon to testify. He reported spending some $38,000 in Missouri and accounted for it. But upon examining Emmerson's account book the committee found two checks listed that had not been accounted for in his previous testimony. These were for $2,500 each, and were made out to Nat Goldstein and Robert E. Moore, two minor Missouri politicians. Both were delegates to the approaching convention. Emmerson was unable to give a satisfactory explanation, admitting that he did not know the men very well or what they had done with the money. Goldstein and Moore gave conflicting testimony; Goldstein declared that he would refund the money if he didn't vote for Lowden at the convention. The committee left it there, adjourning June 5th, three days before the Chicago convention.

No one during the hearing had accused Lowden of complicity, and he immediately issued a statement saying he had instructed Emmerson to be ethical in his expenditures, that he knew nothing about payments to Goldstein and Moore, and that he would refuse to accept their votes at Chicago. Some time later Irving Brant, an editorial writer for the St. Louis *Star*, a paper which had supported Wood and led the outcry against Lowden, wrote to Lowden that he had been victimized by Senators Reed and Spencer who had deliberately trapped and ruined him.

Regardless of Lowden's innocence or the committee's motives, certain unpalatable facts remained. Goldstein and Moore had gotten the money from Emmerson, and no one had been able to explain what for, or how it was used. There was a case for the charge that delegates had been bought. The Johnson and Wood camps shrieked corruption; the Democrats joined in. The Chicago *Herald and Examiner*, owned by Hearst who was backing Johnson, cried virtuously, "You don't have to hire 'em for Hiram." In a Bryanesque statement Senator Borah declared that the convention must not nominate a candidate who had used improper means to obtain the nomination. Although he mentioned no names he was obviously referring to Lowden. Since he had already committed himself against Wood, it did not leave him much of anywhere to go should his own candidate, Johnson, prove impossible to nominate. Unless, of course, he ate his words, and Borah was not one to do that. Accepting Harding was preferable.

The money scandal did not destroy Lowden's cause, nor by itself could it have prevented his nomination; but he himself was to declare, "The real cause of my defeat was probably the Missouri revelation." If this is true, it is guesswork. Certainly it hurt him—particularly in his claim to business efficiency. He hadn't been efficient enough to know what Louis Emmerson was doing in Missouri. Would he do better in Washington?

The last primary was held May 21st and an assessment of the popular strength of the candidates could be attempted. By their measure Wood was ahead in delegates, Johnson in popular votes. Lowden was third, and Harding, who had run last in every race he had entered except that of his home state of Ohio where he had split the delegates with Wood, had made such a miserable showing that most of those who had toyed with the idea of supporting him lost interest.

The pattern that emerged from a *Literary Digest* poll corresponded with the primaries except that Herbert Hoover was in third place, ahead of Lowden and just behind Johnson and Wood. Harding was sixth, behind Hughes, who wasn't running, and Governor Calvin Coolidge of Massachusetts. Betting odds were quoted at even money on Johnson, 8-5 on Wood and 7-5 on Lowden. Harding's chance at 1-5 was rated as less than Hughes' and even with those of a cluster of favorite sons.

Despite disappointing primaries and the money scandal, Lowden was not in bad shape. The bitterness between Wood and Johnson was greater than that of either toward Lowden; he could reasonably hope that one or the other would turn to him in a deadlock. He still appeared to be a logical choice for the old guard, and indeed the more primaries Wood and Johnson won the better Lowden might look to nervous bosses. So ran the hopeful Lowden political arithmetic.

But when all the hopes and guesses of the rival camps were done with, the outlook was not too bright for any of them. No one had emerged with impressive popular strength; dissension had created ill feeling between the leading candidates; no one had nearly enough pledged delegates to win the nomination. Unless some sort of coalition emerged from the Wood-Lowden-Johnson triangle the balance of power would rest with the un-instructed delegations from large boss-controlled states. Anything could happen.

The Republican National Convention assembled in Chicago, Tuesday, June 8th. The delegates found the city steaming, with the temperature hovering around 100 degrees. But the heat did not smother activity on the part of candidates, most of whom were in Chicago working for delegates. Lowden was doing double duty. As governor of Illinois he welcomed delegation leaders to the state, as a candidate he sought their votes. The roles were not incompatible because he was not aggressive in pushing his cause. He believed, or hoped, that he had suffi- cient second-choice strength to win when favorite sons dropped out and old guard leaders made their decisions. Until then he could afford to be patient, but his forces were far from idle. He took a suite in the Blackstone Hotel and conferred there with his managers. His supporters were everywhere. The main Lowden reception center was in the Congress Hotel but there was also a Young Men's Lowden Club, a Lowden Center at the Hamilton Club, and a Woman's Hospitality Room where cor- sages of roses and sweet peas were presented to Ladies for Lowden. There were Lowden cigars, Lowden armbands, Low- den buttons, Lowden badges, Lowden banners, Lowden plac- ards, and Lowden automobile stickers. There were two bands to make Lowden music.

Other camps were equally busy. Red and green turkey feathers, symbols of allegiance to Wood, were plentiful and a Wood newssheet appeared daily. Johnson activities were less flamboyant—he had less money—but his headquarters were busy. Harding's Harry Daugherty brought a glee club from Columbus to serenade not only delegates but rival candidates as well. He said it was to make "sweet atmosphere" for Har- ding.

Political forces were not the only ones present in Chicago. If politics was the business of the convention, the convention was the business of industry and its princes. Among those present were Samuel Vauclain of Baldwin motors, Ambrose Monell of Monell Metals, Dan Hanna for iron, Gary for steel, Vanderbilt for railroads, Henry Byllesby for public utilities, and William Boyce Thompson for copper. J. P. Morgan partners kept in close touch with George Harvey, who having failed to make and control a Democratic President was trying his hand with the Republicans. It was Harvey's suite at the Blackstone that was to become famous as Harry Daugherty's "smoke-filled room."

But most ubiquitous of all the business interests was oil. William Allen White, who was in Chicago, wrote that the 1920 convention was one in which "the Senate group" was "somewhat, if not largely, dominated by a rather large personal interest in large campaign contributions, which were presumed to be available if the new oil group was satisfied. . . . Jake Hamon, national committeeman from Oklahoma, a particularly odoriferous gentleman who was killed by his mistress, was much in evidence around the place . . . the Sinclair interests and the Doheny interests were conspicuous . . . oil had a room in an office building and presumed to summon potential presidential . . . candidates. . . ."

One more factor that influenced the convention—amorphous yet crystal hard in its impact—was the conviction that the election was already won. "Any good Republican can be nominated for President and can defeat any Democrat," Boise Penrose, most powerful and able of the old guard, proclaimed. Although he was ill in Philadelphia when the convention met, his confidence was shared by the smaller men into whose laps the power of decision finally fell. Somewhere along the way, however, they dropped the qualification that the nominee should be "good." Despite previous doubts Penrose sanctioned the omission.

Certain of victory, the old guard, ignoring other elements of the party, rammed its choice of Henry Cabot Lodge as temporary and permanent convention chairman through the National Committee. Earlier the plan had been for Albert Beveridge of Indiana, an old Roosevelt Progressive, to be temporary chairman and deliver the keynote address, but Beveridge was shunted aside in favor of Lodge, who called the convention to order and delivered the keynote address.

Henry Cabot Lodge was a man of breeding, education, wealth and intellect. However, his self-esteem outstripped his intelligence, and Woodrow Wilson had unwisely ignored him as a leader of the Republican opposition and senior member of the Senate Foreign Relations Committee. In 1920, Lodge was animated primarily by animosity toward Wilson, and secondarily by a determination that the new President would not be one who would disdain the greatness of Henry Cabot Lodge. His keynote address, called by the New York *Post* "a hymn of hate," embodied the bitterness that corroded his spirit. It sounded more like an offended monarch demanding the attainting of the person and blood of a traitor than an American statesman addressing his party.

"Mr. Wilson and his dynasty, his heirs and assigns, or anybody that is his, anybody who with bent knee has served his purposes, must be driven from all control, from all influence upon the government of the United States," he cried.

The diatribe was well received by the delegates. It had spirit; it lambasted the Democrats; it was a call to battle. Having emptied himself of his bile, Lodge adjourned the convention until the next day.

Wednesday and Thursday were spent in speeches, in committee work and the presentment and adoption of the party platform. Interest centered about a plank on the League of Nations. The irreconcilable isolationists had threatened to make trouble if the party's stand was too soft, while elder statesmen of the party such as ex-President Taft, Charles Evans Hughes and Elihu Root, former Secretary of State, were to some extent internationalist and probably represented the sentiments of the rank and file of the party. The platform committee rose to the occasion with a plank that approved the Senate's recent rejection of the League Covenant—and then added a jumble of words superficially lucid but senseless: The United States would call for an international association to preserve the peace without compromising national sovereignty. Since the problem of civilization was to find a means to substitute judicial processes for war in settling international disputes, the refusal to compromise national independence, including the independent right to make war or aid in the prevention of war, was a total rejection of the concept being dealt with.

Other platform planks promised a simplified tax system, government reorganization and protective tariffs. The progressives were conceded resolutions favoring collective bargaining rights for labor and child labor legislation. Action favoring agriculture, reclamation and highway construction were promised.

Lowden fitted the platform better than any of his rivals. His achievements as governor of Illinois had included tax and budget reform and governmental reorganization. He favored collective bargaining for both farmers and workers, and had been liberal enough to win the support of Illinois progressive Republicans. As a farmer he could claim firsthand knowledge of agricultural problems. His stand on international affairs was more or less gibberish, but as reflected in the platform, that was the party's stand. On the whole, if it intended to wage the campaign on the principles enunciated in the platform, Lowden was the Republican party's logical candidate.

By Friday morning the convention was ready for nominating speeches. Lowden's name was presented in a twenty-minute address that proclaimed him a "man of visions but not visionary, a man of ideals but not an idealist, a man of works and not of words." A forty-six-minute demonstration followed.

None of the nominating speeches was memorable, but Senator Willis of Ohio did manage to set the tone of the convention when he prefaced his case for Harding with the chummy appeal: "Say, boys and girls, let's nominate Harding."

When the speeches were finished, in addition to Lowden, Wood, Johnson and Harding, a number of favorite sons were in the race. They were not expected to win, but they could be used as a depository for votes until their ultimate expenditure had been determined.

The first ballot ran true to predictions. Wood led with 287½, Lowden was second with 211½, and Johnson third with 133½. Harding had only 65½, but his strength was somewhat greater than that; Daugherty was loaning delegates to Lowden, partly in order to kill off Wood, partly to create "a sweet atmosphere" in the Lowden camp. During the next three ballots Lowden picked up 81 votes and Wood only 27. Johnson's strength held steady but it was evident that, despite his success in the primaries, the men who controlled the convention votes would not have him. Harding had gotten no place and was so discouraged that he told Nicholas Murray Butler that he couldn't afford to keep his hotel rooms any longer and was giving them up.

This was the situation when, after a whispered conversation with Chairman Lodge, Senator Reed Smoot of Utah moved for adjournment until Saturday. The motion was greeted by a roar of noes by delegates who were anxious to finish their work and get out of Chicago. Lodge was not that anxious. He ruled that the motion had been carried and adjourned the convention until ten o'clock the next morning.

One of the most famous nights in the annals of American party conventions followed. Other nominations have been decided by activities carried on while the convention was not in session. In fact, nearly all of them have been, but usually the decision is reached not in one but in many smoke-filled rooms, not by a single group of men representing a very narrow group of interests, but by many groups appealing to varied interests and by discussions often including whole state delegations.

The night of June 11-12 was not the consequence of a farsighted plan. The men involved were neither powerful nor skilled enough to precipitate such an opportunity, but they were at the right place at the right time, and when no strong trend developed they seized the chance they had hoped for. And given the circumstances, they did choose the candidate. Smoot explained it to the correspondent, Mark Sullivan, while riding downtown immediately after the Friday adjournment: "Oh, there's going to be a deadlock and we'll have to work out some solution; we wanted the night to think it over."

That was true so far as it went, but though the group he

spoke for did not make the deadlock, they might have prevented it by releasing the delegates they controlled to one of the major candidates. Or they could have been less exclusive in their consultations on how it was to be broken.

The Lowden camp had not objected to the adjournment, but neither did it admit that there was a deadlock. There were grounds for such a point of view. In the first four ballots Lowden had increased his vote more than any of the others; Wood had shown almost no second-choice strength; Harding was so discouraged that he had wired a lieutenant who was standing by in Columbus to enter his name in the Ohio senatorial race; Johnson had not increased his first ballot strength; no dark horse had appeared. All in all, it appeared that Walter Lippmann's "logic of Lowden" might result in his nomination.

But a far different set of premises than those stipulated by Lippmann motivated the men seeking the solution Senator Smoot mentioned to Sullivan. They had not come to Chicago with a plan to nominate Warren Harding; some of them had other preferences. Nor is there evidence that there was a preconceived plan to get together that night. It started at a dinner shared by Senators Lodge, Brandegee of Connecticut and Curtis of Kansas, and George Harvey. Harvey's only claim to participation in Republican party decisions seems to have been self-election—and he, too, wanted to get even with Wilson, who hadn't appreciated him. The four discussed the situation, and after dinner went to Harvey's suite at the Blackstone. Old guard Senators and others joined the conference; they came and went. Interestingly, Harry Daugherty was not there. He was not important enough.

In a general way these "Senate elders" knew what they wanted in a candidate. They had their own logic. Their man must be willing to accept the role of "weak President"—one who would go along with Congress rather than attempt to assert the prerogatives of his office. He must have been regular in 1912; he must be opposed to the League Covenant, but could not be an irreconcilable isolationist; he must be acceptable to the industrial and financial interests that contributed heavily to the party on the national as well as state level.

These requirements ruled out Johnson on almost every count, and the first of them eliminated Wood, who had a reputation for being imperious and had given clear evidence of being a President in the image of Theodore Roosevelt. Lowden was not so clearly ineligible, but he had been a strong governor of Illinois, and had asserted legislative leadership. The elders were looking for men of lesser stature. That was the crux of their problem—to find a man smaller than themselves. They had to dig deep. Many names were mentioned but none seemed quite right. They kept coming back to one: Warren Harding. No one was enthusiastic about him but no one was antagonistic. As Senator Wadsworth of New York explained, years later:

> They [he was one of them] were like a lot of chickens with their heads off. They had no program and no definite affirmative decision was reached. If they came to any decision at all it was a decision to let the Harding suggestion go through, the fact being that they did not have anyone else to propose.

At about two o'clock in the morning they decided to call Harding in. No other presidential candidate in history has been ordered to appear and make application to a group of petty self-appointed bosses for the position of President of the United States. Few would have obeyed. Certainly not Leonard Wood, Hiram Johnson or Frank Lowden. The first two would probably have told them to go to hell. Lowden might have been more courteous, but he would have refused. (This is one reason none of the three was asked.) But Harding obeyed. They quizzed him about all sorts of matters, his personal life included. In fact it was his personal life that seemed to bother them most. Various accounts of the colloquy differ about the exact words Harvey spoke to Harding. But whether it was an ultimatum of magisterial authority (as Mark Sullivan claimed) or a matter-of-fact warning, Harding apparently was asked to consider his past in relation to any possible scandal it might bring upon himself or the party if he were elected President. To make his decision he was given ten minutes or so to commune with his conscience (perhaps even with God) in another room. He probably thought less about his conscience than about the chances of getting caught, and less about God than about Nan Britton, his mistress, who had borne his child and was even then in Chicago. But he decided to risk it and assured his inquisitors that there was nothing to bar his acceptance.

The board of bosses accepted the applicant. The only remaining task was to obtain the confirmation of the convention. They intended to do it slyly, so that there would be no taint of bossism attached to the nomination. Wood and Lowden would be given a few more ballots in which to attempt to break the stalemate. Harding would be brought forward as a compromise when they failed. They would fail. This would be made reasonably certain by withholding the votes controlled by the cabal. Reasonably rather than absolutely certain, because if the two leaders could get together they might be able to control a majority of the convention, or if Johnson swung his strength to either of them it would probably start an irreversible tide. But the first was improbable, and Borah, Johnson's manager, by continuing to harp upon the money scandal, had made it virtually impossible to deal with either Lowden or Wood. That very night he was talking darkly about a bolt should either Lowden or Wood be nominated. Thus the situation which had thrust the Senate elders into power appeared likely to remain unchanged long enough for their purpose.

Their strategy did not—could not—require secrecy. A certain amount of revelation was part of it. Wood and Lowden were to be advised by friends that they had been judged by their peers and found wanting in availability; rumors were to be set afloat that Harding was the man so that wary and weary delegates might be ready to board the bandwagon when it was launched. Reporters were told it was unlikely either Lowden or Wood could win and Harding would probably be the nominee. The spokesmen delivering this message confessed that Harding was "no world beater" but claimed that he was of "impressive appearance" and the "best of the bunch." A striking thing about the selection of Warren Harding is that no one pretended he was really any good. The best George Harvey could say of him was that he would "go along"; Senator Brandegee defended the choice on the grounds that the country did not need a strong President; Senator Harry New of Indiana made the best of it by rejoicing that Harding was not a "master mind."

Other camps had not been inactive while the conference at the Blackstone was in session. A Wood-Johnson ticket was proposed to Borah, who curtly rejected it and tried to deal with the cabal for an East-West ticket of Philander Knox for President and Johnson for Vice-President. The elders refused. They apparently had no insurmountable objection to Johnson as Vice-President (it was offered to him on the Harding ticket) but they were determined that the presidential nominee should be a creature bounden only to them. They did not need Borah's help, and since he had painted himself into a corner from which he could not deal with Lowden or Wood, they were not afraid of him.

Two supposed Lowden supporters, Colonel Alvin T. Hert of Kentucky and Senator Medill McCormick of Illinois, had attended at least part of the meeting of the cabal. Apparently neither one of them made any effort to protect Lowden's interests, but rather accepted, if they did not participate in, the choice of Harding. When the meeting was over, Hert carried the bad news to Lowden and suggested that he release his delegates. Lowden refused, but was unable to devise any countermeasures and, strangely enough, continued to trust Hert.

Balloting on Saturday was about as anticipated. Lowden passed Wood on the fifth roll call, 303 to 299. On the sixth,

seventh and eighth the two remained about even. Meantime
Harding was fed enough votes to forge slowly but not indis-
creetly forward. On the seventh ballot he passed Johnson. The
eighth ballot was the beginning of the end. Both Wood and
Lowden lost votes; Harding continued to climb. The former
two, in order to gain time, joined forces to get a recess that
lasted from 1:40 to 4 P.M. During the interim Lowden and Wood
met. They talked but failed to agree on anything save that
their managers should get together at once. The managers met
in Lowden's room, and Lowden was urged to accept second
place on a Wood-Lowden ticket. He refused. He did not want
to be Vice-President; he probably preferred Harding to Wood
and he admitted that he could not deliver his delegates to the
General even if he wanted to. After Procter, the soap king and
Wood's manager, left, Lowden said that he would release his
delegates, but to no rival. They would be free to go where
they pleased. Procter upon hearing this hurried back to the
Blackstone and urged Lowden not to make such a move but,
instead, to join Wood in forcing a continuation of the recess
until Monday. On Sunday both camps could further consider
their positions. Lowden consented, but warned that if the recess
move failed he would release his delegates. He had, in effect,
thrown in the sponge.

If they could control their delegates, and this was by no
means certain, Lowden and Wood had the votes to win a
further adjournment. But their authority was never put to a
test. Lowden believed Procter would make the motion; Procter
delegated the responsibility to Hert; Hert double-crossed both
Lowden and Wood by the simple expedient of staying away
from the floor of the convention until the ninth ballot was
under way, when it was too late for him or anyone else to make
the motion. Except for Lowden, who continued to insist that
Hert was blameless, everyone agreed that it was a deliberate
betrayal.

Harold L. Ickes, who had recommended Hert to Lowden as

a floor manager, was unsparing in his criticism of Hert's treachery. He wrote:

> The next morning, uneasy delegates flocked early into the hot and stinking Coliseum. Something was in the air besides foul smells. . . . Our former Western manager of the Hughes campaign, "Tobe" Hert of Kentucky . . . had been told that it was Lowden's wish that the convention should adjourn over Sunday, but others had reached Hert too. Arrogantly, he swept Lowden and his political hopes into the dustpan. It was he who helped to stampede the convention and to deliver its prize to the ineffable Harding. It was alleged at the time that the piece of silver offered him was the promise of a place in Harding's Cabinet. . . .

Hert—who was not given a cabinet position and died a year later—excused himself on the grounds that Harding was sure to win anyhow. He was probably right, as there is no reason to believe that Lowden and Wood could have come any closer to an agreement on Sunday than they had on Saturday.

So the roll calls continued. Lowden, who had gone to the auditorium, was puzzled. "I could not understand then," he wrote later, "and I have never learned since why the motion to adjourn was not made." But it had not been made and, pursuant to his plan, he released his delegates.

Having thus officially surrendered, he retired to a private room of the auditorium where a group including Harding was keeping up with the progress of the balloting by means of messengers sent from the floor. When the news came that on the tenth roll call "the boys and girls" had nominated Warren Harding, Lowden was among the first to congratulate the victor. Harding is reported to have replied that he was not sure but that he would have been happier if he were congratulating Lowden. In the end he would have been.

Defining "right man" as one who can be elected, Harding was the right man—or, at least, not the wrong one. He was elected by a large majority of both the popular and electoral vote. But

Lowden, Wood or Johnson could also have won. It was a Republican year: any nominee was the right man. This was the chief factor leading to the nomination of the worst man. The party system works best when the party leaders are obliged to cast a wide net in fishing for support. The breakdown does not come when decisions are made off the floor—they almost always are—but when they are made by too few men representing too narrow a segment of the public interest. This occurred in the Republican convention of 1920. The deal did not involve the sort of compromise of interests that is the health of democratic politics; it was engineered by a small group of leaders representing their own ambitions and the interests of a very narrow sector of the American people. Nor did the elders bind Harding with promises concerning public policy. They did not have to; they would determine the policy after he was elected. They were choosing a lackey, not a leader; they were searching for weakness, not strength. And they knew their man. They themselves were on the whole of modest stature, but when the strong men failed to get together it left an opening through which the mediocre slipped to the seats of power.

The elders were not dishonest or even insincere. Some of them were cynical, but even these honestly believed in their own ability to guide the affairs of the nation, and they most earnestly believed that a President who was a menace to the prerogatives of the legislature was a menace to the American system of government. Nor is it necessary to accept William Allen White's thesis that there was a deal between the elders and oil. There may have been one, but White offers no acceptable evidence, and besides none was necessary. As the cabal knew that it would be obediently served by Harding, so American business knew that it would be served by the cabal. Its members had served big business for years. They believed in big business. They could be trusted to choose a President.

Of a group of successful and able men—but not overwhelmingly strong candidates—Lowden was the best man for the Presidency. He had an unusually good record as governor, and although he was by no means a brilliant politician he knew the art and practice of politics far better than Wood. He had some of Harding's weakness as a judge of men (witness Louis Emmerson) but none of his weakness of character. For the most part he had kept the parasites who served him out of the government at Springfield. He would probably have made a good though not a great President. It was not a time for greatness. Given the mood of the country and the 1920 orientation of the Republican party, he was the logical candidate. But he could not be counted on as pliable. He was a man of character and a proven executive and legislative leader. So the Senate elders rejected the best man for the worst man, and they did it knowingly and with full freedom of choice. It was one of the most dismal lapses in the history of American political parties.

Lowden decided against running for a second gubernatorial term and retired to Sinnissippi. Harding offered him a cabinet position or an ambassador's post. He refused both. In 1924 he was nominated by the Republican National Convention as Calvin Coolidge's running mate. He declined, and when the convention recessed to give him time to reconsider, he reconsidered and declined again.

Yet he was not quite through with politics. In 1928 he entered and easily won the Illinois Republican presidential primary. He did not campaign nationally, however, and after the 1920 experience he was cautious in the expenditure of money. It added up to being receptive—putting himself in a position where the lightning might possibly strike. But it struck Herbert Hoover instead. Once more Lowden was urged to try for the Vice-Presidency. As usual he refused. At last he was through with politics. The road he had taken had led a long way from Sunrise, but not quite to the White House.

The Democrats

1924

WHEN the Democratic National Convention was called to order on June 24, 1924, the party problem was clearly defined. To beat the Republicans in November they would have to capitalize on the recent exposé of the Harding regime as the most corrupt in American history. And they would need to offer a liberal program as an alternative to the reactionary policies of Harding's successor, Calvin Coolidge. The right man to nominate for the Presidency would be one who could arouse the conscience of the American people, and rekindle the spirit of economic and social liberalism that had animated Theodore Roosevelt's "Square Deal" and Woodrow Wilson's "New Freedom."

But if the party's problem was clear, the difficulties in the way of its successful solution were equally well defined. The Republicans were embarrassed but they were far from prostrate. The unfortunate Harding was dead and Calvin Coolidge had succeeded him. The guilty were being brought to justice. Some were in jail, others had killed themselves. This, the Republicans contended, removed corruption as an issue in the coming election. The G.O.P. was not to be held responsible for the misdeeds of Republican officials, appointed by a Republican President. Although a complete repudiation of the principle of party responsibility, this was as good a defense as could be devised. And in the mid-twenties, when the mood of the American people was not attuned to moral preachment, it might prove to be good enough.

The Democrats also faced the challenge of convincing the public to change parties in an era of financial security. The farmers were in trouble, but commerce and industry were booming and wages were relatively high. Republicans warned the voter against tinkering with prosperity—"Keep Cool with Coolidge."

This then was the situation when the party convention assembled in New York City's Madison Square Garden. It added up to a chance to win the Presidency. How good that chance was depended on the delegates. They must nominate the right man— and go home a united party keyed to a fighting campaign.

That was the rub. Not since 1860 when slavery had split them had Democrats been so divided. On one side were the industrial cities of the East and North, on the other the towns and farms of the South and West. The cities were wet in principle and, despite prohibition, in practice. The farms and towns voted dry. The cities were crowded with immigrants and the children of immigrants who had come from southern and eastern Europe. Like the Irish who had preceded them they were Roman Catholic, and like the Irish they became Democrats. In the towns and on the farms most Democrats were "native American" and staunchly Protestant. Many were members of the Ku Klux Klan which was riding again. The new Klan was strong in the Midwest and West as well as the South, and was dry and opposed to sin, especially city sin. It was dedicated to hating Catholics and Jews as well as Negroes.

Divided into two fundamentally antagonistic groups, the party needed a nominee committed to neither. Unfortunately the two leading candidates, William Gibbs McAdoo and Alfred Emanuel Smith, were committed. They were the symbols of the rival hosts, and each side saw in the other's champion the fleshly materialization of all its nightmares.

McAdoo represented rural Democracy; Al Smith was the darling of the urban masses. McAdoo was dry; Smith was wet; McAdoo was the Klan's candidate; Smith was a Roman Catholic. McAdoo's forebears had fought in the American Revolution; Smith's parents were Irish immigrants. McAdoo had grown to manhood in rural Georgia, Smith on the sidewalks of New York. McAdoo attacked city bosses and city machines; Smith was a Sachem of Tammany Hall.

The lines were drawn and the warriors were in the list. The ensuing battle was the longest and one of the most turbulent national conventions in the history of America. It was not a battle of maneuver; its fundamental decisions were not made in smoke-filled rooms. It raged on the convention floor itself. The issues were not policies but cherished beliefs and angry prejudices. They slugged it out for sixteen hot noisy days and an incredible one hundred and three ballots. Then with both sides embittered and exhausted and the stalemate still unbroken they called it a draw. Party leaders made a choice when it was no longer of value to any but those who valued control of the party. They selected a good man—one of the most distinguished ever to run for the Presidency of the United States. But it was too late by at least a week and sixty or seventy ballots. The chances for winning in November had been dissipated in the heat of the savage midsummer battle. Coolidge was safe in the saddle for another four years.

McAdoo vs. Smith

No boss could control the party. No Steering Committee could suppress its convictions, no secret conference could issue orders. It was a real Convention of profoundly interested men and women.

—The Literary Digest

The Democratic delegates who came to New York to nominate a man who might lead them to victory over Coolidge and the Republicans have stayed through the second sweltering week for the sole purpose of destroying each other! . . . The convention has become a nightmare.

—STANLEY FROST

WILLIAM GIBBS McADOO was tall and rawboned. He had shrewd heavy-lidded eyes, a large nose, a wide grin and a mop of hair which he wore slicked down and parted in the middle. He gave an impression of canniness and energy. A Midwestern delegate from Sauk Center seeing him at Madison Square Garden in his white summer suit would have recognized him as a familiar type—a small-town banker or businessman from back home—a go-getter.

McAdoo was small-town, all right. But he was the boy who had gone to the city and made good in a big way. He built the first tunnel under the Hudson River. He helped nominate Woodrow Wilson for President of the United States. He married the President's daughter. From 1913 to 1918 he was Secretary of the Treasury and helped establish the Federal Reserve System, headed the Liberty Loan drives, and directed the nation's railroads when the government took them over as a war measure. Now, in 1924, he was reaching for the final prize, the Presidency of the United States.

The fourth of eleven children, William Gibbs McAdoo was born in a comfortable house on Powder Springs Road, a few miles outside Marietta, Georgia. He was of British stock—English, Scotch and Welsh. The McAdoos had come to Virginia in the seventeenth century and from there followed the pioneers' trail to North Carolina and through the mountains to Tennessee. They fought in the Revolution, the War of 1812 and the Mexican War. Mary Faith McAdoo was a Floyd of Georgia. Her great-grandfather was a Revolutionary soldier; her grandfather served in Congress; her father fought the Cherokee Indians and helped remove them from Georgia.

A campaign biographer quoted McAdoo as saying that "his first definite impression was of the passage of a victorious [i.e. Sherman's] invading army" in its march through Georgia. His mother—with her husband absent in the Confederate army —had fled with her family to Midway, a suburb of Milledgeville, Georgia. If he did remember he was a remarkable baby. He would have been only about one year old.

At the end of the war McAdoo's father moved his family into an old house that had been a hotel. It was large, rambling and run-down. The only light at night was from flaming pine cones. Here William spent his childhood. Life was hard in the postwar South, but McAdoo believed that this was good for him. He was even grateful to General Sherman.

> I was brought up in Georgia, in the path of General Sherman's famous march to the sea. . . . I feel that I owe General Sherman a debt of gratitude. I believe that character is produced and developed to the highest extent by hardships, suffering and poverty.

Hardship there was, but McAdoo probably knew little of real suffering or poverty. His father built up a successful law practice in Milledgeville, and in 1877 the family moved to Knoxville, Tennessee, where the elder McAdoo accepted a position as adjunct professor of English and history at the University of Tennessee.

Young McAdoo attended the university two years before quitting to take a job as deputy clerk of the United States District Court at Chattanooga. He also read law and in 1885, a few months after his twenty-first birthday, he was admitted to the bar. The same year he married Sarah Houston Fleming, who was to bear him five children before her death in 1912.

McAdoo did not attain distinction at the bar. He was far more attracted by finance and politics, and in these areas he was something of a plunger, suffering notable successes and some failures. His first financial venture was to buy with his own slender savings and borrowed money the shaky Knoxville Street Railway Company. It failed and he was left heavily in debt. The result was a momentous decision. He tells of it in his memoirs:

> . . . Reflecting on the possibilities of my Chattanooga law practice, I came to the conclusion that I would never earn enough money in that or any other small city to pay off my indebtedness. It seemed urgently necessary for me to get into a larger field, so I decided to go to New York. . . .
>
> I raised five thousand dollars on the house [his wife's], with considerable difficulty. In June 1892 we turned towards New York with all the high hopes and buoyant optimism that go with youth.

A correspondent, writing in 1924, pictures him upon his arrival in New York as "a lean and hungry southern carpetbagger, northward bound." Whatever his role, he rented a house on Long Island for his family and went in search of an office in the city. He found two small rooms in a building which faced Wall Street. Then he waited. "Day after day I sat in my silent office and wondered what I ought to do." In October he moved his family from Long Island to a furnished flat on the fifth floor of a five-story apartment building on West Eighty-seventh Street. There was no elevator but the five-flight climb was rewarded by a fine view of Central Park. In addition to climbing the stairs McAdoo got exercise by frequently walking to and from work. It was five miles each way but he saved the ten-cent carfare. So he, too, in his fashion, learned to know the sidewalks of New York.

After two years McAdoo was still not making enough money to meet the needs of his growing family. To supplement his income he entered the security business with Francis Pemberton, another Southerner who had come North to make his fortune. The venture did not make him rich but he did do well enough to move his family to Yonkers. He also continued to practice law and in 1897 entered into a partnership with another William McAdoo. The two McAdoos were not related. They had become acquainted through the confusion of receiving each other's mail. The partnership lasted for about four years, at the end of which William Gibbs virtually retired from the law in order to devote his whole time to the Hudson River tunnel.

The Hudson tunnel made McAdoo. Without it he might have remained a moderately successful New York attorney. Or, being a "lean and hungry" man, he might have found some other project with which to hoist himself out of the rut. But it was not another project; it was the Hudson River tunnel.

It was not McAdoo's idea. Men had been trying to build a tunnel from Manhattan Island to New Jersey for years, and by the time McAdoo became interested the unfinished segment of an abandoned project was half buried in the mud of the Hudson. "It was dead, indeed, but not dead beyond the power of resurrection," he wrote. He got permission from the representatives of the defunct bondholders to look at it, and accompanied by an engineer entered the abandoned tube under the river. He describes it. "It was not a ghost, or a skeleton, but a carcass. I felt as if I had seen the body of some long and enormously heavy animal that had lain down and died." But he would bring it to life. "I never doubted that I would get possession of it and complete it."

Careful estimates indicated a need of six million dollars, five of which would have to be raised before the work could start.

His plan for financing was sound but as he himself wrote later, "The weakest spot in it was myself. I had no money, few influential friends, and no experience or record which would justify the financial community in turning over to me such a tremendous undertaking." Nonetheless, he got the money. The New York and New Jersey Railroad Company was organized with McAdoo as president. His salary was fifteen thousand dollars a year.

With the necessary capital the tunnel was built. That it should be was inevitable, but that it was done so at this particular time was due to McAdoo's vision, energy and boldness. Although he did not, as rumored, become a millionaire, the tunnel did bring him a large income. He estimated it at an average of about fifty thousand a year in stocks and money for the eleven years he was president of the tunnel's companies. But more important than money in shaping his subsequent career was his transformation from an obscure lawyer to "the man who built the Hudson River tunnel." He was given a welcome in political circles that would not have been accorded McAdoo of McAdoo and McAdoo, attorneys-at-law. Moreover, it made him affluent enough to send his son to Princeton, which in turn led to an accidental meeting with Woodrow Wilson and, later, William McCombs.

He met Wilson in 1901 at a railroad junction while on the way to see his son who was ill with diphtheria at the Princeton infirmary. Their conversation was casual but it led to a relationship that grew quite cordial during the next ten years. When Wilson was nominated for governor of New Jersey in 1910, McAdoo offered his support.

The next step came in the spring of 1911. Wilson had won the gubernatorial contest and although he had not formally announced himself as a candidate for the Democratic presidential nomination, a small group of supporters was working with his blessing to that end. Among these was William F. McCombs, an Arkansas-born, Princeton-educated lawyer.

McAdoo met McCombs in the fall of 1908 on the rear platform of a crowded football train returning to New York after the Princeton-Yale game. The acquaintance developed into a full-fledged friendship. Since McAdoo by 1911 was a person of some prestige, it was natural for McCombs to suggest that he join the group working for Wilson. McAdoo accepted and threw himself into promoting Woodrow Wilson with the same vigor that marked his promotion of the Hudson River tunnel. As a Wilson floor leader at the Democratic National Convention, he held his forces firm in the face of the Champ Clark onslaught which for a time threatened to be overpowering. When McCombs wavered and suggested that the New Jersey governor withdraw—Wilson himself was ready to throw in the sponge—it was McAdoo who insisted he stay in the race.

After Wilson's nomination McAdoo was appointed vice-chairman of the Democratic National Committee. By this time he and McCombs, who was the new national chairman, were engaged in a bitter feud which was to continue until McCombs' death. McCombs, however, was ill during most of the campaign, and McAdoo was in charge.

Wilson was elected President in November. In early February, a month before he was inaugurated, he asked McAdoo to enter his cabinet as Secretary of the Treasury. McAdoo accepted. His political rise had been even more rapid than his ascent in the business world. In the spring of 1911 he had been virtually unknown to politics and politicians. In the summer of 1912 he was a Wilson floor leader; in the autumn he was vice-chairman of the Democratic National Committee. In March, 1913, he became the Secretary of the Treasury of the United States. It all happened in less than two years.

Among the nation's Secretaries of the Treasury, only a handful—Benjamin Bristow, Alexander Hamilton, Salmon P. Chase and Andrew Mellon—have become so well known to the public as William Gibbs McAdoo. He owed his fame to the Liberty Loan drives and to his work as wartime director of the nation's railroads and intercoastal shipping. His marriage in 1914, two years after the death of his first wife, to Eleanor Wilson, the

President's daughter, brought further publicity. Thereafter he was frequently referred to as the crown prince or heir apparent. It was not kindly meant, but to the ambitious statesman any fame short of infamy is likely to help more than hinder. Voters like familiar names and faces.

At the end of World War I, McAdoo resigned from the public service. He gave his reasons as exhaustion and the need to rehabilitate his personal finances which had suffered sadly in Washington, where he had spent more than he made. Wilson accepted his resignation in a cordial letter saying that the country had never had a more able Secretary of the Treasury. *The New York Times* agreed that McAdoo had indeed established a reputation which entitled him to be considered one of the outstanding Secretaries of the Treasury. After a three-month vacation he returned to New York and resumed the practice of law. But he was not done with politics. The great trial lay ahead.

In February of 1920 a group of political writers voted on the probable presidential nominee of the Democratic convention to be held in June. McAdoo was first, Wilson second. It is strange that experienced observers cast such a vote. Neither McAdoo nor Wilson was available. Wilson was an invalid unable to perform the duties of his office. His party could not repudiate him but, although there were grounds for believing that he wanted to run for a third term, neither could it risk nominating him. McAdoo's situation was different but as difficult. He might be the right and the best man, but it was the wrong time. He had married Eleanor Wilson; his enemies were already charging that he sought to "inherit the throne." It was silly and vicious, but to politicians who sagely counsel a candidate to always "run scared" it constituted a serious liability. It is generally believed that, despite the Adams family, Americans do not like dynasties. Paradoxically McAdoo's position was further weakened by the fact that at no time did his father-in-law offer the slightest sign of endorsing him. Identified as he was with Wilson and Wilson policies, he needed a

Wilson nod of approval. Failing to get it he fell between the two stools of pro- and anti-Wilson sentiment.

Analyzing his position more shrewdly than the writers who voted him the man most likely to be nominated, McAdoo refused to enter the presidential race. A few days before the convention he formally announced that he was not a candidate. Nevertheless, his name was placed in nomination and he led the field by a good margin in the early balloting. But he would not be enticed. When enthusiastic supporters at the convention called him long-distance he would not even talk to them. Eventually his strength ebbed, and Governor Cox of Ohio was nominated on the forty-fourth roll call. The Democrats were snowed under in November. The plunger had cannily refused to plunge.

Of course he still intended to be President of the United States. This became evident when shortly after the election of 1920 he moved from New York to California. He said it was because the opportunities to practice law were greater in Los Angeles, and that the climate would be good for his bronchitis. The knowing ones disagreed. Mark Sullivan wrote:

> . . . The cynical among us were ready to say, and even the humorously friendly among us counted it as an entirely harmless political euphemism, that Mr. McAdoo's change of residence was suggested no less by the greater salubrity of the California climate, than by the greater political salubrity of the California Democratic organization.

Oscar Underwood of Alabama was the first to announce candidacy for the 1924 Democratic presidential nomination. McAdoo was not far behind. Six months before the convention he admitted that he was in the race. Strategy demanded that he come out early. He knew that his forces could not control the convention on the first ballot, but hoped that if he could show sufficient strength the big states that held the balance of power might swing to him as the only candidate with enough popular support to beat the Republicans. Since politicians generally prefer to win with the right man rather than lose with their own favorite, the strategy was sound. And it had historic justification. Numerous conventions had seen the bosses put aside their particular candidate for an apparent winner. The Democrats had done it as recently as 1912 when they abandoned Champ Clark for Woodrow Wilson.

The problem was to amass the strength needed to convince a stubborn opposition that McAdoo was the right man. For the effort he had certain advantages. He was better known throughout the country than any prospective opponent. "Say 'McAdoo!'" wrote John Owens in the *New Republic,* "and an image rises in the mind of every literate man. Underdog and upperdog sees an eye with fire in it; each sees a jutting nose and daring chin; each recalls, the one with hope and the other with fear, a record for 'bustin' through' and doing things." The image is a valuable asset in a country which traditionally admires a fighter and a go-getter. McAdoo had other political capital. As director of the railroads he had raised wages, improved working conditions and effected a policy of equal wages for equal work regardless of race or color. The first two steps won the friendship of labor; the equal-pay policy made him more popular with Negroes than any Democrat since the Civil War. This plus identification with Wilson's social legislation entitled him to claim strength with workers and progressives in every party. Yet he was not far enough to the left to alienate the stable middle-class Democrats of the small towns and cities who constituted the bulk of his strength.

His farm-town-small-city strength was augmented by prohibitionists and the Ku Klux Klan. Prohibitionists were for him because he emphatically declared himself a bone-dry. His relations with the Klan were not so direct. He was not a member; he at no time spoke favorably of it; nothing in his record indicates that he was either a racial or religious bigot. But he was a Protestant of native stock, and the sheeted brotherhood had no better place to go. Oscar Underwood denounced them; Al Smith was a Catholic; other prospective candidates were either very dark horses or the protégés of big-city Catholic bosses. Henry Ford was nearer to Ku Klux ideals, but though mentioned he was never a serious candidate. Only McAdoo was left. He was not the Klan's man but he was its best bet, and while McAdoo himself held aloof his lieutenants courted the Kleagles.

McAdoo also drew some support from the business world. The Memphis *Commercial Appeal* declared that he had done "big things in a big way," and the Cleveland *Plain Dealer* editorialized that in business and politics he had a record of exceptional achievement. This record converted no Republican captains of industry and finance, but some Democrats such as Bernard Baruch found it good.

In further support of his availability McAdoo could point to the 1920 convention. Refusing to campaign or even admit that he was a candidate, he still got upwards of three hundred votes, and led in the early balloting. No opponent could offer evidence of such grass-roots strength.

Naturally McAdoo also had weaknesses as a candidate. Four years of prohibition had left the cities of the East as wet as the South and West were dry, and the wets despised McAdoo as earnestly as the drys loved him. It was the wet sentiment as much as anything else that solidified the forces opposed to him. Most formidable was the antagonism of the city machines. He had earned their enmity. From his first appearance on the national political scene he had denounced them; as Secretary of the Treasury he had starved them. He represented the "country" wing of the party which they regarded, rightly, as inimical to their interests.

In November the three most powerful Democratic bosses in America—Tammany's Charles Murphy, Illinois' George Brennan and Indiana's Tom Taggart—met at French Lick Springs, Indiana. Newspaper headlines spelled out the reason: DEMO-CRATIC CHIEFS SEEK DARK HORSE, DISCARD MCADOO; PARTY CHIEFS LAY PLANS TO SMOTHER BOOM FOR MCADOO; MURPHY RALLIES WETS FOR SMITH TO BEAT MCADOO. The New York

Tribune explained Murphy's attitude, one undoubtedly shared by the others. Murphy wanted "to force the nomination of someone who will treat Tammany better than Woodrow Wilson treated the battle-scarred organization between 1913 and 1921."

In general big business disliked McAdoo even more than the city bosses did. As Secretary of the Treasury he had not been tender of its interests; as director of the railroads he had been too sympathetic toward labor; he represented Wilsonian reform which among other things meant an increasing amount of governmental regulation. Since most business leaders were Republicans, this opposition might not seem too dangerous to a Democratic candidate, and it was not as lethal as to a Republican. Nonetheless it was damaging. As Republicans must have some votes from workers, Democrats must get money where it is, and just as there are many poor Republicans so are there many rich Democrats. In 1924 with union funds not yet tapped, it was the rich who paid the greater part of campaign expenses. They could not be ignored, and with some notable exceptions they did not want McAdoo.

Neither did a good many loyal Wilsonians. He was sound enough on social and economic issues, but he straddled on foreign policy. He declared that he was not an isolationist but hedged on the League of Nations. "We can go into Europe to help stabilize their institutions without involving ourselves in entangling alliances." Since the League with its entanglements was the heart of Wilsonian idealism, this was totally unacceptable to its devotees. Wilson died in February of 1924 without endorsing his son-in-law's candidacy.

Then came oil. At the end of 1923 the scandals of the Harding administration were beginning to emerge, and Democratic strategy required that these should be clearly identified in the public mind as Republican scandals. On January 24, 1924, the most sensational single episode in the unrolling drama of corruption was enacted. Edward L. Doheny, oil magnate, admitted before a congressional investigating committee that he had secretly sent $100,000 in a little black satchel to Albert B. Fall, Harding's Secretary of the Interior. Thus Doheny became one of the blackest villains in the oily melodrama. A few days later it was learned that McAdoo had had business relations with Doheny. Recalled to the stand, Doheny testified that soon after McAdoo's retirement from Wilson's cabinet he had employed him as an attorney at a $25,000-a-year retaining fee for a period of five years. It developed later that there had also been a contingency fee of $900,000, and that Doheny expected McAdoo to earn most of his fee doing work in Washington during the closing years of his father-in-law's administration.

To McAdoo's enemies all this was heaven-sent. The hostile Eastern press insisted that it made him unavailable as a presidential candidate. How could the Democrats accept Doheny's attorney as their standard-bearer? they screamed. And for once the liberal journals of opinion joined forces with the conservatives. These were supporting Robert La Follette of Wisconsin, whose strength, like McAdoo's, was largely in the West. The Doheny affair gave them a case against their champion's most dangerous rival. The *New Republic* summed it up:

> Just what Mr. Doheny hoped to get in return [for the $900,000 contingency fee] remains to be explained, but it looks as if it might have been something not unlike personal political influence. If this is true, Mr. McAdoo was converting his former public position . . . into a source of enormous private profit.

McAdoo fought back. He demanded and got a hearing before the congressional committee that had heard Doheny's testimony. His defense was straightforward. He had been retained as a special counsel in connection with the Doheny oil interests in Mexico which were threatened with confiscation by the Mexican government. He had attempted to use no influence in Washington. He had never been involved in oil leases in the United States. He had not only resigned as Doheny's lawyer as soon as he learned of his dealings with corrupt Republican officials, but he had also returned one year's retainer.

His critics could not pretend that he was involved in any corrupt practices, but they were not silenced. The New York *World* admitted that he had given a satisfactory account of his relations with Doheny, but insisted that he was nonetheless unavailable for a campaign in which the methods of the Dohenys and the records of the Falls would be issues. The *New Republic* was more caustic:

> They whitewashed an innocent man, whose only crime was bad luck, the bad luck of a virtuous citizen who orders lemonade in a saloon which is raided before he finishes his drink. . . . No candidate is possible for the Democrats who has any connection with oil, however blameless.

McAdoo did not agree. He continued his vigorous campaign, and his solid core of Western-Southern supporters remained loyal. If their champion had been indiscreet it was easy to forgive him. Oil, Mexico, even Washington, were far away. Black satchels containing a hundred thousand dollars and contingency fees of almost a million were not very real to them. But saloons, foreigners and the political menace of Roman Catholicism were nearby and frightful. Besides, they were not very much impressed by indignant screams from the brawling, drunken, un-American cities. Certainly they were not ready to take lessons in virtue from Sodom.

McAdoo showed undiminished strength in the late winter and spring primaries. New York's Governor Smith beat him badly in wet, German-Catholic Wisconsin but elsewhere he did well. When the pre-convention books were closed in June he led all opponents by a comfortable margin. But it was no longer McAdoo against a nondescript field. The city throngs had found their champion. It was McAdoo against Al Smith.

Alfred Emanuel Smith was ten years younger than McAdoo. He was born in New York City in the shadow of the Brooklyn Bridge. His childhood was in the right tradition for an American boy destined to be President. His family was poor; he made his own way in the world. But there was a difference. He was not in the frontier or rural tradition. He did not trudge behind the oxcart, or split rails, or live in a house lit by burning pine knots. He did not walk dusty miles to a country or village school to win an education. What little schooling he obtained was in a New York City parochial school. He was not a country boy— which is to be virtuous—but a city urchin—which is to be miscreant. And he was Irish Catholic, the son of Irish-Catholic parents who had migrated to America.

His father died when he was thirteen years old, leaving a widow with five children to support. Young Al drove a truck awhile and then got a job as stall keeper in a Fulton fish market. In his spare time he hung around the political club of Tom Foley, the Democratic district leader. In time he was rewarded for his political activity with the job of clerk in the office of Commissioner of Jurors of New York City. This was in 1895. The job paid well enough for him to marry. His bride was Catherine Dunn; she, too, was Irish Catholic. They had five children.

Al Smith was a professional politician. Mark Sullivan describes him in the role:

> To everyone in his district, Smith was a kind of combination of friend, adviser, feudal chief and ever ready to help in time of need. When any of them lost his job, had trouble with his landlord, needed coal for the winter, wanted advice about getting forward in the world, was concerned with education for his children—in every material or spiritual complication that persons of simple lives run into, they turned to Smith for help; and Smith had the personality which included both the capacity for practical help, and pleasure in the act of helping.

Here is the portrait of a Tammany chieftain that rural America did not see and would not look at. That it did not and would not goes far to explain what occurred in the 1924 Democratic convention.

Smith, however, was more than a professional politician. He was a career politician who earned his living from public office. And it was well earned. Few political professionals and fewer political amateurs have served their employers so well. From 1903 to 1915 he was a member of the New York State Assembly. He was its Democratic leader in 1911 and its Speaker in 1913. His record was so remarkable that when he was nominated for sheriff of New York County—a job which reputedly brought in $100,000 a year—the Republican New York *Tribune* declared it would be wise for the state to pay him $100,000 a year to keep him in Albany where he had done more good than all the other legislators put together. He was elected sheriff and served until 1917 when he assumed the duties of president of the Board of Aldermen. In 1918 he ran successfully for governor of the state. He was defeated in 1920. In 1922 he tried again and won. He was re-elected in 1924 and 1926.

As legislator and governor Smith advocated increased government support of public health and sanitation, tenement house regulation, workmen's compensation, child welfare, prison reform, public power and better public education. These were reasonable grounds for protesting McAdoo's claim as the Democratic liberal champion. It is significant, however, that Smith's was the new liberalism of the cities rather than the radical Western Democratic agrarianism. It aimed primarily at improving life in the swelling urban areas, and held little appeal for farmers and the inhabitants of small towns. So just as there were two images of a Tammany politician at the convention in Madison Square Garden, so were there two conceptions of a liberal—Al Smith, the urban liberal; William McAdoo, the rural liberal.

Despite a brilliant legislative and administrative record, Smith faced almost insurmountable barriers as a candidate for the presidential nomination. The Eastern wing of the party to which he belonged was in the minority. Time, Franklin Roosevelt and John Kennedy might alter this, but that lay in the future. In 1924 most Democrats were in the South and rural West, and most Democratic electoral votes came from there. In fourteen elections since the Civil War the Democratic candidate for President had come from New York seven times. But

New York was not grateful. It had cast its electoral vote for the Democrats only three times. This situation was reflected in other Smith territory. He was strongest in Republican country. The Democratic states were for McAdoo or favorite sons.

The greatest source of Smith's weakness was that the opposition to him was charged with emotion. He was wet; he was an Irish Catholic; he was a Tammany politician. He wore a brown derby hat and talked with an East Side twang, and occasionally in an East Side idiom. Even the songs his supporters roared were alien and disquieting to rural ears: "East Side, West Side, All Around the Town"; "The Sidewalks of New York." Or they were Irish, and hence to a nativist or Klansman suspect: "Sweet Rosie O'Grady"; "Little Annie Roonie."

"Let's look at the record," Smith was wont to say in his campaigns for office, and in New York the voters looked and found it good. But at Madison Square Garden his opponents would not even look. They were not interested in what he had done, but in what he was—a wet Irish-Catholic Tammany Sachem—the symbol of all they hated and feared.

Perhaps Smith knew this, although as a native New Yorker he may have been characteristically provincial and ignorant of sentiment in the hinterland. Whether he knew it, most Democratic leaders did—including bosses Murphy, Brennan and Taggart. But Smith was their stopper, their one hope of keeping McAdoo from running away with the nomination on an early ballot. When McAdoo was disposed of they could get together on someone, and they knew it couldn't be Al Smith. In this design the machine bosses were joined by big business interests. Industry, banks, railroads, metropolitan newspapers, disliked McAdoo, and had an exaggerated fear of his radicalism. So urban politicians, urban progressives and urban conservatives closed ranks, and the Smith-McAdoo fight was not only a clash between sections, it was also big against little business. Although big business did not want Al Smith (it wanted Cal Coolidge), he was better than McAdoo and at best he could be used as a cat's-paw to drag the chestnuts out of the McAdoo fire and into the lap of a compromise candidate of their own choosing.

Smith himself stuck to his job as governor, and did not campaign for the nomination. He made no speeches and entered no presidential primaries. Nonetheless he was an acknowledged candidate and state conventions chose delegates instructed for or favorable toward him. In Wisconsin he won the primary from McAdoo even though he had not entered it. In the spring Smith headquarters were opened in New York City. At about the same time, Tammany boss Charles Murphy died. Murphy's death was hailed by Smith's opponents as a blow to his prospects, but his supporters believed that it enabled him to emerge from the boss's shadow and run on his record of honest, progressive government. Both views were the product of wishful thinking. On the one hand the New York organization remained unshaken in its loyalty to Smith, on the other he was still a product of machine politics, and an unabashed member of Tammany.

On May 1st Franklin D. Roosevelt took active charge of Smith's campaign. Smith wanted him because of the Roosevelt name. As the 1920 Democratic vice-presidential candidate Roosevelt had national stature; he was Protestant, rural (Hyde Park), and at that time dry. He would broaden the appeal of the Smith cause. Roosevelt apparently entered the campaign with some reluctance. He and his political confidant, Louis Howe, did not believe that Smith could be nominated or that 1924 was a Democratic year. But when urged he consented, and in doing so increased his own stature within the party. Even Smith's opponents came to admire him during the course of the convention.

The Smith strategy was to wear down McAdoo as Wilson had worn down Champ Clark in 1912, and then, if possible, to stampede the convention. The Brooklyn *Citizen* explained that Smith was ". . . the one man so far named whose personality evokes genuine enthusiasm—the one man who could, under certain conditions, cause a spontaneous stampede in his direction." The certain circumstances that were to cause a spontaneous stampede were to be helped along by a vociferous pro-Smith gallery. This guaranteed a disorderly convention.

If a deadlock between Smith and McAdoo developed, other candidates were available. There was Senator Samuel Ralston, an Indianapolis machine politician with a small-town background. Labor and the Ku Klux Klan liked him, and so did the politicians and conservative business interests. The forces opposing one another in the persons of McAdoo and Smith were reconciled in Sam Ralston. Besides, McAdoo was splashed with oil, Smith with alcohol. Sam Ralston was unbesmirched, and Tom Taggart had him groomed and ready.

John W. Davis was as cosmopolitan as Samuel Ralston was provincial, as distinguished as Ralston was commonplace. He was born in West Virginia and educated at Washington and Lee University. At twenty-six he was the Democratic leader in the West Virginia legislature. He served in the United States House of Representatives, and later as Solicitor General of the United States. Before the Supreme Court of the United States he was a brilliantly intellectual trial lawyer. In 1918 President Wilson appointed him Ambassador to Great Britain. He served until 1921. Upon his return, he joined a New York law firm and soon was recognized as one of America's leading lawyers. Intellectually Davis was eminently qualified for the Presidency, and there were other things in his favor. He had experience in legislation and politics; his service as ambassador entitled him to claim a better understanding of international affairs than that of his rivals; he was a Protestant of native stock; he was untouched by scandal.

But despite his distinguished career the name John W. Davis rang no bells. William Jennings Bryan denounced him as a Wall Street puppet. Davis made no pre-convention campaign for delegates and none was made for him until a week or two before the convention, when friends established Davis headquarters in a room in the Waldorf.

The conservative's favorite was Oscar Underwood of Alabama, an ardent champion of states' rights and an enemy of woman's suffrage and prohibition. Other names were mentioned during the spring: Henry Ford, Charles Bryan, governor of Nebraska and brother of William Jennings, and other favorite sons who were used merely to keep delegates uncommitted. Nineteen of them were to receive votes on the convention's first roll call.

The 1924 Democratic National Convention was called to order in New York City's Madison Square Garden on June 24th. Hendrik Van Loon said the garden looked like the inside of a cheap candy box. Other observers noted that its ventilation was bad and that it was a firetrap. Many recalled prophetically that it was the home of circuses and prize fights. In the case of the 1924 Democratic battle, however, the fight was not confined to the ring. It boiled out over the whole city. Movie houses showed Smith's picture; theatre orchestras played "East Side, West Side." Irving Berlin wrote a Smith song and New Yorkers sang it all over town. Babe Ruth consented to serve on a Smith committee. Hotel employees wore Smith buttons; taxi drivers regaled their fares with praise of Smith; the New York press paid him tribute and pictured McAdoo in cartoons and editorials as oil-smeared and Klan-controlled.

McAdoo, in enemy territory, was not cowed. He had come to New York a week before the convention and established two headquarters, one in the Vanderbilt Hotel and another across the street from Madison Square Garden. He issued statements assailing the machines and their bosses, and branding the metropolitan press as a creature of the predatory interests. He talked to delegates. His lieutenants and publicity agents were everywhere. He could not match Smith on the sidewalks of New York, but he had his allies who made sure that the voice of the countryside should not be drowned out by the shrill din of the city. A rain of telegrams from Anti-Saloon League leaders all over the country deluged delegates; Cyclops and Dragons, Klokards and Klybees warned them against succumbing to big-city blandishments. Anti-Catholic literature was distributed. Most of this was without McAdoo's consent, but he did not repudiate it, and it would have been nonetheless effective had he done so.

Both sides overplayed their hands, hardening rather than softening the lines of resistance—making a stampede more difficult, a deadlock more likely. And the favorite sons and the dark horses were ready. Sixteen avowed candidates had come to New York for the convention. John W. Davis was already in the city. He stayed away from the convention but was in touch with his managers.

Senator Pat Harrison of Mississippi was the keynote speaker. Flamboyant and intemperate, he attacked Republicans as creatures of corruption. The speech was supposed to set a pattern for the fall campaign, but the delegates failed to respond with more than conventional enthusiasm. For the time being they were not much interested in fighting Republicans; they were taking one another's measure.

McAdoo was placed in nomination by Senator James Phelan of California. It was midafternoon and hot and sultry, and Phelan's speech was long and dull. Not even McAdoo delegates paid much attention. But when Phelan had finished they were ready. They paraded and demonstrated for nearly an hour. With many of them wearing cowboy outfits the Western motif was marked—a challenge to the sidewalks of New York. The sidewalks, represented by the Smith-packed galleries, responded with boos and a unified chant of "Oil! Oil! Oil!" Their hostile demonstration appeared to be organized; if so it was a blunder. It only angered the anti-Smith delegates, and confirmed their low opinion of the city, its people and its candidates. It also set the note for the convention.

When it was Smith's turn Franklin Delano Roosevelt came to the rostrum on crutches. It was his first major political appearance since his polio attack. His speech was the most effective of the convention. He appealed for party unity, cited Smith's record, and in one of those felicitous phrases of which he was to become a master he called Smith the "Happy War-rior" of the political battlefield.

The violent demonstration that followed Roosevelt's speech was not a tribute to it. It had been organized long before. Several thousand Tammany warriors were in the gallery. Tammany captains were in their places around the Garden. A Tammany general was on the speakers' platform. Noise producers from lungs to automobile sirens were ready. The ensuing uproar was such that McAdoo leaders, who controlled the convention machinery, considered adjournment to another city. However, when it had lasted just 50 percent longer than McAdoo's, the demonstration was called off and order restored.

Nominations mounted to seventeen and stretched on into the third day before the platform was brought in. The Resolutions Committee had recognized the dangers besetting the party and worked cautiously. Republicans were unequivocally condemned, most other issues were straddled. These included prohibition and the League of Nations. The prohibition compromise, not endorsing it but saying it should be enforced, was acceptable to the whole committee, but the League issue was carried to the convention floor.

The plank declared that the Democratic party was willing to submit the question of entry of the United States into the League of Nations to a national nonpartisan referendum. It did not say that it would advocate entry, just that it would be willing to have the people vote on it. League advocates rejected the plank but were voted down. Only the peace of the world was involved, and at the moment no war was imminent. On this question the Smith and McAdoo leaders were in agreement. They were both afraid of losing votes.

The Ku Klux Klan was not so easily disposed of. It claimed over a million members and had great political power. It elected mayors, governors, United States Senators and Representatives. It controlled state legislatures. Its greatest strength was in McAdoo territory; it was weakest in the East where Smith was strong. In Klan country both Democratic and Republican politicians accepted Klan endorsement. Many of them joined the order. But nationally neither party accepted its principles of bigotry and hate. The platform committee presented a discreet plank that did not mention the Klan by name but did condemn "any effort to arouse religious or racial dissension." This was sufficiently obscure to keep the Klansmen in McAdoo's camp happy. McAdoo's opponents struck back instantly, insisting that the plank was not enough. The Klan must be denounced by name. This stand against bigotry was noble in principle but purely political in motivation, directed less against the Ku Klux Klan than William Gibbs McAdoo. If McAdoo forces accepted the explicit denunciation, it would weaken him in areas of his greatest strength; if they rejected it, it would further identify him with the Kluxers. After wrangling all night the committee gave up. At six o'clock Saturday morning it agreed to submit alternate planks to the whole convention. Both of these condemned Klan principles, but only one of them mentioned it by name.

In the debate that followed, William Jennings Bryan led the McAdoo delegates. He did not defend the Klan or admit sympathy for its activities. But he said that naming it would only exaggerate its importance. The Smith galleries jeered and hissed. Bryan replied with a plea for tolerance and party unity. He, too, was sincere, but he, too, had ulterior motives. He was for McAdoo and, even more, he was against Smith. After long and bitter debate the convention voted. It was one o'clock Sunday morning. Stanley Frost, *Outlook* correspondent, described the scene:

> . . . A thousand blue-coated policemen . . . held the floor of the . . . Convention, so that the vote . . . was taken with every delegate's head in reach of a nightstick. . . . The policemen were no stage effects. They were needed. The tension between the two factions of the Democratic Party, which had been piling up for months, became raw and ugly as the delegates gathered and wrangled. There were fist fights in plenty; some

threats that implied guns, an intense irritation that might have broken out into a conflagration at any moment. The leaders of the Convention were so alarmed that they decided at one time to clear the galleries of all spectators before allowing the Klan question to come up. The police were the alternative precaution; it is probable that they alone made it possible to take that vote without riot and perhaps without bloodshed.

There is some doubt regarding the exact count on the vote. Some authorities say that the plank omitting the name of the Klan carried by less than one vote out of 1,089; others give it a majority of as high as five. But all agree that it carried. The Bryan-McAdoo forces had triumphed over those of Smith. But it was a Pyrrhic victory. The gulf that had opened between the factions was as wide as the winning majority was thin.

The remainder of the platform was adopted without controversy, and the balloting began. The first roll call gave 431½ votes to McAdoo and 241 to Smith. A walloping 461½ votes went to seventeen minor candidates, none of whom received as many as sixty votes. But their accumulated strength constituted a third force potentially strong enough to be decisive. It was not, however, a unified block. George Brennan of Illinois and Tom Taggart of Indiana were important elements in it, but they did not direct or dominate it. Nor could Smith or McAdoo. It was an unbossed convention.

The balloting ground on day after day. It was trench warfare with the rival forces deeply dug in. The watchword was not "Victory or Death," but "They Shall Not Pass." After thirty ballots Roosevelt said Smith would withdraw if McAdoo would. McAdoo wouldn't. Before the thirty-seventh, William Jennings Bryan tried to start a swing to McAdoo. The attempt fell flat. On the sixty-ninth ballot McAdoo reached his peak—530 votes. He lacked only twenty from having a simple majority but he was still 202 away from the two-thirds needed for nomination. He hovered around the 530 mark for a few more roll calls—and then he began to fall back. On the eighty-seventh ballot Smith passed him. That should have been exciting, but it wasn't. McAdoo had lost, but Smith hadn't won. He had only 368 votes, 364 short of nomination.

Naturally there was activity behind the scenes. McAdoo was trying hard to win support from favorite-son delegations. He felt that if he could just make a breakthrough on one or two fronts the opposition might collapse. But he could not make the breakthrough. In some cases minor candidates did not want to end the stalemate until both leaders collapsed, giving them a chance. In others it was a matter of not wanting McAdoo. Smith was a political realist. He knew after a few ballots that he could not be nominated, but was determined to stop Mc-Adoo at any cost, and win the nomination for the Eastern wing of the party. After fifty ballots he offered to back Oscar Under-wood if Underwood could get the support of two Southern states besides his own Alabama. Superficially this might appear to be a marriage of incompatible interests. In reality it was not. Underwood was wet and anti-Klan, and he was conservative, which made him acceptable to the Eastern financial interests. But compatible or not, the wedding did not take place. Un-derwood asked for twenty-four hours to win over the required two states. He failed to get even one. During long service in the Senate he had lost touch with the South. In a few years he would quit public life, not to return to Alabama but to live near Washington.

After the eightieth ballot a conference of representatives of all the candidates was held in the Waldorf Hotel. Once again Smith offered to withdraw if McAdoo would. McAdoo again re-fused. Governor Albert C. Ritchie of Maryland, himself a fa-vorite son, then suggested that all delegates be released from the instructions given them by their respective states. While requiring no candidate to withdraw, this would break the dead-lock and open up the race. The minor candidates and Smith consented, but again McAdoo representatives held out.

Although he was hanging on, McAdoo was through. And so, in effect, was the convention. Having failed to produce a strong candidate, it now fell into the hands of the party leaders. They knew it was too late to beat the Republicans, but a party bolt might be avoided, and there was always the question of the control of the national party organization. Party control had been the objective of the urban leaders since the Klan resolution had revealed the depth of Democratic fission.

The day after the meeting at the Waldorf, the plan to release delegates from state instructions was presented to the whole convention and accepted. Even McAdoo delegates voted for it, and McAdoo strength began to crumble on the next ballot when delegations previously bound to him switched to other candidates. On the one hundredth ballot McAdoo got only 190 votes, Smith 351½ and John W. Davis 203½. On the one hundred and second roll call Smith went over to Davis. On the one hundred and third Davis was nominated.

Why Davis? It was not because he was picked by bosses meeting in a smoke-filled room, or riding in a carriage in Central Park. Davis was not the product of machine politics, nor of urban Democracy; nor was he the champion of rural America. The Ku Klux Klan did not love him; Sauk Center would not recognize him as its own. He was chosen because by the one hundred and third ballot he was the right man, the man who could prevent a party bolt—and lead the Democrats to honorable defeat. He was brilliant. Although not popularly known he was respected and even honored by the well-informed. His record of public service was distinguished and unimpeachable. Summing him up, one newspaper editorialized that never had a faster horse been nominated on a slower track. The slow track helped make Davis the right man.

Technically his selection was a triumph for the Eastern wing of the party—the city conservatives and Catholic bosses. It insured that the national party organization would be in their hands. Since the Eastern wing was the minority faction in 1924 and seldom delivered electoral votes, this was a very real victory. Some observers saw it as an amusing variant of the city slicker taking in the country bumpkin. William Hard wrote in the *Nation*:

> Nothing was charminger to the delighted observer of human behavior in this vale of tears and guffaws than the McAdoo delegates in the New York Democratic Convention, who, having wept and prayed and shouted themselves hoarse and worried themselves sick over McAdoo and progressivism, led the march on the convention floor toward Davis and what William Jennings Bryan had denounced as an alliance with Wall Street.

This is only partially true. The McAdoo delegates knew what they were doing when they accepted Davis. In terms of practical politics his nomination was a defeat for them, but they cared less about practical politics than certain new forces in American life they neither liked nor understood. For one hundred ballots they grimly voted against Al Smith—against Catholicism and whiskey and foreigners. From such evils Davis offered sanctuary. He lived in New York but he was from West Virginia, and country people, especially Southerners, never forget where folks are from. He was dry and of sound American native stock. To many delegates and millions of small-town and rural Americans these things were more important than winning control of the national organization. They might not love John W. Davis; in the West they might even scratch him for Bob La Follette, but they would remain Democrats and vote for local and state Democratic candidates.

So on July 9th, after fifteen days of fighting, Davis was the right man with whom to lose. By that time there was no chance to win. If there ever had been a right man for winning it was neither McAdoo nor Smith. McAdoo could have carried the South and might have done well on the West Coast, but that would not have been enough. In the face of weakness in the East he would have had to win all the West—the 1916 Wilson feat—and with La Follette in the field he did not have a chance. Smith would have been even weaker than McAdoo. He was probably weaker than any man who received a vote in all the

one hundred and three ballots. That is a matter of record. Four
years later—even with dry and Klan strength ebbing—he was
nominated for the Presidency by acclamation after only one
ballot. He had a nominally united party behind him in a campaign during which he was acclaimed by frenzied crowds in
cities all over America. And on election day he was slaughtered.
He couldn't even carry his own state of New York. In the East
only Rhode Island gave him a majority; he lost every Western
and Midwestern state. Part of the South broke away—the rest
voted for him only because it hated General Sherman and radical reconstruction more than it did the Pope. Smith might have
been the right man in 1960. In 1924 he was thirty-six years
before his time.

But if an extraordinary political career marked by solid
achievement is the best preparation for the Presidency, Smith
was the best man. He was among America's most brilliant
graduates of the vocational school of practical politics. He
might have been a great President. And yet there are reservations. He was a master technician who understood New York's
problems. Was he a great statesman? Did he understand America beyond its urban borders? Did he comprehend the changes
that technology was bringing to the world? His post-1936 career
and final haven in the Liberty League raise grave doubts. It has
been said that Tammany has no foreign policy. Did its greatest
son have one? On this and most other current issues no one
knew just where he stood. By tangible measurements Smith
was the best man. By intangible ones there remains a question.

By no measurement was McAdoo the best man. Politically
he had occupied a high position on the general staff, but he had
not been the general. On the record he was a good man, in
some years he might have been the best one, but not in 1924.

John W. Davis was the most distinguished of the candidates,
and in terms of intellectual capacity the best. He was a brilliant
attorney and an able ambassador, but America has not been
particularly happy in the men elected President because of

excellence in nonpolitical endeavor. Like Smith, he was uncommitted on most of the issues of the day. This increased his availability as a compromise nominee; it makes assessing his qualities as a President more difficult.

Viewed in the light of the future, the nomination of John W. Davis may have deeper significance than could have been apparent in 1924. If it meant that control of the party and its future was to be in the hands of its Eastern wing it may have portended Roosevelt's New Deal alliance between the city machines and the A.A.A. farmers. It foreshadowed 1960 and John Kennedy. Without realizing what was happening, the Democratic melee at Madison Square Garden suffered out the birth pangs of a new era in American politics, one which was going to witness the evolution of the Democratic party in ways which were vaguely sensed but not understood by the warring factions as they waged battle.

McAdoo was sullen in defeat. Three days after the convention was adjourned he went to Europe. Upon his return he gave Davis only enough support to keep his status as a party member in good standing. He was later elected United States Senator from California, and he played an important part in Franklin D. Roosevelt's 1932 presidential nomination. But he was realistic enough to put away his own presidential dream. He knew he was numbered among the unchosen.

The Republicans
1952

THE 1952 Republican National Convention was characterized by paradox. Senator Robert Taft, "Mr. Republican," was defeated by Dwight Eisenhower whose political affiliation, if he had one, had been unknown until a short time prior to his candidacy, and whose service to the Republican party was nil. Robert A. Taft was defeated primarily on the grounds that "Taft can't win" yet he lost only one election during his whole career. He was known for an almost brutal honesty, but at the '52 convention his opponents shrieked, "Thou shalt not steal," and declared him morally unavailable for the nomination. Taft was not only the Republican party's foremost statesman, he was also its foremost champion of business; he was the Taft of the Taft-Hartley Act. Still when he lost the nomination the Chicago Tribune voiced a fairly common sentiment when it listed Wall Street as one of the factors in his defeat.

Nonetheless, there was logic in the convention's contradictions.

When the Republican National Convention met in 1952 the party had lost five successive presidential elections. Depression and Franklin Roosevelt had transformed it from the country's majority to its minority party. It was not on its deathbed but one or two more Democratic sweeps might put it there. It was more important than ever to nominate the right man, and the right man was the one who could get the most votes. If he was also the best man so much the better; if not, then the best man was a luxury the party could not afford. That was the mood of Republican politicians throughout the country. It was the mood of the convention.

Just who this right man might be was a question that stirred sharp difference of opinion. One wing of the party was certain he was Taft, another wanted General Dwight D. Eisenhower. The opposition to Taft was based in part on very real doubts that he could be elected, but it was more than that. It was rooted in a party division that dated back to 1936.

In 1936 Alfred M. Landon, the Republican presidential nominee, challenged the New Deal in principle and act. The result was the worst drubbing in the history of presidential elections. One consequence of this disaster was the emergence of what Taft was to refer to contemptuously as the "me-too" wing of the Republican party. This segment accepted the basic innovations of the New Deal, and centered its opposition on its administration, asserting that Republicans could do the job better. After World War II it also accepted the necessity of vigorous American leadership of the free world, and attacked the Democrats not on their foreign policy but on botching it. In addition to "me-too," this faction was also labeled the "international" and the "Eastern" wing of the party. It called itself various things—"the new conservatives," "the new Republicans." Sometimes it even seemed to hanker after being the "new liberals." New was always the key word, the abracadabra that wrought the transfiguration. Its front, though not its es-

sence, was the product of Madison Avenue. It had no pre-eminent leader, but at every national convention after 1936 it did have a candidate for the presidential nomination: Willkie in 1940, Dewey in 1944 and 1948, and Eisenhower in 1952.

The opposing wing of the party was known as the "old guard"; its members were "standpatters." To a considerable degree the labels were justified. Out of necessity it, too, accepted much of the New Deal as irrevocable, but it also rejected much and attacked the principles as well as the acts of Roosevelt and Truman. It sought to reduce rather than merely control governmental power. It did not covet the appellation new, and although it bore a resemblance to nineteenth-century laissez-faire liberalism it was proud to be known as conservative. Before 1942 this wing was isolationist; after 1942 with isolationism dormant it was nationalist. Its greatest strength was in the Midwest. Unlike the "me-tooers" the old guard did have a recognized leader. He was Senator Taft. He was their candidate for the presidential nomination in 1940, stepped aside for his Ohio colleague, John Bricker, in 1944, and tried again in 1948. Each time he and his legions were beaten by the Easterners. He knew that 1952 was his last chance.

These were the forces that clashed at the 1952 Republican National Convention. The party had not faced such a grave crisis since 1860 when Horace Greeley stalked the Wigwam croaking, "Seward can't win." It was Taft against Eisenhower, but it was something more. It was the Middle West, the old Republican heartland, against the East; it was intransigence against accommodation. Some believed it was the last stand of the old guard.

Taft and the old guard lost the battle. Who can say they lost the war! Dwight Eisenhower won the nomination and the Presidency. For eight years he was Mr. America, but Robert Taft remains Mr. Republican. And the voice of Goldwater is heard in the land.

Taft vs. Eisenhower

The question is not where they were but which way they were going. Were their faces set forward or backward?

— MACAULAY

Taft can't win.
Thou Shalt Not Steal.

As the delegates to the Republican party's twenty-fifth national convention converged on Chicago it is possible a few recalled that it was the thirteenth to be held in that city. Some may have reflected on the change that had taken place since Lincoln's 1860 nomination. The most significant innovation was television, for this was the first political convention to be nationally televised. There would be sixty-seven hours of televising at a cost of ten million dollars. Approximately seventy million people would view the proceedings. There were other changes undreamed of ninety-two years before. The Wigwam had been almost unbearably hot: the International Amphitheater, site of the 1952 convention, though still uncomfortable, was air cooled. Loudspeakers made most of the proceedings audible.

Outside the convention hall the hoopla designed to prove the popularity of candidates had changed little in spirit but had increased in intensity and fatuity. The brass bands of 1860 were supplemented by sound trucks; banners, once strung across the streets, were borne aloft by blimps and helicopters.

The trappings at candidates' headquarters had changed little. In 1860 Thurlow Weed had dispensed lavish hospitality at the New York delegation headquarters. In 1952, at Taft's $115-a-day Hilton Hotel suite, refreshments were served to the music of Sammy Kaye. Two floors above, at Eisenhower headquarters, delegates were showered with attention, gifts and campaign propaganda. The Eisenhower people had more flowers and hats, but with his "Belles for Bob," Taft had more girls to give them out.

Beneath the trappings, however, candidates' headquarters had undergone a century of radical change. In 1860 the rivals remained ostentatiously at home, awaiting the call to duty. It was a sham but it had advantages. The principals themselves avoided the posture of quarreling fishwives; unsavory deals might be made in their names but they were not personally involved. By 1952 such aloofness was a thing of the past. The presidential primary forced candidates to declare themselves and to campaign. The national convention was the culmination of the campaign.

In 1952 the rivals were both in Chicago with headquarters only two floors apart. Taft arrived a week early, saying he had a hard core of 510 delegates, less than a hundred short of the 604 necessary to nominate. He appeared confident and possibly was. In politics he had always tended toward optimism, foreseeing triumph because he willed it. He was often wrong but never totally disillusioned. There was a good reason. Like many of the unchosen he did triumph in all save his ultimate ambition.

Robert Alphonso Taft was born on September 8, 1889, in Cincinnati, Ohio. The Taft family, English in origin, had been in the United States for eight generations. Robert's grandfather served as United States minister to Austria-Hungary and Russia. His father was William Howard Taft, Secretary of War, Governor General of the Philippines, Chief Justice of the Supreme Court, and President of the United States. Robert Taft's is no saga of hardship. He did not have to struggle to the top; he was born there and maintained his position almost effortlessly by virtue of birth, intellect and character. Except for four years in the Philippines he grew up in Cincinnati. He was a quiet, shy boy, but there is no hint that his childhood was unhappy. If he was often alone it was from preference. During his father's Presidency he was in college. He got his B.A. from Yale and his law degree from Harvard, graduating from both with honors. He began his law practice in Cincinnati.

In 1914 he married Martha Bowers, the daughter of President William Howard Taft's Solicitor General. A brilliant woman, she was to play an important part in her husband's political career. The young couple bought an old rambling clapboard house at Indian Hills thirteen miles from Cincinnati and remodeled it. It was to be Taft's Ohio residence for the rest of his life. Here, at Washington and at a summer "cottage"—eighteen rooms and eight baths—at Murray Bay on the north shore of the St. Lawrence River, the Taft family lived. Taft did some amateur farming, played golf and read detective stories. Like hundreds of thousands of other successful business and professional men, he commuted to his office in the city.

World War I interrupted his law practice. He volunteered twice but was rejected each time because of nearsightedness. In 1917, however, he was appointed Assistant Counsel for Herbert Hoover's United States Food Administration. He did his work well enough to earn decorations from the governments of Poland, Finland and Belgium. Following the Armistice, Hoover took Taft with him to Europe. He was in Paris during the peace negotiations, and supported American participation in the League of Nations. It was his one wholehearted fling at internationalism.

The association with Hoover was to prove fruitful. The two had much in common: intelligence, a passion for marshaling facts, a sense of public responsibility and impatience with opposition. Above all they were both conservative. They also had a common lack of grace in their public relations and an inability to dramatize public issues. All this made Taft the political as well as the spiritual heir of Hoover. The legacy was of little value—the depression had rendered Hoover politically bankrupt.

After the war, Taft returned to Cincinnati. There, in 1920, he launched his political career. His rise was rapid if not spectacular. In 1921 he was elected to the State House of Representatives. As a legislator he was hard-working, effective and colorless. Later he was elected to the State Senate, but in 1932 he shared his party's fate and was beaten for re-election. It was his one defeat by Ohio voters.

For the next six years he practiced law and earned in his own right a position as one of Cincinnati's leading citizens. He was on the board of directors of numerous corporations, and his law firm was one of the best known in Cincinnati.

In 1938 he returned to politics as a candidate for the United States Senate. Two great obstacles stood between Taft and his goal. In the primary he had to defeat a candidate backed by the Republican State Chairman. Then, if successful, he would have to unseat the Democratic incumbent, Senator Robert Bulkley, who had already served two terms, and was backed by the prestige and patronage of the New Deal.

In the primary, Taft and his wife worked out the plans for his campaign, wrote the speeches and starting in different directions stumped the state. In their speeches Robert talked about issues, Martha talked about Robert. In a sense the wife's task was the hardest; Robert Taft was an honest product but not very attractively packaged. Martha Taft was equal to the occasion. Combating the myth that poor self-educated boys grew up to be the best Presidents, she said: "My husband is not a simple man. He did not start from humble beginnings. He is a very brilliant man. He had a fine education at Yale. He has been well trained for his job. Isn't that what you prefer when you pick leaders to work for you?"

Taft won the primary and was ready to take on Bulkley. This was only two years after Roosevelt had pulverized Landon, and other Republican candidates had gone down in droves. Unimpressed and unafraid, Taft made a frontal attack

on the New Deal, beginning with six joint debates with Bulkley. During the first he was booed but he kept on talking. He
talked through hundreds of speeches, some thirty thousand
miles of travel and two hundred thousand dollars' worth of
campaign money. He beat Bulkley by 170,597 votes.

Taft was forty-nine years old when he took his seat in the
United States Senate. He was about six feet tall with a large
bony frame. His hair was thin; he wore rimless glasses and a
derby hat. In private he was unassuming and open-minded,
but in public life he was often dogmatic, assertive and tactless.
Reportedly he once said it was dishonest to be tactful. He also
disapproved of political glamour. Perhaps this was sour grapes
—as one critic remarked, he had "all the glamour of a pint of
branch water."

This is not the portrait of a popular leader. He was not one.
He lacked Roosevelt's buoyant charm, Truman's earthiness,
Eisenhower's charismatic aura. He was not an orator such as
Henry Clay or William Jennings Bryan. He made little effort
to conciliate or to please. He was a solemn, stubborn man
whose very integrity had a jagged cutting edge. He was the
antithesis of a democratic politician. Yet he was "Mr. Republican." This was in part because of circumstances. In 1938 the
Republicans were so weak that any member who won a major
victory attained status as a national leader. Taft had won such
a victory. He had scarcely taken his seat in the Senate before
he was being mentioned as presidential timber.

When Taft entered the 76th Congress, only twenty-three of
the ninety-six United States Senators were Republicans. Small
as the band was, it constituted the nucleus of an opposition.
Taft's destiny was to lead this opposition, and it was in this
role that he was most effective. He was fitted for it by tempera-
ment and his devotion to conservative principles. Taft's credo
was that the opposition's function was forever to oppose the
majority with rocklike determination on matters of principle.
His unrelenting antagonism toward Thomas E. Dewey and the
group he represented was based on the conviction that they

had gone whoring with the New Deal. He, too, wanted to be President, but not that much.

His chief New Deal target was unnecessary spending. In this category he lumped both extravagance and expenditure for what he regarded as improper purposes. He favored balancing the budget by cutting government expenses. He did not admit to being antilabor but he did distrust Roosevelt's labor policies. On the whole he would not repeal the New Deal, but he would stop it in its tracks.

Throughout his career a troubled uncertainty—totally at variance with his certitude on domestic issues—marked Taft's views on foreign policy. Perhaps he recognized that facts, which he profoundly respected, were often in conflict with his deep-rooted isolationism. In 1920 he had favored American entry into the League of Nations, and on first entering the Senate in 1939 he supported Roosevelt's proposals for revision of the neutrality laws. But as time passed and war pressed closer he became more and more isolationist. He voted against peacetime conscription, Lend-Lease, extension of the draft, and, changing his earlier stand, against a revised Neutrality Act. Until Pearl Harbor he opposed United States entry into the war, and never seemed to have been fully convinced that our participation in it was necessary.

In 1936 Ohio's political bosses had advanced Taft as a favorite-son candidate for the presidential nomination. Their purpose, however, had been only to hold the state's delegation uncommitted, and he was not, in fact, placed in nomination. Nor had he considered himself a candidate. In 1940 he was a candidate and when he entered the race his chances seemed to be as good as anyone else's. Depression and defeat had so flattened the Republicans that the old leadership was discredited. This left room for new faces, and of these Taft's was the best known.

But there were others. The first to formally enter the field was Thomas E. Dewey, the New York City District Attorney who had won national prominence as a prosecutor of hitherto immune gangsters. In 1933 he had been beaten for governor by the Democratic incumbent Herbert Lehman. Lehman, however, was extremely popular and the vote was close enough to stamp Dewey as a good vote getter. Nonetheless, he had lost while in Ohio Taft was winning, and he had held no elective office while Taft was a United States Senator with years of political experience. Dewey had able managers and was well financed, but he was not quite ready.

If Dewey was not ready, Wendell Willkie's claim to Republican leadership appeared fantastic. Willkie was born a Democrat and remained one until 1938. Although his activity in politics had been limited, he had served on a Tammany committee and supported Franklin Roosevelt's foreign policy. A hundred Republican congressmen denounced his candidacy by implication when they demanded that the party nominee be a man whose views were consistent with the party's record in Congress. In the eyes of the old guard, if Dewey went whoring after the New Deal, Willkie was one of the whores.

Willkie was forty-eight years old in 1940. He was born on an Indiana farm and educated in the state's public schools. After graduating from Indiana law school he went to Akron, Ohio, where he practiced corporation law until he moved to New York. In 1933 he was elected president of Commonwealth and Southern, a utility holding company. In this capacity he clashed with TVA and the New Deal, drawing attention as a man willing to slug it out with F.D.R. at a time when most Republicans were running for cover. He was not a politician and to many Americans that was an asset. Maybe a businessman could beat Roosevelt.

The Willkie boom was launched early in 1940 with the formation of Willkie clubs. At first old-line politicians stood aloof and big business, although benevolent, stayed in the background. It was a businessman's grass-roots movement. But it was not spontaneous. On the contrary, it was launched and carefully nurtured by a well-financed organization. The political strategists were, as the fall campaign was to prove, political amateurs, but they were masters of public relations. Wendell Willkie, relatively obscure on Christmas, was a national figure by Easter.

Taft, too, was working hard. He concentrated on winning the support of political leaders and stayed out of the primaries. This does not mean that he neglected appeals to the public. Accompanied by his wife he visited twenty-eight states. They followed the Ohio campaign pattern, Robert talking on issues while Martha worked at humanizing Robert. Unfortunately Taft usually destroyed the image created by his wife. Although the favorite of old-line politicians and conservatives and respected by Republicans and Democrats alike, he was not loved by the people. Roosevelt said "my friends" and millions of men and women felt they had a friend and were comforted. Taft just couldn't do it.

On the eve of the national convention, Philadelphia was engulfed by carefully nurtured turmoil. Sound trucks rolled through narrow downtown streets, self-conscious delegates organized impromptu parades, the Union League Club, Republican almost to a man, strung electric bulbs that spelled out LOVE OF COUNTRY LEADS and WELCOME G.O.P. This was pro-Republican, anti-Democratic sentiment, but there was civil war as well. The rival candidates were waging a fierce publicity battle.

Outside Taft's headquarters at the Benjamin Franklin Hotel were two papier-mâché elephants adorned with red and yellow blankets labeled TAFT. One nodded sagely; the other wriggled its trunk. In the hotel ballroom there was a third elephant with a pretty girl posed on its back. The Republican Glee Club of Cincinnati toured streets and hotels playing Taft songs.

The Dewey camp, not to be totally eclipsed in the elephant department, distributed postcards with two of them nuzzling trunks and saying, "Do we want Dewey? We do." But the Dewey masterpiece was the $20,000 "highway pullman," stationed in the parking lot outside his headquarters. It had seven beds, a kitchenette, bathroom, and a medicine chest. Delegates who visited it were warmly welcomed.

Willkie's troops were working hardest of all. Shortly before the convention, five hundred "salesmen" arrived to "sell" Willkie—the climax to a campaign that for days had showered delegates with letters, postcards and telegrams. A booklet called *Win Wilkie as a Boy* described him as a young hell-raiser who upset privies and gambled away Sunday-school cards, and who was a radical enthusiast for Theodore Roosevelt's trust busting and Jack London's socialism. Trust busting and London's fuzzy ideas left a lot of Republicans cold. But the booklet did set Willkie apart from his chief rivals. It is difficult to picture Dewey, the great prosecutor, gambling away Sunday-school cards or Robert Taft upsetting a privy.

Ironically the publicity stunts and propaganda paid even smaller dividends than usual. Men's eyes, even those of the delegates were fixed elsewhere. On June 21st Marshal Pétain met Adolph Hitler in the forest at Compiègne. On the 22nd, Britain and the Netherlands were bombed. On the 23rd, Pétain signed the truce with the Reich. France had fallen. *The New York Times* squeezed hard to get in adequate convention coverage, and being the *Times* it did so. But stories that would ordinarily have been splashed all over page one were on page eleven or sixteen, with only a capsule account up front.

Despite the heightening European crisis, Taft refused to comment on foreign policy. Dewey in a pre-convention statement had advocated aid to the Allies without violating international or domestic law, or entering the war. Willkie had gone a step further by supporting reciprocal trade agreements and aid to Great Britain. Did the disasters in Europe affect the selection of the candidate? William Allen White, reporting from Philadelphia, believed the impact to be negligible:

> Upon foreign policy. . . . there is neither discussion nor purpose nor any consciousness of the terrible reality just ahead. . . . It is unthinkable that 1,000 men and women who have in their hands the destiny of their country should be entirely innocent, so puerile in their political attitude. . . .

As the convention opened, all indications pointed to a Dewey lead on the first roll call with Taft second and Willkie a poor third. No one expected the first ballot to be very significant, however; it was recognized that Dewey's following was so unstable that he might become a victim of polarization with his supporters falling off to Willkie on the left and Taft on the right. Should all three leaders fail, favorite sons and dimly visible dark horses were available.

The first ballot went about as expected. Dewey led with 360 votes, Taft was second with 189 and Willkie third with 105. The remainder was scattered among eleven candidates. With the second ballot a trend developed which was never to be checked. Dewey's strength waned, Taft gained slowly and Willkie shot up. By the end of the fourth roll call the contest was between Taft, 254, and Willkie, 306. On the fifth each gained 123 votes. The balance of power now rested with Michigan which had been voting for Senator Vandenberg, Pennsylvania which had remained uncommitted by casting its ballots for favorite son Governor James, and a scattered Dewey vote.

On the sixth ballot no decisive break occurred until Michigan was reached. Michigan voted for Willkie. Pennsylvania was next; she boarded the now fast-rolling bandwagon. When the roll call was complete Willkie was nominated with 655 votes. Three hundred and eighteen delegates stayed with Taft to the end.

Although Taft was to come much closer to the nomination later, 1940 set a pattern of frustration that was to be repeated. Willkie was the first of the "me-too" candidates. Dewey and Eisenhower were to follow. Willkie was a political upstart; Dewey was not but Eisenhower was. In 1940 Taft had promising frontline strength but lacked secondary strength. This was to be true later. A final characteristic of the recurring pattern was that the Taft following was so inelastic that it could not maneuver effectively. Stubbornly loyal to its leader, it would not combine with other groups to stop a rival or select a compromise candidate. Thus to the paradox of Mr. Republican's failure to be nominated for the Presidency is added the one that he had no influence on who was chosen. He was neither king nor kingmaker.

In 1944 Taft did not try for the presidential nomination, stepping aside for his Ohio colleague, Governor John Bricker. The sacrifice was not great—Dewey and the Eastern wing of the party had the nomination sewed up. Dewey won on the first ballot and Bricker settled for the vice-presidential consolation prize. Since Roosevelt beat the Republicans for the fourth time it couldn't have been much consolation. Taft was well out of the picture.

He himself had a narrow escape. Apparently overconfident, he did not campaign hard for Senate re-election and scraped through with a margin of only 17,000 votes. Yet he did win while Dewey was beaten, and he returned to the Senate, as one of the few prominent Republicans on the national stage.

In 1946 the Republicans won control of Congress for the first time since 1930. Taft moved from the opposition to the informal leadership of the majority. It was an opportunity not only to demonstrate his capacity for constructive statesmanship but also to build a record for another attempt at the presidential nomination. He did all this in the 80th Congress, but it probably hurt more than it helped him. President Truman denounced the 80th as the "do-nothing" Congress and made it an issue in the 1948 presidential campaign. The President's charge was inaccurate. The Congress did not do the things that Truman believed needed doing but it did do things. The Taft-Hartley Act was passed and the Knutson bill reduced income taxes—but mostly in the interest of the upper income brackets. Though it couldn't have been passed over Truman's veto without Democratic help, Taft-Hartley further alienated labor from the Republican party and spurred the unions to greater efforts in behalf of the Democrats. Knutson himself described the political consequence of his tax bill: "The Democrats said my bill was a 50-50 bill—gave a horse to the rich man and a rabbit to the poor man." He believed that it helped to "lick him." It undoubtedly helped to lick other Republicans. A third political blunder of the 80th Congress was to reduce the money available to the Commodity Credit Corporation. This resulted in a lack of funds to build cribs for the storage of corn and in turn forced farmers to sell at low prices. Truman was to win the election in the corn-hog belt.

All this is hindsight illuminated by the outcome of the 1948 elections. Before the election the Republicans were confident, more so than in any year since 1920 when they nominated Warren Harding. There were good reasons for optimism. Roosevelt was dead and few observers, including many Democrats, believed Harry Truman to be politically formidable. This opinion was further fostered by a poor Democratic showing in the 1946 congressional elections. It appeared that the voters were ready for a change.

With the Presidency seemingly a sure prize for the Republican nominee, and Dewey's 1944 defeat leaving the party with only a nominal leader, there was no dearth of aspirants to the nomination. Taft announced his candidacy in October, 1947. He had two important rivals: Dewey, somewhat rehabilitated from the '44 defeat by re-election as governor of New York, and Harold Stassen, former governor and Senator from Minnesota and recently released from service as an officer in the Navy. Other possibilities were Senator Vandenberg of Michigan, Governor Earl Warren of California and two general-heroes, Dwight Eisenhower and Douglas MacArthur. Eisenhower put himself out of reach in January. After receiving a notification that a movement was under way to line up delegates for him in New Hampshire, he "pondered a reply for a week," then declined:

> . . . I am not available for and could not accept nomination to high political office. . . . Unless an individual feels some inner compulsion and special qualifications to enter the political arena, which I do not, a refusal to do so involves no violation of the highest standards of devotion to duty. . . . It is my conviction that the necessary and wise subordination of the military to civil power will best be sustained and our people

will have greater confidence that it is so sustained when lifelong professional soldiers in the absence of some obvious and over-riding reasons, abstain from seeking high political office. This truth has a possible inverse application. I would regard it as unalloyed tragedy for our country if ever should come the day when the military commanders might be selected with an eye to their future potentialities in the political field rather than exclusively upon judgment as to their military abilities.

MacArthur, too, remained on the job, in Japan. He did permit his name to be entered in the Wisconsin and Nebraska primaries but his showing was not strong enough to keep his cause alive. For 1948 the military was out.

Both Taft and Dewey disliked primaries but Stassen, whose slim chance for nomination lay in demonstrating overwhelming popular strength, forced them to the hustings. Stassen challenged Taft in the latter's own Ohio. Taft stumped the state and won handily, but although he carried his case directly to the voters when forced to, most of the pre-convention campaign was conducted in states where there were no presidential primaries.

In 1948 the Republicans again held their national convention at Philadelphia. It was slated to open on June 21st. On the 20th Taft drove in from Washington. At his first conference he correctly predicted the race would be between himself and Dewey. He also said that he would get 312 votes on the first ballot and had a very good chance to win. As usual he was optimistic.

A spirit of genuine confidence marked the 1948 Republican National Convention. The New Deal's heyday was over, and the G.O.P., no longer on the defensive, was ready to tear Harry Truman to pieces. Governor Dwight H. Green of Illinois set the tone. Sweating under the bright TV lights, his collar wilted, he shouted:

"The New Deal party can have no real program, because it is no longer a real party. It mustered its majorities from a fantastic partnership of reaction and radicalism. For years this strange alliance was held together by bosses, boodle, buncombe and blarney. Such a party is all things to all men. The New Deal was just that. Its offspring was the sorriest series of broken promises in the history of our nation. . . . The New Deal party invited the lunatic fringe to share its feast of power. . . . The New Deal lived with those radicals in unholy intimacy for many years. . . . That group of crackpots was never competent to hold responsible office. . . ."

Not since 1924, when Senator Pat Harrison spewed forth abuse on the Republicans, had a national convention heard a more intemperate attack. But new depths were reached when the Connecticut congresswoman, Clare Booth Luce, photogenically standing in the floodlights, seemingly as fresh and unperturbed as if she were at a garden party, gave the country a foretaste of McCarthyism. Her phrase to describe the Democratic party was that it was "a mishmash of die-hard warring factions." According to Doris Greenberg of *The New York Times*:

> She identified these factions as the extreme right, or Jim Crow wing; the left or Moscow wing containing most of the nation's "political bubble-heads" and a "dangerous core of labor racketeers, native and imported Communists and foreign agents of the Kremlin"; and the center, or Pendergast wing, run by the "wampum and boodle boys, the same big city bosses who gave us Harry Truman in one of their more pixilated moments."

Since the "Jim Crow" wing was to secede from the Democrats to form the States' Rights (Dixiecrat) party, and the "Moscow" wing led by Henry Wallace was also to bolt, only the "wampum and boodle boys" would be left for Truman to rally in November. It was to be enough, but the Philadelphia delegates were unaware of the catastrophe that awaited them, and Mrs. Luce left the rostrum amidst volleys of applause.

By the fourth day the convention was ready to choose a candidate for the Presidency. Taft, Dewey, Stassen, Warren, Vandenberg, MacArthur and Governor Baldwin of Connecticut were placed in nomination. Taft got the longest and loudest ovation. It was his only triumph.

On the first ballot Dewey led with 434 votes; Taft was far behind with 224. On the second roll call Dewey's vote rose to 515. Clearly Dewey would win unless all other candidates united. A motion to adjourn was made and carried after confident Dewey managers declared that they had no objection.

The adjournment lasted for about three hours. During that time it was impossible to form an anti-Dewey coalition. Taft had previously refused to combine with Vandenberg in a pre-convention stop-Dewey move and Warren's views were closer to Dewey's than to Taft's. Stassen and Taft were separated by personal ill-feeling as well as policy differences. Nevertheless they did meet. The conference was held in a freight elevator to insure secrecy. Nothing came of it and when the convention reconvened, John A. Bricker read a message from Taft:

"A careful analysis of the situation shows that the majority of delegates will vote for Governor Dewey. I therefore release my delegates to vote for Governor Dewey, and to nominate him now."

Other candidates followed Taft's lead. Dewey was nominated by acclamation. It was the first time the Republican party had chosen a standard-bearer who had been previously defeated.

Taft accepted the verdict of the convention stoically. He said that Dewey would make a great Republican President, and campaigned for him in the South and West. But his heart could not have been in it. Registration figures and election returns notwithstanding, he stubbornly clung to the conviction that the Republicans could win without Democrats. They had only to get out their own party vote. According to the Taft thesis they were failing to do this because conservative Republicans, discerning no difference between "me-tooers" and New Dealers, stayed home on election day. They could be lured to the polls only by a hard-hitting, uncompromising REPUBLICAN campaign.

In spirit, although on a higher level, he was with Governor Green and Congresswoman Luce and could regard Dewey's soft sell only with contempt.

Dewey's second defeat at the hands of Truman finished him as a presidential candidate. It may have been equally lethal to Taft's ambitions. The reason for this is to be found in the nature of the campaign. In the opinion of Taft, Dewey lost because he failed to hit hard enough at Democratic vices and extol highly enough Republican virtues, including the record of the 80th Congress. Just as it is hard to quarrel with a winner so it is difficult to defend a loser, especially when, as Dewey's detractors claimed, defeat had been snatched from the very jaws of victory. Dewey waged his campaign and lost. Obviously his strategy had failed. But that is not proof that Taft's would have succeeded. Harry Truman campaigned as much against Taft as Dewey. He directed his sharpest barbs against the Taft-led 80th Congress. Might not Dewey's defeat have been caused less by his own mistakes than by the Taft millstone around his neck? He refrained from saying so but other anti-Taft Republicans were less reticent. It was about this time that the "Taft can't win" cry began to be heard.

This was in 1948. In 1950 Taft confounded his dismal critics. He was re-elected to the United States Senate by a landslide of 437,000 votes. Enemies attempted to discount his triumph by pointing out that his opponent was weak and that Republicans in general had gained in the off-year election. It was true, but the thumping 437,000 vote victory remained—the largest majority ever polled by an Ohio senatorial candidate. Taft had won.

Before the senatorial election his supporters said that if he won by as much as 250,000 votes he should try again for the presidential nomination. Twice burnt he did not commit himself immediately after his triumph, but in the spring of 1951 he did agree that it would be a good thing to sound out sentiment throughout the country. The resulting reports were encouraging. On October 16, 1951, he took the plunge, announc-

ing that he had agreed to run in the Wisconsin primary and permit the use of his name in Ohio. He added:

> I am going to run because I believe I can conduct the only
> kind of campaign which will elect a Republican to office. I
> believe we can extend to the entire nation the methods which
> we used in Ohio—a forthright presentation of our case to the
> people of this country, to the farmers and the workmen, to the
> businessmen and to all of those who accept American prin-
> ciples; a determined organization of every enthusiastic sup-
> porter to interest the voters who have stayed at home in such
> large numbers, but who can be interested and persuaded to vote
> if there is enough enthusiasm on the part of Republican sup-
> porters.

Taft said that he had received "more than 2,000 letters, telegrams, telephone calls, urging me to run, from numerous state
chairman, national committeemen, Senators, Congressmen,
publishers and other party leaders." It was something more
than the usual statement. Taft was saying: "We've had enough
of 'me-too' candidates. The party needs a gut candidate. One
who will go out and slug, not play around as Dewey did in 1948.
What do they mean Taft can't win? Look what I did in Ohio.
I can do it in the nation."

Taft was the first to announce but there were plenty of others
ready and willing. Earl Warren and Harold Stassen were anxious
for another try; Senator Dirksen, a Taft man, was an eager
understudy should his principal falter. The "Easterners," un-
converted and unrelenting, surveyed a field that ranged from
mediocre to great: Governor Driscoll of New Jersey, Senators
Lodge and Saltonstall of Massachusetts and Duff of Pennsylvania, and James Conant, ex-president of Harvard. And in
Paris, apparently uninterested, was General of the Army Dwight
D. Eisenhower.

The Eisenhower candidacy did not bloom overnight. It was
the consequence of assiduous cultivation. After Dewey's defeat
in 1948, his name was again brought forward and Dewey himself became an early Eisenhower convert. A year before Taft's

announcement, he was quoted by the New York *Herald Tribune* as saying that he would recommend that the New York delegation support Eisenhower in 1952 if the General would accept a draft. The next day, the General, who had written in 1948 that he was "not available for and could not accept nomination to high political office," said that he had not changed his sentiments. But the earlier message had also said that soldiers should not seek high political office "in the absence of some obvious and overriding reasons." This left a loophole. The draft-Eisenhower move was not abandoned.

By the summer of 1951 it was obvious that the obstacles to a draft were insurmountable. Unless Eisenhower came home, got out of the army and campaigned, he could not be nominated. The Easterners had no one else with whom they could beat Taft, so they increased the pressure on Eisenhower. All summer long congressmen, governors, Senators, visited Paris. They failed to get a commitment, but neither was the door slammed in their faces. They continued to work and hope. In September Roy Roberts of the Kansas City *Star* declared that his old friend Eisenhower had "confided in him that he was 'a good Kansas Republican.'"

Despite these indications, it was January, 1952, before there was any change clearly discernible to the public in Eisenhower's posture of aloofness. After a Paris meeting with the General, Senator Henry Cabot Lodge held a press conference in the lavish Eisenhower for President headquarters at the Shoreham Hotel in Washington. With TV and newsreel cameras whirring away, he told the fifty newsmen who were able to squeeze into the room—there were as many more outside—that Eisenhower was "a candidate to the full limit that Army regulations permit." In clipped, almost arrogant, phrases, he added that the General's name would be in the New Hampshire primary "to the finish," he would not be "running for exercise," and they could check his statements for themselves at the Supreme Headquarters near Paris. Lodge was emphatic: "I am speaking for the General and will not be repudiated."

At Eisenhower's Rocquencourt headquarters the first response to newsmen's inquiries was silence, but one of Eisenhower's staff meaningfully hinted that "silence is sometimes more eloquent than any statement." *The New York Times,* the New York *Herald Tribune,* the Chicago *Sun-Times,* the Providence (R. I.) *Journal* and *Life* magazine came forth with endorsements. Then Eisenhower, through his chief press officer, released a characteristically qualified statement:

"Senator Lodge's announcement of yesterday as reported in the press gives an accurate account of the general tenor of my political convictions and of my Republican voting record." He went on to say: "Under no circumstances will I ask for relief from this [NATO] assignment in order to seek nomination for political office and I shall not participate in the pre-convention activities of others who may have such an intention with respect to me." Then the hedge. "Of course there is no question of the right of American citizens to organize in pursuit of their common convictions. I realize that Senator Lodge and his associates are exercising this right in an attempt to place before me next July a duty that would transcend my present responsibility. In the absence, however, of a clear-cut call to political duty, I shall continue to devote my full attention and energies to the performance of the vital task to which I am assigned."

It was enough for his backers to go on, and if he knew it or not, General Eisenhower had taken a road from which he would not turn back. He was still angling for a draft but that failing he must hit the campaign trail.

The Eisenhower candidacy resulted in the Republicans' bitterest pre-convention contest since 1912. Until March it appeared that Taft would at last get the nomination, but with spring—and the New Hampshire primary—came a change. Eisenhower, Taft and Stassen were entered. Eisenhower beat Taft by over ten thousand votes; Stassen was a poor third. It was a setback for Taft, but his camp was not unduly discouraged, and when the General's aides said that the voice of the people had at last been heard over those of conniving politicians, Taft spokesmen pointed out that Eisenhower had had the support of Governor Sherman Adams' state machine and of seven other ex-state governors. New Hampshire was thus discounted as an index to popularity. Minnesota, which held its primary a week later, could not be. Here only Stassen, who was backed by the state organization, was formally entered. Eisenhower supporters waged a write-in campaign. The result was unparalleled in the history of presidential primaries. Stassen scraped through but his margin was only 20,000 over Eisenhower, who had polled 106,000 votes; Taft got 24,000. When told of the result Eisenhower was reported to have asked if that was good. The story may be apocryphal, but whether Eisenhower knew or not, Taft did. He knew it was appallingly good, and that he was in for another knockdown fight with the Easterners.

Minnesota and New Hampshire were particularly harmful to Taft. They gave force to the "Taft can't win" cry which had been raised again by his adversaries. This endangered the source of his greatest strength. Outside of the East, most state and local politicians preferred Taft. As organization men they resented Johnny-come-latelies who stepped in to snatch the prize that someone else had earned. So the boys in city hall, courthouse and capitol were for Bob and they didn't like Ike. And yet . . . many of them had to run themselves; to most, local office was more important than the Presidency. They wanted someone at the top of the ticket who would attract votes to those running at the bottom. Maybe that was Ike. Besides, Eisenhower elected was preferable to Taft defeated. In one case they might not get their fair cut of the victory pie. In the other there wouldn't be any pie to cut. This sort of talk put Taft on the defensive. He had to dissolve doubts as to his ability to win. It could only be done by beating his opponents in the primaries.

Even before the Eisenhower menace had become threatening, Taft had chosen Wisconsin as the proving ground of his ability to get votes. The selection had been carefully made. Wisconsin was the testing place for Republican presidential candidates. It had knocked out Wendell Willkie in 1944. In 1948 it put an end to an infant MacArthur boom and forced a too-complacent Dewey into an active campaign. A Taft victory in Wisconsin could be hailed as survival in a trial by ordeal. Actually the ordeal was not too terrifying for Taft. He had the support of Tom Coleman, the old-guard boss, and with the decline of the La Follette dynasty and the rise of Senator Joseph McCarthy Republican progressivism was on the wane.

The Eisenhower managers, recognizing their man's disadvantages in Wisconsin, kept him out. But since Stassen and Warren entered, Taft could claim that the state's primary would be a fair test of his ability to win. Taking no chances, he campaigned hard, addressing some hundred and fifty thousand people in over a hundred speeches.

Another crucial fight was being waged in Nebraska. Only Stassen had formally entered the primary, but both Taft and Eisenhower followers worked hard on a write-in campaign. The vote would mark the first direct test of strength between the two since the New Hampshire primary. It was important to Taft that he reverse the earlier verdict.

Both Wisconsin and Nebraska voted on April 1st. It was Taft's greatest day of the campaign. In Wisconsin he won twenty-four of the thirty delegates to Warren's six. Stassen was shut out and knocked out. In Nebraska Taft not only beat Eisenhower, but Stassen as well. Taft *could* win. He had survived the crisis and stalled the Eisenhower bandwagon. It would be a fight to the finish.

April 1st was also important to Eisenhower. It was his first lesson in politics. He was never a very adept pupil in the art, but he could master the elements when he had to, and with the Wisconsin and Nebraska reverses he learned what every politician must know, and did what every politician must do. He ate his words. On January 7th he had said, "Under no circumstances will I ask for relief from this [NATO] assignment in order to seek nomination for political office." On April 2nd he asked the Secretary of Defense to be relieved. The request was granted.

He would be relieved June 1st. That gave him about a month to campaign.

So, at the beginning of April the fairest dreams of both camps were shattered. There would be no easy victory for Mr. Republican; there would be no irresistible wave upon which Ike could float into power. Both sides girded for battle. It was waged fiercely, sometimes bitterly, always ruthlessly, both in the primaries and in local and state party conventions. By mid-April *Life* magazine's tally of committed delegates was Taft 201, Eisenhower 88. This was deceptive. New York's vote alone, not yet officially committed, would bring Eisenhower nearly even.

Eisenhower formally retired from the army June 2nd, voluntarily surrendering $19,541 annual retirement allowance in keeping with his high ethical standards. He was now free to campaign. On June 4th he made his first campaign address. It appeared to justify the Taft camp's prediction that when exposed to the heat of politics the war hero would be revealed as a fumbling statesman. Carroll Reece, strong for Taft, said unkindly that Eisenhower seemed to be for "mother, home, and heaven." Reece's error was in not realizing that so are the American people, and for father as well. And father had come home.

The campaign continued throughout June with neither candidate gaining a decisive advantage. Taft continued to pick up delegates and came out ahead in pledged votes, but Eisenhower won the battle of the public opinion polls. Taft had polled 2,785,990 primary votes in twelve states, Eisenhower 2,115,430 in nine; on the eve of the convention the Associated Press tabulated 458 delegates for Taft, 406 for Eisenhower. On the other hand, a Gallup poll report on trial runs between the two and Adlai Stevenson showed Eisenhower winning by a landslide 59 percent to 31 percent and Taft losing by a hair 44 percent to 45 percent. This nourished the "Taft can't win" theme. It is little wonder that he branded Gallup "just a propagandist for Eisenhower."

The last word of the experts appeared in *Newsweek* on June 30th. Fifty of the nation's "top political writers" divided 25 for Taft, 24 for Eisenhower, 1 for Warren. A month before, the same prophets had given Eisenhower a 35 to 11 lead with Governor Warren getting 3 and Senator Dirksen 1.

Primaries, polls and experts might agree that the race was close, but both sides continued to pretend great confidence. Taft claimed 603 or 604 votes (604 was the magic number); Henry Cabot Lodge declared, "The jig's up for Senator Taft." Both were whistling in the dark. Taft was far short of 604 votes, but neither was the jig up for him. It would be soon enough, however, for in the Texas issue his downfall was in the making.

The problem involved in the Texas contest was not new to Republican national conventions. Since 1872 the party in the South had been moribund. The only real reason for its being was to feed on crumbs of patronage from Republican Presidents. As a consequence, intraparty rivalry centered on controlling the delegations to national conventions in order to merit recognition and spoils. Few conventions had been without rival Southern delegations. These contests were generally settled to the satisfaction of the convention by its National Committee and Credentials Committee, but occasionally a minority report was carried to the floor of the convention. In such cases party rules provided that in a vote on contested delegation all delegates temporarily seated could vote on all contests except their own. Naturally these Southern contests caused trouble from time to time, but generally after a pained cry of "We wuz robbed," the storm passed. Not so in 1952.

Charismatic leadership—the one qualification no one denied Dwight Eisenhower—requires perfect virtue in the leader. Correspondingly the opposition must be impure. The Democrats were to find this out in 1952 in a campaign that was mounted as a crusade of the righteous. This posture of perfection was more or less successfully maintained through vicissitudes that included vicuna coats, the revelation that the candidate for Vice-

President had been, while a Senator, subsidized by a business group, and the resignation of key administrators charged with conflict of interest. Democrats found it irksome and even unfair, but they should remember that the first victim of the great crusade was not a Democrat at all; it was Mr. Republican, whose admirers also called him "Mr. Rectitude."

Robert Taft was not only the first victim of the great crusade; he was the burnt offering necessary for its launching. The Republicans knew from the start that no Democrat existed who could beat Ike in the general election. But securing the nomination was something else. In a fight confined to Republicans—and some Texas Democrats—Taft *could* defeat Eisenhower—and he almost did. At Aulis, Agamemnon sacrificed his beloved daughter Iphigenia that the ships might sail to Troy. At Chicago the Eisenhower faction—dispensing with the Greek king's grief—sacrificed Mr. Republican that the Eisenhower crusade could begin to roll. They picked up a few fagots for the sacrificial fire in Louisiana and Georgia, but most of them came from Texas.

It grew out of the closeness of the race. With every vote needed, the Eisenhower camp could not afford to give Taft anything by default. It was decided to raid his instructed delegations. In Georgia and Louisiana troops for a counterattack were at hand. In Georgia there had been two Republican factions for years. The then-dominant one was for Taft. Through control of local conventions it had named a Taft delegation to Chicago. The dispossessed—and steam-rollered—were naturally ready to board the Eisenhower train. In Louisiana, too, a rival faction was trying to wrest party control from the regulars who were for Taft.

Texas was different. Oil and industry had created powerful business interests in the state. These had accommodated themselves to the Democratic party, and had not done badly. Still they were not altogether happy. Texas Democratic politicians in Washington looked after strictly Texas interests, but on problems of broad national policy they had a deplorable

habit of voting like Democrats. Actually Texas Democrats, unlike their brethren in the Deep South, were not bound to their
party by pathological thongs of loyalty. There the classic Southern tradition was diluted by that of the West. In Fort Worth,
Houston, Amarillo, El Paso, the fragrance of magnolias and
crepe myrtle mingled with the smell of cow dung and oil. Consequently the Texas conflict was more than the clash of two
impotent factions of a moribund G.O.P. The Eisenhower Republicans were trying to build a Republican party that would
make Texas a Republican, or at least two-party, state. They
were backed by business interests that aimed at rewards far
greater than crumbs of patronage. They included thousands of
men and women who had previously been Democrats. This
fusion was facilitated by the fact that Texas had no party registration system, and that the laws regarding party membership
were vague.

In all three states, Georgia, Louisiana, Texas, the fight followed a somewhat similar pattern. Rival local factions named
rival delegations to state conventions. There pro-Taft officials
threw out enough opponents to give them control and name
Taft delegations to Chicago. It was an old game sanctioned by
custom. But in Texas a new defense was presented. There the
Eisenhower delegates were branded as Democratic wolves in
Republican sheep's clothing. Their only Republican credential
was a card they had signed saying that they were Republicans.
As such they were welcome to the party, but only as privates,
not as generals to take it over. The Eisenhower side retorted
that their procedures had been legal (which was true) and
that the new party members were entitled both legally and
morally to be considered bona fide Republicans.

The state convention was held at Mineral Wells on May 27th.
The Taft faction controlled the party machinery and threw out
enough Eisenhower delegates to give them a majority. They
then elected a Taft delegation to the Chicago convention. The
Eisenhower people held a rump convention and elected an
Eisenhower delegation.

To Taft and his command these southern civil wars were only fights for control of the party machinery being carried on along traditional lines. If they resulted in contested delegations the Republican National Committee, the Convention Credentials Committee, and if need be the convention itself would at the proper time take proper action.

But the Eisenhower camp was in search of a crusade as well as delegates. In Texas they found it, and exploited it brilliantly and unscrupulously. Before the Mineral Wells meeting Henry Cabot Lodge announced that it would hold unusual significance. After it the cry of theft was raised. It was not merely a matter of votes; it was also a matter of morals. The moral issue was emphasized throughout June. It crested, as planned, the first week of July. Before he left Denver for Chicago on a leisurely whistle-stop tour in his thirteen-car special train, Eisenhower avowed that he was going to "roar out across the country for a clean, decent operation." As he barnstormed along, he referred to the "back-room schemings" to thwart his nomination. On July 4th there were three speeches at Ames, Iowa. In one of them, televised nationally, he declared that there was a "straight-out issue between right and wrong." Mindful that it was a patriotic holiday, he added, in a lofty tone: "Political integrity and majority rule are the cornerstones of American Government. Those who seek to ignore them or scoff at them or destroy them, do damage not only to our party but to the nation. It is because these issues are at stake that I am in this fight." In other rear-platform statements he charged the Taft faction with using "chicanery" and "crookedness."

When Taft arrived in Chicago for the convention, he was greeted by a brass band, a crowd of friends, TV cameras and hurly-burly which caused him to snap out with the remark that such confusion was a good reason for not televising national committee meetings. The Eisenhower entry into the convention city was far otherwise; it was carefully planned to send him to the annual reunion of the 82nd Airborne Division, where "amid flickering candles and muffled drums for the dead,

Eisenhower wept." The father image had been projected to perfection.

Meantime, about a week before the convention, the Republican National Committee met to prepare a report on the temporary convention roll of delegates to be submitted to the Credentials Committee. A telegram from Herbert Hoover urged compromise on the disputed delegations and suggested that a panel of distinguished Republicans arbitrate. A letter from Taft followed. He too suggested a compromise on the Texas issue, 22 votes for himself and 16 for Eisenhower. This seems to have fairly represented Texas sentiment, as reflected by the local conventions. But the Eisenhower command would have none of it. Even before the National Committee acted, Lodge issued a statement from Eisenhower headquarters at the Hilton Hotel. "There will be no compromise. . . . The American people will not stand for smoke-room tactics." Disregarding Lodge's warning, the National Committee voted 60 to 41 to accept the Taft proposal.

The next assault on Taft came from the annual Governor's Conference which was being held in Houston. This is a nonpolitical gathering designed for the discussion of state problems. But most of the Republican governors were there and their party convention was a week away. It was not to be expected that they could resist politics. They didn't. On July 2nd, just five days before the national convention, they issued a manifesto. Just who cooked it up is not generally known, but it was signed by twenty-three Republican governors. It declared that contested delegates should not be allowed to vote on any contest until the convention itself had seated them.

On the surface it was merely a resolution on procedure. But it was intended to damage Taft and it did. More of his than of Eisenhower's delegates had been seated by the National Committee. Under the existing rules contested delegates could not vote on their own contest but could vote on those of other states. In a close roll call these votes might determine who was to be seated, which in turn might determine who was nominated.

The manifesto also had a psychological effect that hurt Taft. It made it appear that the twenty-three governors who had signed the manifesto were against him, and added fuel to the accusation that Taft was trying to steal the nomination.

Guy Gabrielson answered for Taft. He pointed out that the existing rule had been in effect since 1912 and had the authority of time and use. He asked why, if it was so bad, the rule had not been changed in 1944 or 1948 when the Dewey (Eisenhower) faction of the party was in control of the convention machinery. He was answered by shriller cries of "Thou shalt not steal."

On the day before the convention, the "Citizens for Eisenhower Committee" placed a full-page advertisement in the Sunday edition of Colonel Robert R. McCormick's Chicago *Tribune*. (McCormick was using his paper for Taft.) This advertisement was addressed "To *all* Republican delegates." It then declared:

> The eyes of the nation are on you. The nation may *differ* as to WHO should be nominated. But the nation *agrees* that there must be no shadow of doubt that the winner of the Republican nomination—no matter who he may be—was *honestly* nominated, in a *free* and *unrigged* convention. . . . Unless the American people have confidence that they were not cheated of their votes and that our nominee was duly and freely chosen in an *unrigged* convention, this convention might better never have been held."

Young Eisenhower supporters carried the THOU SHALT NOT STEAL standards onto the convention floor.

The convention was called to order on Monday, June 7th. After the opening formalities Senator Bricker made the routine motion to adopt the previous rules. It was not routine on this occasion. Governor Arthur B. Langlie of Washington immediately offered an amendment that provided that no contested delegate if seated temporarily by less than a two-thirds majority of the National Committee could vote on any other contested delegation until he himself was seated by vote of the whole convention. That it was a maneuver in the Eisenhower quest for delegates rather than a reform in the rule is made clear by the fact that it was to apply only to the 1952 convention. Taft emphasized this in his *Analysis of the Results of the Chicago Convention* written after his defeat:

> . . . The Eisenhower press made a moral issue of the change in rules, although it was contrary to all parliamentary procedure, and was admittedly proposed only for this Convention because of the danger of making it a permanent rule.

The Langlie amendment was debated for two hours. In the course of the arguments Congressman Brown of Ohio, a Taft delegate, proposed an amendment to the Langlie amendment which would exclude seven Louisiana delegates from any contest on the grounds that they had been declared the legal delegates by the Louisiana Republican State Committee. As a consequence, although both sides knew that it was the Langlie amendment that was at stake, when a vote was taken it was on the Brown amendment. Taft lost, 658 to 548. The Eisenhower delegates had been re-enforced by Warren's, Stassen's and most of those not yet committed. This did not mean that they were lost to Taft on the decisive nominating roll calls, but it was ominous in that they had temporarily committed themselves to the Eisenhower crusade. Having once donned the garments of purity it is difficult to discard them. Recognizing that the first battle was lost, a Taft delegate moved the adoption of the Langlie amendment. The motion carried unanimously.

Taft was by no means through. On Tuesday and Wednesday the Credentials Committee, dominated by the old guard, ruled on all contested seats. It awarded Eisenhower all but two of the Louisiana delegates and Taft all of Georgia's. It accepted the Taft compromise on Texas. Including minor contests the total score on contested seats was Taft 76, Eisenhower 21.

As expected, when the committee report was brought to the convention for approval, an Eisenhower delegate offered a minority report recommending seating Eisenhower's Georgia delegation. It was a test vote. As Georgia went so would Texas. In the subsequent debate Senator Dirksen entered the lists as the Taft champion. His speech was the most dramatic of the convention. Millions of people watching television saw him point an admonitory finger at Governor Dewey who was sitting with his New York delegation and cry scornfully: "We followed you before and you took us down the path to defeat." Millions of people saw Dewey stare back impassively, and heard boos from delegates. Whether the boos were directed at Dewey or Dirksen could only be surmised.

When the debate was over the roll was called. Taft lost again, 607 to 531. The danger of theft (at least by Taft) had been averted.

Taft's defeats on the Langlie amendment and Georgia deegation contest were significant beyond the number of votes involved. They indicated to those uncommitted delegates who were eagerly sniffing the air to detect which way the winds of victory were blowing that Eisenhower was probably their man. Taft wrote that because of these two defeats "our prospective strength on the first ballot fell well below [Eisenhower's] strength, and he had all the bandwagon advantage which we otherwise would have had."

The losses on the first roll calls were caused in part by earlier reverses. They were less spectacular than the battle of Texas but possibly more decisive. There were 128 uncommitted votes at the convention—enough to determine the nominee. The two largest blocks were Michigan and Pennsylvania. Taft had hoped for at least twenty-seven Michigan votes, and, less confidently, for substantial support from Pennsylvania. But the bosses, Michigan's National Committeeman Summerfield and Governor Fine of Pennsylvania, were against him. Although he got some votes from each state the total fell considerably below expectations.

Pennsylvania was following a familiar pattern. From 1860, when she plumped for Lincoln, to 1952, it, more than any key state, had held off committing its votes until it could be reasonably sure it had chosen a winner. Upon occasion it has waited too long, but in 1952 most of the state's delegates were safely aboard before the opening day of the convention, and voted against Taft on the Langlie amendment and Georgia contest.

In Michigan there had been no pre-convention Taft-Eisenhower fight. Of the forty-six delegates sent to Chicago thirty-three were uncommitted, the others divided about evenly. Presumably the delegation was willing enough to land on the winning side, but there was a more pressing problem. Governor Williams and the United Auto Workers were in the process of transforming Michigan from a banner Republican to a Democratic state. As a result Michigan Republicans were more anxious than usual to get a presidential candidate who would bring votes to the whole ticket. They had to beat "Soapy" (they never did) ; this was more important than any presidential smiles or patronage that might accrue. "Taft can't win" turned the scales. They needed Ike.

Candidates were put in nomination on the night of June 10-11. Senator Dirksen proposed Taft. He called him Mr. Republican, Mr. Integrity, Mr. America. He said he was the trustee of the American legacy which came down from Lincoln and he again attacked Dewey as a leader of lost causes. Governor McKeldin of Maryland presented Eisenhower's name. Warren and Stassen were nominated as expected. General Douglas MacArthur was an added starter. It was long after midnight when all the nominees were duly entered. The convention adjourned until next morning.

On Friday morning Chairman Martin called the convention to order. A few minutes later the roll call began. It was a massive two-man fight. When it was over Taft had 500 votes, Warren 81, Stassen 20, MacArthur 10. Eisenhower had 595, only nine short of a majority. Stassen promptly switched 19 votes and it was all over. Taft was again unchosen.

Analysis of the roll call by regions is suggestive. Taft led 232 to 112 in the Middle West; in spite of the Georgia, Louisiana, Texas reverses he won the South 119 to 103; Warren had 71

Western votes, of the remainder Eisenhower nosed out Taft, 79 to 78. But in the East, Taft was slaughtered, 301 to 71. The Internationalists and "me-tooers" had done it again. There is meat for further conjecture. In 1952 and again in 1956 Eisenhower carried the East handily, but the Republican vote increased there less than in any other section of the country. As long as Ike was running it didn't matter, but the 1960 election raises an interesting question. Does the Eastern wing of the G.O.P. party choose the candidate, while it is the Middle West and West, with a little help from the South, that must elect him if he is to be elected?

After his nomination General Eisenhower's first political move was to visit Taft in his headquarters at the Conrad Hilton Hotel. As he entered the corridor leading to Taft's room he was booed. It did not often happen to him in America. Taft met him at the door.

> EISENHOWER: "I came over to pay a call of friendship on a great American. His willingness to cooperate is absolutely necessary to the success of the Republican party in the campaign and of the Administration to follow."
>
> TAFT: "I want to congratulate General Eisenhower. I shall do everything possible in the campaign to secure his election and to help in his administration."

Taft kept his promise. He did campaign for Eisenhower and he did help in his administration. In fact he virtually took over its legislative program. Publicly he urged his friends to have tolerance and avoid recrimination. But privately he was bitter. His resentment boils over in his private analysis of the reasons for his defeat:

> The whole strategy of the other side was to change the rules and get enough votes to steal all the contested delegates. . . .
> If there was a moral issue, my suggestion that I be allotted only the district delegates clearly not contested, and that representatives of both sides discuss the whole matter in detail, district by district, certainly should have destroyed the issue.

But the press was completely unfair in their treatment of it. Adverse national committeemen frankly admitted that they could not even sit down and talk about the merits of the various Taft contests, because it would deprive them of the smear issue.

Thus he charges that the authors of the "Thou shalt not steal" issue were themselves thieves, and that such cries as "corruption," "chicanery" and "no compromise" were utilized as a protective cloak by hypocrites bent upon a smear. It is a grave and bitter indictment, but Taft himself had been subjected by the pro-Eisenhower press and Eisenhower headquarters to greater abuse that had less justification.

General Eisenhower was the right man. Taft *might* have won but Eisenhower did win. Facing a crisis which required that the party should not lose a sixth successive national election, the Republican delegates could not afford to gamble on Mr. Republican. Available data indicated that there were not enough Republicans to win. Independent and Democratic votes were essential, and as the symbol of dyed-in-the-wool Republicanism, Taft would not attract them. Eisenhower, a war hero, a transparent man of good will whose Republicanism was of too recent vintage to have engendered partisan antagonism, would. Taft's appeal was that the country needed a strong Republican President; Eisenhower that it needed a savior. The times were troubled; the people wanted to be saved.

Viewed from Chicago, 1952, Taft was the best man. He had political experience; he was familiar with every aspect of national policy; he understood the function and responsibilities of the presidency. Eisenhower, by reason of his training and preoccupation with his duties as a soldier, had less knowledge than the average informed American layman of the operation of the country's political system and of the country's social and economic needs. His brief experience as president of Columbia University gave no grounds for confidence in his capacity or will to adapt himself to unfamiliar responsibilities. The Eastern wing of the Republican party branded Taft a standpatter. He was, but this is more meaningful as a description of his source of political strength than as a means of distinguishing him from Eisenhower. *Newsweek* said on June 23, 1952: "On the issues Taft and Eisenhower were taking similar, if not identical positions in most areas." Only on fiscal matters was there a sharp difference. Here Eisenhower expressed the opinion that the budget could be cut $40,000,000,000 in a few years. As skeptical of Republican as Democratic pie-in-the-sky, Taft ridiculed the figure as much too high, and cited it as an example of Eisenhower ignorance. History proved him right.

Eisenhower's command made much of his experience with international politics, and compared it to Taft's provincial isolationism. If foreign affairs are to be carried on through personal contacts, Eisenhower did have the advantage. He knew many of the leaders of the nations of the world, most of whom probably had greater confidence in him than in Taft. If, however, foreign policy were to be formulated and carried out by the Secretary of State—and under Eisenhower it was until the death of Dulles—there probably would have been less difference between Eisenhower's and Taft's conduct of international affairs than might at first appear.

In 1951 Taft published a book, *A Foreign Policy for Americans*. In a pre-publication article in *Look* magazine he summarized his principal arguments. He castigated the Democrats for past sins but approved the Truman-Acheson policy of containment if only it could be made more "affirmative." He wrote:

> There is much more agreement on the general character of the strategy to be adopted than is generally supposed. For the present our policy may be said to be one of containment; but it certainly carries the hope that we can develop an affirmative policy which will constantly extend the doctrine and the power of liberty.

This could have been written by Dulles and said by Eisenhower.

On the whole Eisenhower and the men around him were the best choice if only foreign policy were to be the issue, but the advantage was not great enough to compensate for Taft's superiority when all aspects of presidential responsibilities are considered. It must be repeated that this is the view from Chicago in 1952. The convention delegates took the man most likely to win. In doing so they rejected the one best fitted for the Presidency.

Robert Taft's futile quest for the Presidency ended July 11, 1952. He was not, however, done with politics. In the short time left to him he rose to new heights of power and prestige, and put the finishing touches on the legend of Mr. Republican.

After the convention he went to his summer home at Murray Bay for a rest. Upon his return he met Eisenhower at Morningside Heights in New York City, and presented him with a policy manifesto. After a two-hour conference the General signed the document subject to a few minor changes. This does not mean that Eisenhower had abandoned his principles. He had always been as conservative as Taft.

Taft next turned to the Senate. He organized it while his erstwhile opponents were still preening themselves on their victory, and considering in what honorary moth bag they would enshroud poor old Bob Taft. He got himself elected minority leader of the Senate, and his followers appointed to the important committee posts. Senators who had worked hard for Eisenhower found themselves shunted to one side. Henry Cabot Lodge was not among these. He had been beaten for re-election to the Senate by Representative John F. Kennedy. Kennedy could probably have done the job without Republican help but he got some from angry Taftites.

Early in the spring of 1952, Taft led a group of Republican congressional leaders to a White House conference. They did not go to be briefed, but to consult with the President and give him advice. The best man was instructing the right man regarding the responsibilities of his job. The two worked together amiably and understandingly, if not intimately. Walter Lippmann said that Taft was beginning to act as a kind of prime minister for the President. Other observers remarked upon Taft's loyalty to his chief. He was loyal to President Eisenhower, but in a larger sense he was being loyal to himself and what he considered to be the real Republican party. He was serving the party by trying to convert the President to its historic principles. He was not wholly successful, but as a veteran statesman he knew and practiced the art of getting what he could. "[The Eisenhower program] certainly isn't all I'd like it to be . . . but I think I can go along with it most of the way. When I can't I guess I'll just say so and be satisfied with getting myself on the record."

So to the end he compiled his record. It was the record of Mr. Republican.

He died of cancer on July 31, 1953. They buried him in the Indian Hill Episcopal churchyard near Cincinnati where he was born. But it is not Robert Taft of Cincinnati who is remembered. It is United States Senator Robert Taft of Washington, D. C. There a memorial tower stands on the Capitol grounds. It houses a twenty-seven-bell carillon. At its base is a bronze statue of Robert Taft.

In 1959 the United States Senate established its own Hall of Fame. In it are portraits of Henry Clay, Daniel Webster, John C. Calhoun, Robert M. La Follette, Sr., and Robert A. Taft. They were chosen by a selection committee headed by Senator John F. Kennedy of Massachusetts. The committee reported that it had not attempted to select the five greatest senators but the five who represented:

> . . . to the extent possible the most significant periods in the history of the Senate; the highest traditions and qualities of the Senate and its members and the great political and regional movements of the past—men whose statesmanship, transcending

party and state lines, left a permanent mark on our nation's history and brought distinction to the Senate.

Taft was chosen as the outstanding representative of the conservative movement of the twentieth century. Perhaps his fame is more secure in that role than had he been President.

The Democrats

1952

IN 1952 the Democratic National Convention rejected Senator Estes Kefauver of Tennessee as its presidential nominee, and chose Illinois governor Adlai Stevenson. Kefauver entered the race early and traveled over fifty thousand miles in quest of the nomination; Stevenson would not even say he would accept it if drafted. Kefauver entered sixteen primaries and won fourteen of them; Stevenson entered none. Kefauver came to the convention with some two hundred and fifty pledged delegates; Stevenson had forty-one and a half, all unsolicited. Kefauver's name was known throughout the nation; outside his own Illinois, Stevenson's was relatively unfamiliar. Nevertheless the convention took Stevenson. It appears capricious, but as in the case of Robert Taft's rebuff at the hands of the Republicans two weeks earlier, there was sound logic behind Kefauver's defeat.

In July, 1952, the Democrats were approaching the end of

266] THE DEMOCRATS—1952

twenty years of presidential power. During most of that time they had controlled both branches of Congress and occupied the governor's mansion in most of the states. The Democratic party had become the nation's majority party. Yet it faced the probability of defeat in the approaching presidential election. Voters grow tired of a party too long in office, or perhaps they sense the value of periodic change; authority entails responsibility for action and every action is distasteful to some segment of the electorate. In twenty years, the accumulation of grievances becomes ominous. These are perils inherent in long tenure in office. In 1952 the Democrats had additional troubles. Scandals in the Truman administration had been revealed, the Korean War was unpopular, the cost of living was high, General Eisenhower, a glamour candidate with strong popular appeal, had just been nominated by the Republicans. In the face of these handicaps only a firmly united party led by the right man could hope to win.

Unfortunately the party was not firmly united. The Dixiecrats were once more calling themselves Democrats but their allegiance was of doubtful quality. After their thrashing by Truman in 1948 they were unlikely to embark on another third-party adventure, but if the wrong candidate were to be chosen they might sulk or bolt to Eisenhower whose Republican affiliation was so recent as to be relatively inoffensive. The Henry Wallace Progressive movement was dead, but the left wing of the Democratic party was very much alive and determined not to compromise its principles, particularly in regard to civil rights. The right man must be acceptable to them as well as to the South. Between the extremes was the majority that wanted first of all to win and was ready to compromise in order to do it. It was this center group that judged Estes Kefauver unavailable and turned to Adlai Stevenson. It was the only draft in the history of the Democratic party.

Kefauver vs. Stevenson

This coon has rings in his tail, but I want you to remember I have no ring in my nose.
                                                    —ESTES KEFAUVER

This is a convention in search of a candidate.
                                                    —ANNE O'HARE MCCORMICK

ESTES KEFAUVER was born in Madisonville, Tennessee, on July 26, 1903. His paternal ancestors came to America from Alsace-Lorraine in the middle of the eighteenth century. His mother, Phredonia Estes, was of distinguished Italian stock. Members of the Estes family migrated to America before the Revolution and fought in that war. Robert Cooke Kefauver, Estes' father, was one of Madisonville's leading citizens. He owned a hardware store, built the town's only hotel, bought real estate and engaged in local politics. He was mayor of Madisonville for twenty years. In 1912 he stumped the country-side for Woodrow Wilson. Estes accompanied his father during this campaign, nailing posters on trees. It may have been his earliest political activity.

Kefauver was a leader in both high school and college. He was on the high school basketball and baseball teams, was secretary-treasurer of his class and editor of the yearbook. At the University of Tennessee he was editor of the college paper and president of the junior class and of the All Students Club. In his senior year he was president of the Southern Federation of College Students. He was also on the varsity football and track teams. Somewhere along the way he found time to study.

Following graduation he taught school and coached the football team in Hot Springs, Arkansas, where he had taken his mother for her health. A year later he decided to study law. He chose Yale and worked part of his way through by waiting on tables. Upon his graduation he returned to Tennessee and entered a prominent Chattanooga firm as a junior partner. In 1932 he was named East Tennessee vice-president of the Tennessee Bar Association and later was a member of the American Bar Association's central council. During the depression years of the thirties his income from his practice—largely insurance and corporation law—rose to $25,000 a year.

In the summer of 1934 Estes Kefauver met green-eyed, red-haired Nancy Pigott. Miss Pigott's father was an American marine engineer who went to Scotland and stayed to eventually become manager of a British shipbuilding firm. In time he designed the engines for the *Queen Mary* and *Queen Elizabeth* and was knighted. Nancy graduated from the Glasgow College of Art, studied art in Paris and worked in London as a "dress designer, book illustrator and interior decorator." She was visiting an aunt in Chattanooga when she met Kefauver. They were married in Scotland in 1935 and returned to Chattanooga where they first rented and then bought their own house on Lookout Mountain. Nancy Kefauver came to share her husband's political interests. During his campaigns she worked almost as hard as he did. In response to a comment that he was a "Red," Kefauver once said, "The only thing Red about me is my red-haired wife, Nancy."

Estes Kefauver entered politics as an apostle of reform and an enemy of bossism. It was in this role that he was to become known first in Tennessee and then throughout the United States. It was the source of much of his success, but it also played an important part in his failure to win the Democratic presidential nomination. It carried him to the United States Senate and into the race for the Presidency. But although American Presidents have wrought reform, neither major political party has ever nominated a man whose chief claim to recognition was reform. It was under the aegis of George Fort Milton, the brilliant historian (author of *The Eve of Conflict* and *The Age of Hate*) and civic-minded publisher of the Chattanooga *News,* that Kefauver made his start in politics. Many of Kefauver's early political attitudes—on social legislation, constitutional reform, the TVA and other liberal measures— were influenced by the genial but dynamic Chattanooga publisher. In later years, Kefauver's emotional spur in championing the TVA may well have come from his knowledge that it was Milton's support of TVA which induced the Tennessee Electric Power Company, a subsidiary in Wendell Willkie's Commonwealth Southern Utilities empire, to drive Milton out of the newspaper publishing business. The episode cast a permanent blight upon Milton's later career and life.

Among Kefauver's earliest campaign in Chattanooga was a war on a city commissioner of streets and sewers (Kefauver accused him of unethical relations with contractors) and a fight for reform of the state constitution. In 1938 he made his first run for public office—the State Senate. His canvass set a pattern that, except for magnitude, was not to vary much in subsequent campaigns. He presented a program and talked issues, but relied more on personal appeals. Wherever people were—at factory gates, in stores, at picnics or spectator sports —Estes was, smiling, shaking hands, asking for votes. In the 1938 contest, the machine opposed him. He lost by about 307 votes out of 15,000. He has never since lost an election in Tennessee.

The next year when the incumbent congressman from his district died, Kefauver ran for the unfulfilled term. The Democratic organization again opposed him, but during the course of the campaign it fell victim to internal war and his opponent withdrew; Kefauver won by default. In the general election he beat the Republican candidate by a wide margin.

As a congressman, Kefauver was generally to be found among the moderates of the Democratic left. It was said that he tried to be known as "a liberal who does not antagonize the conservatives." He favored reciprocal trade agreements, federal aid to education, and became a proponent of TVA. In the Wilsonian tradition, he opposed economic monopolies. As a member of the House Small Business Committee, he had a part in establishing the Smaller War Plants Corporation. The committee also came out with a significant report on cooperatives. Kefauver was chairman of its subcommittee on monopoly, and for a time he seemed to accomplish little except to incur the distrust and contempt of businessmen. But he was not dissuaded from his "trust-busting." *Business Week* noted in 1946:

> Specifically, Kefauver and his staff feel that the sporadic pokes by government agencies at industrial firms or industries are next to useless. What he wants is a general tightening up of the antitrust laws and their enforcement so that a wholesale attack on bigness seems possible.

He was not, however, always on the side of the reform angels. He made the mistake of writing a public letter which implied that members of the One Thousand Club (donors of $1,000 to Democratic campaign funds) could expect special treatment in Washington. Opponents naturally made the most of his fall from virtue and it probably hurt him, but not much.

In Washington, Kefauver amplified the political techniques that had made him famous. He substituted letters to his constituents for handshaking. He not only personally answered letters from the folks back home but ordered his hard-worked staff to scan the newspapers for notices of births, marriages, birthdays, high school graduations.

His congressional record and the tending of his flock brought him re-election to the House four times. In 1940 he crushed his primary opponent, 17,000 to 1,500; in 1942 and 1944 he had no primary opposition and won in the general election. In 1946, however, the Democratic county organizations in his district coalesced against him. The ensuing campaign was bitter. Among the charges made against him was that he had a New York "pink" on his staff. Kefauver stood on his record, shook hands, asked for votes and smashed the bosses by a 9-1 majority. He was now ready for bigger game and higher office. In 1948 he ran for the United States Senate and challenged state boss Ed Crump.

Crump was the "seventy-three-year-old monarch of Memphis," who in 1948 boasted: "I have been elected 26 times without being defeated. I have assisted others 87 times without defeat. Altogether 110 times in 45½ years." Crump had suffered some setbacks, too, but it could not be denied that since he had won his first mayoralty campaign in Memphis in 1909, he had controlled its city government through many of the years. A son of a captain in John Hunt Morgan's Raiders, young Crump had built his political machine largely through his ability to win the confidence of Negroes and lower-class whites. He used his personality and ruthless efficiency to weld Memphis and Shelby County into a solid bloc. His influence swayed and then controlled Tennessee politics. Charles Edmundson, in 1948, described the power tactics of the Crump machine:

> The machine was so powerful that only a little overt intimidation was required to keep the restless in line. An ambulance operator who spoke out against the Boss found his drivers harassed and arrested in a way that threatened to destroy his business. A Negro druggist who wanted the Negroes to vote independently saw his business fall toward zero—policemen stationed outside his door searched customers as narcotics suspects. A country-wide mass meeting of the Parent-Teacher Association was called and expelled a woman leader who questioned the wisdom of one-man government in Shelby County. An outstanding high-school principal who refused to paste on his car stickers of the Crump candidate for governor was banished to a position as instructor in a remote school. . . . For several years the Boss barred CIO organizers from Memphis by simple edict. In this period a stranger was occasionally hauled into police headquarters on suspicion as a subversive character because the masthead of the *New Republic* or the *Nation* showed above his coat pocket. . . . When Crump was young, the machine permitted a wide-open city. Crump grown older

frowned on sin, and the bawdy houses and bookie joints were closed tight. He says, possibly in exaggeration, "Sin is out in Memphis."

In 1948, power was beginning to slip from Crump's grasp. Tennesseans were discontented with the 2 percent sales tax the old boss had rammed through the state legislature. In the senatorial primary he at first considered "ox-blood red" Kefauver no more than a political nuisance. But as the campaign developed, it became clear even to Crump that Kefauver was not one to be pushed out of the way. Kefauver defended his liberal record in Congress, accused Crump's machine of Communist-like tactics, rang doorbells and shook hands in typical Kefauver fashion. Using old University of Tennessee annuals for reference, he made a list of all the alumni living in the state; he then called upon them personally. He chatted with prominent citizens in every town, but he was also willing to talk with anyone on Main Street, shaking hands right and left as he went along. Nancy Kefauver was usually close by, taking notes for future use on the names, interests, and affiliations of those with whom her husband spoke. The Kefauvers had an information folder for every community. Kefauver also had a campaign organization, made up mostly of political amateurs, full of zeal for his cause. He used the radio with disarming effectiveness. His first radio talk in the campaign had the title: "Mistakes I Have Made."

Feeling the pressure of Kefauver's popularity, Crump began to revile him in full-page newspaper advertisements costing $18,000 a day. One proclaimed: "Estes Kefauver Assumes the Role of Pet Coon." The simile of a raccoon rifling a drawer with its paws while it appeared to look elsewhere implied that Kefauver, pretending to be a loyal American, was secretly in sympathy with Communism. Kefauver's press agent, Jack Bailhe, suggested the ingenious reply that made Kefauver famous. He acquired a live raccoon—christened D. Boone for campaign purposes—which Kefauver exhibited to his audiences.

"This," said Kefauver, "is a pedigreed West Tennessee coon.

Notice his big bushy tail. This coon has rings in his tail, but I want you to remember I have no ring in my nose."

Soon Kefauver began to don a coonskin cap for his campaign speeches; he even wore a deerskin jacket with fringe on it and called himself a "revival of the independent frontier spirit." When the biggest primary vote in the history of the state was counted, Kefauver was the winner. He had whipped "Mistuh Crump." It was not entirely a bloodless victory. In Polk County three died in election-day violence and the national guard had to be rushed in to restore order. In the November general election, Kefauver defeated B. Carroll Reece, ex-chairman of the Republican National Committee, who campaigned in a Cadillac to the tunes of the Grand Ole Opry entertainer, Roy Acuff. There was, however, a portent of future defeat in Kefauver's victory. When New York publishers asked him to write a book on how he had won, a member of his campaign staff suggested the title "How to Win an Election, and to Hell with the Politicians." No man has ever won the Presidency by telling the politicians of his own party to go to hell.

When Estes Kefauver was sworn into the United States Senate he had served over ten years in the House of Representatives. Ordinarily, however, it takes twenty years and an important committee chairmanship for a representative to make a national reputation, and Kefauver was no exception. Outside of Tennessee and Washington he was scarcely known, and during his first year in the Senate he was just another freshman Senator. Then, on January 5, 1950, he introduced a resolution for a congressional investigation of crime. It was to spread his name all over the country and make his face familiar to millions of television viewers. It was to make him a major candidate for the presidential nomination.

There is no evidence that Kefauver introduced the crime resolution to get publicity or make a national reputation. He has never been a statesman who viewed broadly the whole national and international landscape. Rather he picks certain problems which he worries and pounds until he gets results.

Crime was one of the problems he chose to hammer. Although his legal practice generally had not been in criminal law, Senator Kefauver became interested through reading reports of various State Crime Commissions. They indicated that crime was so firmly rooted and widespread after World War II that it was largely beyond the power of local and state governments. In November, 1949, Kefauver decided to try his hand at federal anticrime legislation by drafting bills to outlaw the interstate shipment of slot machines and syndicated horse-racing information. He doubted that his proposed legislation could even scratch the surface; the tie-ups between crime and politics went far deeper and the public was indifferent because it knew or cared so little about the criminal network. It was to remedy this ignorance and indifference that he introduced his resolution. His announced purpose was to focus attention on the lords of the underworld, not himself.

His resolution passed. A select committee, to be known as the Kefauver Committee, was appointed. Kefauver never tried to give the impression that he was doing it all alone. His staff of eleven specialists did much of the work. The Department of Justice opened to the committee its files on over one hundred suspects. Other government agencies cooperated. The Bureau of Internal Revenue, acting upon direct authority from President Truman, opened its tax records. Kefauver denied that he tried to overdramatize the hearings. He said, "I don't want to master-of-ceremony a circus." But he did believe that public hearings were a means to arouse the public to the significance of crime. Publicity, he believed, would also stimulate local law enforcement. He was right. Among others, Frank Erickson, known as the nation's "biggest bookie," would go to jail as a result of Kefauver's campaign.

The first of the public hearings took place in New York City. The sober *New York Times* captured the scene and the audience.

> The television viewers at home and the hundreds who crowded around sets in bars and radio stores saw yesterday prob-

ably the most remarkable, absorbing and instructive day of video ever presented on the screen.

The opening session of the Crime Investigating Committee was nothing less than a Hollywood thriller truly brought to life. For five and a half hours there were gripping and compelling drama and suspense in watching one of the seamier sides of national life spread out for all to see and hear. . . . At times it was almost difficult to believe that it was real.

The central characters could hardly have been cast to type more perfectly or "played" their parts more vividly. In the committee's chairman, Senator Estes W. Kefauver, Democrat of Tennessee, there was a lanky soft-spoken southerner who ruled the proceedings with an admirable, judicious calm.

Calm was needed as the proceedings continued in the midst of turmoil created by photographers, cameramen and reporters. Frank Costello's lawyer complained it was too much for the delicate sensibilities of his client: "During the entire proceedings powerful blinding Klieg lights were on during all the time, motion picture cameras were grinding and hordes of photographers have been roaming the room as they are at this moment. . . ."

For eleven months the committee continued to unfold a drama that fulfilled the promise of its opening scenes. As Kefauver went from city to city, he subpoenaed witnesses, then sat down to talk with the local police and as many underworld characters as he was able to dredge up. Some of the hearings— in Detroit, St. Louis, New Orleans, San Francisco—were televised; others, such as the three-day hearing in Kansas City, President Truman's own bailiwick, were held behind closed doors. At the end, Chairman Kefauver declared that crime, as a Big Business, was stealing between $17 and $25 billion each year from the American people.

A summation of the committee's findings was presented to the Senate. It reported that there were nationwide gambling syndicates and that the Sicilian society of eight hundred, known as the Mafia, was close to being a national Murder, Incorporated. And with the connivance of politicians and corrupt policemen, the Mafia had muscled into legitimate business.

As a result of the crime committee's activities federal legislation was passed. Another consequence was that Estes Kefauver, who had traveled over 50,000 miles during the course of the investigation, was no longer a relatively unknown junior Senator. He was a national figure—the white knight who had entered the lists against gamblers, dope peddlers, racketeers, corrupt cops and politicos. Under the Klieg lights a candidate for the presidential nomination had been born.

Still, Kefauver was not everybody's hero. He had offended more than the underworld. Alliance between crime and politics had been disclosed in cities controlled by Democratic bosses. Even politicians who were themselves untouched by the investigation felt that it had needlessly brought their organizations into disrepute. They did not believe that the publicity had been necessary. They thought, or pretended to, that just as much could have been accomplished without fanfare. The criticism was ill-founded. Kefauver did not object to spreading his name and fame throughout the country, but if he were to get action the public had to be aroused. The revelation that crime king Frank Costello had, in 1949, donated $25,000 to the Democratic National Committee was undoubtedly embarrassing to the party. Senator Scott Lucas of Illinois felt that publicity concerning Democratic politicians and a corrupt Chicago police officer—"the world's richest cop"—contributed to his defeat in a bid for re-election, and it may have. But neither these nor equally embarrassing disclosures were basically Kefauver's fault. He merely disclosed crime and graft. Responsibility rested with the criminals and grafters. Nonetheless, he had embarrassed the party and he was not to be forgiven by the "pros." At the Democratic National Convention they opposed him almost to a man.

He encountered other obstacles. The majority of the voters of the Deep South disliked him. He was too liberal for the taste of many, and his record on civil rights was unacceptable to most Southern Democrats. This record included advocacy of the repeal of the poll tax and opposition to the filibuster, the South's last defense against civil rights legislation.

Ironically his position on civil rights also made Kefauver unpopular with some voters in the North; the no-compromise liberals of the left were as insistent on undiluted fealty as any white-supremacy Southerner. Although he had gone about as far as a Tennessee Senator could and keep his job, Kefauver had not rendered such fealty. He had voted against antilynching and F.E.P.C. bills. He tried to explain it:

> I would support a properly drawn anti-lynching bill. . . . One of the chief aims of my life has been to better race relationships and to increase the opportunities of all races. I have opposed the F.E.P.C. bill because frankly I do not think it would achieve this end. It is difficult to legislate a change in the habits of peoples. . . . However, if I were the Democratic nominee for the Presidency I would support whatever the platform said in this regard.

It was all in vain. He was spotted with sin and the no-compromise liberals would have none of him. Thus confronted with the opposition of Northern city bosses, Southern county bosses and no-compromise liberal bosses, he had either to forego his ambition or by means of the primary carry his fight directly to the people. He chose the primaries. This entailed offending President Truman.

At the dawn of the new year, 1952, the President had not yet announced his intentions regarding another term. Until he did it would be unseemly for anyone—particularly a brash freshman Senator only recently risen to fame—to reach for the nomination. Aspirants with strong regional or bloc backing could afford to wait, secure in the knowledge that when maneuvering did begin they were at no disadvantage. Kefauver's position was different. His only chance was to show such overwhelming primary strength that he could not be denied. So he had to enter the primaries, and if he waited for Truman's decision it might be too late to get into a number of them. He did the only thing he could do. He went to the President. But Harry Truman would not be hastened or smoked out. He said that he had not made up his mind, and if Kefauver wanted to run, he could anticipate no active opposition from the President. This last was probably not strictly true, but it would have been arrogant for the President to tell a man he couldn't run. Making the most of this blessing, such as it was, Kefauver entered the first of the state presidential primaries—New Hampshire. Truman then permitted his name to be entered. Charles Brannan, Truman's Secretary of Agriculture, declared that with the President entered it would be an insult if Kefauver did not withdraw. Kefauver's reply was to offer to quit if the President would. The Democratic National Committee rejected the proposal. Kefauver and Truman both stayed in.

Kefauver has been criticized by experts for rushing in where wise men dared not tread, and thereby offending the national organization. But there is this to be said. Had he gone to the party bosses he would certainly have been told not to run, or to wait awhile, which for him would have amounted to the same thing. He had gotten where he was by going over the bosses' heads directly to the people. With radio and television to supplement his well-proved handshaking technique he might be able to go farther. It was worth a gamble and he had always been a political gambler. Besides, it was his only chance.

He stumped New Hampshire, once wandering by accident over the border into Vermont. He shook hands, chatted and said he was Estes Kefauver and hoped people would vote for him. His wife, Nancy, was with him. In one town where most of the audience was French-Canadian she addressed them in French. Truman did not campaign, but the state organization, most of the local organizations and organized labor worked for him. It was more or less Estes and Nancy against the world. And Estes and Nancy won. New Hampshire gave Kefauver 20,417; Truman 16,298.

The crime investigation made Kefauver a presidential candidate; New Hampshire made him a force to be reckoned with. True, New Hampshire was a small state with only eight delegates, and Truman had not campaigned, or even said he would accept nomination. Nonetheless, he was the President, the party's most popular leader, the man who had whipped Tom Dewey. Estes Kefauver was now the man who had bested him. It shook the Democratic high command and the bosses everywhere. There was no weakening in the resolve to stop Kefauver, but it was recognized that it would take some doing. He had demonstrated that he was a tough coon who could lick his weight in dogs any day. Maybe so, but even if he managed to do so, dogs and more dogs would keep right on coming.

Kefauver continued to enter primaries. State organizations had no major candidate with whom to oppose him. They had to resort to favorite sons or slates of uninstructed delegates. In Ohio it was ex-Senator Bulkley, in California State Attorney General Pat Brown; in Wisconsin there were two anti-Kefauver slates. He beat them all. Illinois tried a write-in for Adlai Stevenson. Senator Lucas helped and the National Committee put up $40,000. Kefauver, with his name on the ballot, got about 500,000 votes, Stevenson 50,000. Considering that Stevenson denied he was a candidate, 50,000 votes was not a meager showing. But neither was Kefauver's half million. In New Jersey, Kefauver received 100,000 write-ins, the field 100. In Pennsylvania, too, all votes were write-ins; Kefauver got 100,-000 votes, Truman 10,000, Stevenson 1,500. He smashed Senator Kerr in Nebraska. By May 14th he was able to boast in the columns of *The Kefauver News* that in eleven states he had won 65 percent of the primary votes—"nearly six times the popular support of his nearest competitor."

It was impressive and it made him the leading candidate, if not the one most likely to succeed. Yet it was not quite as impressive as appeared at first glance. In many of the primaries his was the only name on the ballot. In the four states where he did have major opposition he only broke even. He won over Kerr in Nebraska and Truman in New Hampshire, but lost to Senator Russell in Florida and Averell Harriman in the District of Columbia.

He had picked Florida as a proving ground for the South. There if anywhere he might show Southern strength. Southern Florida did not fully share the traditions of the Deep South and some of the crime committee's most sensational exposure had been in Dade County (Miami). Kefauver campaigned hard; he carried Miami, but Russell beat him in the North Florida "cracker belt" and won the state by a comfortable majority. In the District of Columbia he was opposed by the regular Democratic organization and had to defend his civil rights record in a heavily Negro area. It was too heavy a burden.

A further Kefauver weakness was that he could not count on all the votes from the states in which he had won. Some of the primaries were only advisory, and while the voters picked Kefauver, unfriendly state conventions picked the delegates to the national convention. His first-ballot strength might, as first-ballot strength frequently does, prove illusory. The real predilection of the delegates might not be apparent until they had fulfilled their nominal obligations. That could be the second or even a later ballot.

Nevertheless when all his advantages were discounted, Kefauver remained formidable. He led in the primaries; he led in pledged delegates; he led in public opinion polls. It is an axiom in politics that you can't beat somebody with nobody. By March, Kefauver was emphatically somebody while the opposition still lacked a declared candidate upon whom it could unite. Despite New Hampshire, Truman could have had the nomination had he reached for it, but in early April he announced that he wasn't running. Kefauver loomed still larger.

Not that he was without declared rivals. Senator Richard Russell of Georgia was quietly and without much effort lining up the South, but in a general election he could carry nothing outside it and probably knew it. A distinguished and respected somebody, he was the wrong somebody. Senator Kerr of Oklahoma stayed in the race even after his Nebraska defeat and picked up a few delegates, but his identification with oil was a handicap and he had little strength outside the Southwest.

On April 22nd Averell Harriman entered the race. He had a record of twenty years of public service. His posts included Secretary of Commerce under Truman, Ambassador to Russia and Great Britain, Chairman of the President's Committee on Foreign Aid and Director of Mutual Security. Regarded as a moderate, he took a stronger stand on civil rights than any of his rivals and thereby became the favorite of the no-compromise liberals. It promoted him from the status of a favorite-son candidate, but it also made him totally unacceptable to the South, and consequently to those who were looking for a nominee who could lead a united party. He was further handicapped by lack of personal magnetism—and he was little known to state and local politicians.

So for one reason or another, none of Kefauver's avowed opponents—Russell, Kerr, Harriman—was the somebody with whom to beat him. Party leaders in search of a candidate had to look further. Wherever they looked the search led to Governor Adlai Stevenson of Illinois.

Adlai Stevenson was born in Los Angeles, California. When he was six years old his family moved to Bloomington, Illinois. For the Stevensons this was coming back home. Jesse Fell, Adlai's maternal great-grandfather, had helped lay out the town, founded Illinois State Normal University and established the *Pantagraph,* Bloomington's first newspaper. A Republican, he worked for Abraham Lincoln's nomination at the 1860 party convention. The Fell family continued to publish the *Pantagraph* and it continued to be Republican. Stevenson's paternal grandfather was also an early settler in Bloomington. He was a Democratic congressman, Assistant Postmaster General, and Vice-President of the United States.

Adlai was educated in the Bloomington public schools, the Choate School and Princeton University (1922). He attended Harvard and Northwestern law schools. He practiced law in

Chicago until 1933, when he was appointed special council to the Administrator of the Agricultural Adjustment Act. Dividing his time between law practice and government jobs, he served as special assistant to the Secretary of the Navy and to two Secretaries of State. He participated in the San Francisco United Nations Conference and was senior adviser to the United States delegation to the United Nations General Assembly. Thus until 1947 his public career was not unlike Harriman's. Both served the country with distinction, but not in roles that attract public attention or lead to familiarity with state and local politicians. In 1947 this changed. The Democrats picked Stevenson to run for governor of Illinois. When he was selected Democratic hopes were dim. Like Woodrow Wilson thirty-seven years earlier in New Jersey, Stevenson was used to lend prestige and respectability to the party in a year when it appeared there was not much else to gain. Two factors changed the picture. One was Stevenson himself. He was revealed as a brilliant orator and a leader capable of arousing genuine enthusiasm. The second factor was the exposure of corruption in the administration of Republican Governor Dwight Green. When the polling was over, Stevenson had been elected by 572,000, the biggest majority in Illinois history.

Stevenson proved to be an able governor and astute politician. He cleaned up Green's mess, took more than a thousand parasites off the public payroll, established a state merit system and persuaded a Republican legislature to enact laws providing for reorganization of the state government. He attracted men of capacity to his own staff and to the public service. By 1952 he had acquired presidential stature. Furthermore he possessed the availability missing in the avowed candidates. He was in the middle on the issues that divided the party. Civil rights: "I feel very strongly that this is the first responsibility of the states themselves. If the states are unwilling or unable, then I presume there is no alternative to having the federal government do so." Social Welfare: "Government through its public assistance and social welfare programs should seek to enhance but not to supplant the duty of the individual. . . ." Taft-Hartley: "Some features of this law seem to me to advance the cause of good labor relations, and other features in my opinion do not." He also opposed higher taxes and increasing the national debt.

He had liabilities. During his term as governor he was divorced; the effect in the Bible Belt was problematical. It was alleged that Charles Wray, his superintendent of foods and dairies, had been bribed to pass horse meat as beef. He dismissed Wray, but his detractors reveled in the "horse meat scandal." He wrote out a deposition on the character of Alger Hiss which was used against the author. Outside Illinois he was not known; in public opinion polls he ran far behind Kefauver. Still, as the pre-convention campaign progressed, Stevenson's net assets increased while those of other presidential possibilities diminished. A poll of local courthouse and city politicians showed that many of the professionals believed him to be the right man.

The only trouble was that Stevenson insisted that he was not a candidate. As early as January Truman sounded him out; he wasn't interested. Colonel Jacob Arvey—who had paved the way for Stevenson's gubernatorial victory—tried to push him; he wouldn't be pushed. A group of political amateurs led by Walter Johnson, a University of Chicago history professor, formed an organization to draft him; he gave them no encouragement. He would not permit his name to be entered in primaries and did not countenance the write-in campaigns made in his behalf. He at no time stated categorically that he would reject a draft, but until July he said nothing to indicate that he would not. Then, early in July, with the convention only three weeks away, he thawed, but only a little. On one occasion he told reporters that "it remained to be seen" if he would accept a draft. A few days later when questioned he complained that the subject was getting tiresome. It was thin gruel for those who were working for him but it kept them alive. It also probably prevented other undecided delegates from going elsewhere. They would wait a little longer.

There have been only two drafts in the history of American presidential nominations. James A. Garfield was drafted by the Republicans in 1880. He was more than willing. That leaves Stevenson's as the only case of drafting a reluctant candidate. Governor Dever of Massachusetts said just before the '52 convention that a genuinely reluctant candidate cannot be drafted. The statement requires amplification. Certainly a person genuinely determined not to run cannot be compelled to do so. The record proves that Stevenson was not, in this sense, determined. Determination and reluctance, however, are not identical and he does appear to have been genuinely reluctant. At this time his reasons must remain speculative. He said that all he wanted to run for was another term as governor of Illinois. This is far from implausible. During his first term he had given a great deal of his time and himself to the state's problems—had made very real sacrifices in its interest. It would not be strange if he preferred a position to which he was already so deeply committed, and in which he had already scored substantial success, to the ordeal of a national political campaign and—in the doubtful event of victory—the far heavier ordeal of the Presidency itself. Or it is possible that he did want the nomination but was too prudent to take it except on his own terms? The terms can be guessed: the guarantee of a genuinely united party behind him; President Truman's blessing without on Stevenson's part an all-out endorsement of Truman policies and the Truman administration; no commitment to any faction of the Democratic party.

Whatever his reasons, Stevenson was reluctant, and his reluctance probably strengthened him. It prevented him from being Harry Truman's candidate, or the liberals' candidate, or the South's candidate. Being no one's he could be everyone's candidate. By spring, no realistic calculation concerning the probable Democratic nominee could omit him. Yet the question mark remained.

In May one more hat sailed into the ring. It was the well-worn Homburg of the Vice-President of the United States, Alben Barkley of Kentucky. No living Democrat had served the party more loyally. Party politicians knew and trusted him. As the Veep he was known and regarded with affection all over America. The moderate and party professionals who leaned toward Stevenson could accept him; so could the South. And he was not at all reluctant. The Presidency would be a fitting and just reward for his many years in the public service. Yet in those years lay his weakness. There had been too many of them. He was seventy-four years old. He would be seventy-eight at the end of a first term, eighty-two if he served through a second. Still, it was reported that the Truman administration would back him for at least a trial run, and other anti-Kefauver elements might fall in line. Barkley responded gallantly to the call. He came to Chicago the Sunday before the convention and went to work. He attended church, put in sixteen hours on radio and TV and visited delegates. He did not claim specific commitments from delegations. His strategy was to make himself available in anticipation of the hour when Russell withdrew and Kefauver had been beaten back. That hour was not to arrive, but on Sunday, July 20th, there appeared to be a reasonable possibility that it might.

Thus when the delegates arrived in Chicago the situation was fluid. If primaries, pledged delegates and public opinion meant anything, Kefauver was the people's choice. But he was not the politicians' choice. Kerr was virtually out; Harriman and Russell had strong backing but were factional candidates; the Barkley boom was in full blast.

Stevenson maintained his posture of reluctance. On the day before the convention, the Illinois delegation—of which Stevenson himself was a member—met in private. Eavesdropping newspapermen reported Stevenson asked not to be nominated, because he preferred to run for another gubernatorial term. The delegates rejected his appeal, declaring that they reserved the right to nominate him if they saw fit. On the same day, Sunday, the big Pennsylvania delegation polled. Stevenson led with thirty-two votes; Kefauver got fourteen. New Jersey, too, put a foot on the Stevenson bandwagon when a spokesman announced that the state delegation did not regard Kefauver's primary victory binding, and that it had a "new interest" in drafting Stevenson. Even New York was so restive that Harriman had to beg the delegates not to weaken his position by talking of Stevenson as their second choice. So the Stevenson draft gathered steam while he himself remained uncommitted. As long as this situation prevailed not only his own position but those of less coy possibilities were obscure. It is difficult to stop a candidate who won't start running—so the others, with a wary eye on Stevenson, turned on one another. Russell and Barkley busied themselves with stopping the front-running Kefauver; Harriman and Kefauver worked at stopping Barkley. Meanwhile the unauthorized Stevenson headquarters at the Hilton Hotel expanded from two to seven rooms; Chicago gamblers made the home entry the betting favorite.

It was about eleven o'clock Monday morning, July 21st, when the band struck up in the convention hall. Delegates straggled onto the floor, visitors into the balconies. The Democratic party, on the American scene for over one hundred and fifty years, was preparing to convene in its thirty-first national convention. The first one had nominated Andrew Jackson for a second term. Since then it had picked 14 winners and 16 losers.

At 11:30 the convention was called to order. The invocation was delivered, the Mayor of Chicago welcomed the delegates, the call of the convention was read. This was routine; what followed was not. The Chairman of the National Committee introduced Adlai Stevenson. He did not come to the platform as a candidate but as governor of Illinois greeting the state's guests. The distinction was oversubtle for many delegates. As he approached the microphone the Illinois standard was raised by delegates on the floor. Stevenson gestured no. Indiana, Colorado, New York, Rhode Island, held up the placards bearing their names. There were a few cries of "We want Stevenson." It was not exactly a demonstration, but it was the sort of thing that could turn into one. Stevenson once again gestured in protest, and admonished his admirers genially:

"I thought I had come here to greet you; not you to greet me."

Then he turned to his prepared address. According to one account he was interrupted by applause twenty-two times. When he had finished there was another tentative attempt at a demonstration. He killed it by turning and leaving the platform. For part of the remainder of the day he sat inconspicuously in the midst of his Illinois delegation. Then he left the hall; the convention was neither to see nor hear from him until it had nominated him for the Presidency.

Stevenson's welcoming speech had not been calculated to stampede the convention. Nor did it do so. But it may have played an important part in his nomination. Many delegates had come to Chicago leaning toward him merely because they were leaning away from someone else, or because they couldn't find anywhere else to lean. They did not know him or very much about him. They were receptive toward a draft but not yet sold. They had not yet seen who or what manner of man he was. His brief address gave him their answer. He could excite his listeners; he possessed the intangible qualities that make for leadership; he could hold the party together. Maybe he could even beat Eisenhower. Maybe the convention in search of a candidate had found one.

Shortly after Stevenson had finished his address Governor Schricker of Indiana announced that he would nominate him with or without his consent. Other state leaders gave approval. Among them were Representative John Kennedy of Massachusetts and Pittsburgh's Mayor Lawrence. By night Jonathan Daniels, newsman and astute commentator, declared that Adlai Stevenson would run because the convention would run

288] The Democrats—1952

him. Other correspondents predicted that it was all over before it had really begun.

The first day of most national party conventions are harmonious. This was not true of that of the Democrats in 1952. On Monday night it became embroiled in a loyalty oath controversy that was not to be finally settled until Thursday. The fight involved North and South, extremists and moderates, and the prospects of candidates for the presidential nomination. Its roots reached back to the 1948 Dixiecrat campaign when the "regular" Democratic organizations of Louisiana, Mississippi, Alabama and South Carolina had taken over the Democratic label and the Democratic party column for J. Strom Thurmond, their candidate for the Presidency. The issue this raised was clear. Either the Democratic party is a national party bound by the action of its national convention, or it is an alliance of state organizations, each of which is free to use the party designation for any candidate it decides to run. Although admittedly the source of American party power is in the state and local organizations, the Southern regulars would carry party organization and responsibility back more than a hundred and twenty-five years to a time when there was neither national convention nor national committee. Theoretically there could be at least one candidate from each state running as the Democratic nominee. The matter came to a head the night of the convention's opening session as the result of a contest over seating contesting delegations from Texas and Mississippi.

In each of these states a group of "regulars" was opposed by "loyalists." The regulars were dominated by former Dixiecrats and undoubtedly represented the majority of the Democrats in their states. The loyalists based their claim to recognition on loyalty to Truman in 1948, and as representing the opinion of a majority of the whole party. As there was no doubt that the regulars had been legally chosen, the National Committee seated them. It more or less invited a floor contest, however, by leaving seats on the convention floor for the loyalist delegation. The invitation was rejected in favor of a loyalty oath.

Northern liberals—the Kefauver and Harriman camps and representatives of labor—formulated the loyalty resolution. In a slightly milder form it was presented to the convention on Monday night. It required that the delegates to the convention should pledge themselves to exert "all honorable means" to see that the candidates nominated by the Democratic National Convention were placed on the ballots in the several states as party nominees. The resolution caused little excitement that night. It passed on a voice vote. The next day the backers of the pledge further softened it by agreeing that it would apply only to the 1952 convention, and would not be required of any delegation representing a state that had laws with which it conflicted.

Nonetheless, the delegations of Virginia, South Carolina and Louisiana refused to accept the pledge. Senator Harry F. Byrd of Virginia said, "We'll just sit here and maybe they'll throw us out." The recalcitrant states were stricken from the convention roll. But though excluded from membership, they stayed there while party members sought for a way to restore them to grace and party responsibility. The Democratic organization was not afraid of another third-party movement. The rebellious regulars would not bare their backs to another whipping such as Truman had administered in 1948. But they might, if pushed too hard and if Republican fields seemed greener, desert to Eisenhower.

The chief excitement on Tuesday was caused by Alben Barkley's withdrawal from the race. After labor leaders rejected him as too old, his friends from the Truman administration decided the trial run had failed to generate enough support to warrant further backing. He accepted the inevitable, but not with his customary grace. Along with notice that he was withdrawing he issued an angry attack upon the labor bosses. He was to be put back in the race on Thursday but his role would be reduced to that of a compromise possibility in the event of a probable deadlock.

James Reston, the *New York Times* correspondent, said that

Wednesday might have been called the "Smear Stevenson day." As the governor's bandwagon gained momentum the smear became so outrageous that Kefauver (although he bitterly accused Stevenson backers of scheming to create a synthetic draft) issued a statement denying any part in the "scurrilous" attacks. The smear, however, was merely a disreputable accompaniment to legitimate attempts to stop Stevenson. The Kefauver and Harriman camps were particularly active in these attempts and kept in touch, but as neither was willing to subordinate its interest to the other, they were unable to make much progress.

On Wednesday night the platform was adopted. It promised among other things to continue on the road traveled by Roosevelt and Truman, favored the repeal of the Taft-Hartley Act and further expansion of agricultural supports. On civil rights it repeated almost verbatim the 1948 plank that had led to the secession of Southern delegates. Now, however, there was no sign of a bolt. After the adoption of the platform the convention adjourned until the next day.

On Thursday the Virginia, Louisiana and South Carolina delegations were brought back into the fold, and presidential candidates were nominated. The party moderates who put unity before principle were responsible for the final solution of the loyalty controversy. A resolution to readmit Virginia because her state laws made the pledge unnecessary was introduced. So far as the choice of a presidential candidate was concerned it made little difference if the sulking delegates were admitted or not. Nor could they influence the platform, which was already adopted. Nevertheless, the move had practical implications and affected the fortunes of rival candidates. It was a rebuke to Harriman and, in a lesser degree, Kefauver. They were accused of trying to arouse a North-South animosity that would force Northern delegates to accept the liberal thesis— which might involve commitment to a liberal candidate—or face the charge of supporting white-supremacy reactionaries. It was even charged that no-compromise elements backing Harriman wanted to drive Southern delegates out of the convention. This would not only be a healthy purge for the party but would benefit Harriman, who had no Southern support. Although there was—and is—some sentiment among Northern extremists for "purifying" the Democratic party by getting rid of its existing Southern wing, there is no evidence that responsible leaders of any faction wanted such a thing during the 1952 convention. The Harriman and Kefauver forces, however, did support the loyalty oath and opposed the resolution to readmit the Virginia delegation. The South, mostly pledged to Russell, solidly backed it. This left the balance of power in the hands of the uncommitted delegations, most of whom were lining up behind or leaning toward Stevenson. Everyone awaited the vote of these delegations. Some were looking for a lead, some for revelation. If the city bosses, including Chicago's Arvey, voted for Virginia's admittance Stevenson could be pictured as the candidate of ex-Dixiecrats and city bosses. On the other hand, if they voted against the resolution it might alienate the South to such a degree that the South would join in stopping Stevenson. Illinois voted 45 to 15 against the resolution, but as the roll call proceeded it became evident that other Northern urban delegations were lining up for it. When Pennsylvania voted 57 ayes to 13 noes the trend was clear. Meantime Illinois had seen, or been shown, the light. Its leaders were working feverishly on the floor. The delegation switched its vote. Others followed its example. When switches and corrections of the roll call were completed, the motion to admit the Virginia delegation had passed, 615 to 529. With the wall breached, Louisiana and South Carolina were admitted on a voice vote. It was past midnight. The convention adjourned.

The defeated Harriman and Kefauver forces screamed that the party had betrayed its principles and pointed to Illinois (Stevenson) as the chief traitor. Their cries of anguish fell on deaf ears—the majority of the delegates had joined in the move to restore the outlawed culprits to grace. Stevenson occupied the middle ground more solidly than ever.

Estes Kefauver was placed in nomination by Governor Browning of Tennessee. The speech followed the usual Kefauver line. He had beaten the bosses in Tennessee; he had exposed the tie-up between politics and crime; he had donned the armor of a righteous cause; he was a liberal; he was not for the repeal of the twentieth century.

The nominating speeches lasted until past midnight. Eleven candidates were placed in nomination. Of these only Kefauver, Russell, Harriman and Stevenson could be considered major contenders, and the fortunes of the first three were on the wane. Any slim chance Harriman and Kefauver had clung to virtually vanished in the smoke of the loyalty pledge battle. By reason of attrition only Stevenson remained, and by the time the convention adjourned early Friday morning he had gotten the final boost—if one was needed—that virtually assured his nomination. Word spread that Harry Truman had finally decided that Stevenson was the right man.

Kefauver never stopped trying. He had spent the last week before the convention in fund raising and arrived in Chicago dead tired. Nonetheless he launched into a grueling series of activities. He called on delegates, appeared on radio and TV, conferred with his own leaders and those in rival camps interested in stopping Stevenson. Attempting to neutralize the effect of Stevenson's welcoming address and keep his own name in the news, he issued a statement attacking Eisenhower as a "pseudocrat" who spoke "liberal one day and reactionary the next." On the second day of the convention he met with Harriman. The two agreed that neither would withdraw without consulting the other. On Wednesday, in the midst of the debate on the loyalty issue, he appeared with his eighty-one-year-old father in a guest box in the gallery. Evidently forewarned, his supporters interrupted the debate with the noisiest and longest demonstration the convention had yet seen.

After the adjournment of the Thursday-Friday night session, Kefauver-Harriman leaders held a final meeting at the Congress Hotel. The object was to stop Stevenson but when the meeting ended at five in the morning no uniform front had been organized. Moreover, Hubert Humphrey, the Senate's most articulate and able liberal, and a Kefauver delegate, had warned that party well-being and the liberal cause must not be subordinated to stopping Stevenson—who was also a liberal. Humphrey further cautioned his colleagues not to permit Stevenson to be nominated by Southern conservatives and Northern urban bosses. This might occur if Kefauver and Harriman delegates—who together could not control half the convention votes—held off too long.

When the meeting was over, Humphrey, following his own advice, let Stevenson know that the Minnesota delegation would break to him after its commitment to Kefauver had been fulfilled. Governor G. Mennen Williams of Michigan followed Humphrey's example. Even Harriman virtually surrendered. At a breakfast with Stevenson he promised to support him in the event Harriman himself withdrew. Russell, too, was prepared to release his delegates to Stevenson although, like Harriman, he was putting off the inevitable just a little longer. Only Kefauver refused to give up. He still had the most pledged delegates; measured by primary votes and public opinion polls he was still the people's choice; he was still fighting.

Friday's business was the nomination of a candidate for the Presidency. On the first roll call Kefauver led with 340 votes, Stevenson had 273, Russell 268, Harriman 123½. The others were scattered. Kefauver was ahead but doomed. Even if he could get all the Harriman votes and 26 that had been cast for Humphrey he would still lack a majority. But from somewhere he summoned shreds of hope. Watching the proceedings on a TV screen in the Stockyards Inn, he declared after the roll call that he still thought he would win. It was wishful thinking.

Many observers and delegates believed the nomination would come on the second ballot. It did not. Stevenson picked up less than a hundred votes and was still behind Kefauver, who had added 22½. Russell held his 268. Kefauver stoutly declared that he saw no sign of a draft. After the second roll call the convention adjourned for dinner—and the larger night-time TV audience.

President Truman had arrived in Chicago during the balloting. He at once sent an aide to suggest to Harriman that he release his delegates to Stevenson. The suggestion was unnecessary. Harriman had already drafted his withdrawal. His statement was read to the convention when it reconvened at 8:45. The chairman of the New York delegation also announced that New York would support Stevenson. On the roll call that followed, Pennsylvania, Arkansas, Michigan and Massachusetts followed New York's lead. Then Kefauver surrendered. With Stevenson only a few votes from the nomination, Tennessee gave him its 21. At the end of the roll call, with 615½ votes needed to nominate, Stevenson had 617½. For the first time in its history the Democratic party had drafted a candidate. Two hundred and seventy-five loyal followers stayed with Kefauver to the end.

Stevenson was the right man. American elections are often determined by the electorate voting for or against one of the candidates rather than choosing between them. Such was the case in 1932 when the American people knew little about Franklin Roosevelt and probably didn't care very much. They voted against President Hoover whom they saw as the symbol of the depression. By 1936 the situation was reversed. Landon was buried in an avalanche of votes for Roosevelt. Any other candidate would have likewise been buried. 1952 was another such election. No one could have beaten General Eisenhower. The people liked Ike and they still liked him with unabated enthusiasm in 1956. Any opponent would have been a lamb led to the slaughter. Stevenson was twice the lamb. Nonetheless he was the right man for the Democrats. He could not come even close to winning, but the party held together. The November election returns offer undeniable proof that many Democratic voters switched to Eisenhower, but there was no general bolt, and no third-party move. With a few exceptions, notably in Texas, the organization men remained loyal. Thus unified, the Democrats won every congressional election after 1952, and a majority of the governorships. In 1960 when the unbeatable Eisenhower no longer faced them they were ready to recapture the Presidency.

It is unlikely that Kefauver could have preserved as great a degree of party unity. He waged his campaign against bosses, yet bosses, especially Democratic city bosses, have to deliver vital votes on election day. Kefauver had the courage to vote for a degree of justice for the Negroes. The Southern Bourbons would not forgive this. They would tolerate it in a Northern infidel; in a Southerner it was heresy. But because he did not go all the way on civil rights, Northern no-compromise liberals condemned him. The Democratic party would not have fallen apart had Kefauver been nominated. But it would not have survived the eight years of the Eisenhower ordeal quite so well. And 1960 required that it be in fighting trim.

Neither was Kefauver the best man. His congressional record reveals him as a man of high integrity and superb courage. He is persevering at any task to which he sets himself. His crime investigations were major contributions to the public interest. Few United States Senators have served the people of the United States as well as Kefauver.

But the Presidency is a different sort of job. It requires team-work and Kefauver has been a lone wolf. He has never succeeded in winning the confidence of politicians. A President lacking such success is lost. Finally, Kefauver's achievements have been largely the result of sticking tenaciously to one job to the exclusion of others. The historian Brooks Adams pointed out that those who would lead a nation must have generalizing minds. Perhaps Estes Kefauver has such a mind but his revealed virtues seem to spring from a specializing one. This was the view from Chicago in 1952. It has not changed since.

Adlai Stevenson's experience—in 1952—had been broader. As governor he had proved himself an able administrator with

greater ability than Kefauver to win friends, and a lesser pro-
pensity to make enemies. He was not to be President but he
was the best man.

Kefauver was hurt and angry at his loss. He felt that ruthless
politicians had thwarted not only him but the majority of Democratic voters who had endorsed him in the primaries. He did
not, however, hold Stevenson responsible for this and campaigned for him.

In 1954 his Tennessee enemies led by Senator Kenneth
McKellar made a supreme effort to beat him. He was accused
of being a Red and somehow abetting the Supreme Court in
the desegregation decision. Kefauver doffed his coonskin cap
and replied in kind. His critics were little Hitlers and little
Stalins. They were beneficiaries of gamblers and gangsters.
He could sling mud with the best—or worst—of them. But he
also ran on his record. He won easily, carrying ninety-one of
the states' ninety-five counties. In the general election he had
only token opposition.

In 1956 he made another try for the Presidency. Stevenson
was an avowed candidate this time and nearly everyone conceded him the nomination. Estes Kefauver never conceded anything without a fight. As in 1952, he chose the primaries as the
only road open to him. Unlike 1952, he found even that road
rough. He started well, winning in New Hampshire and even in
Minnesota, where Stevenson campaigned with the support of
the state party organization. Then the tide ebbed. After Minnesota he lost every primary in which he and Stevenson faced
one another.

By midsummer he knew his cause was hopeless. He had picked
up 165 instructed delegates but it was not enough. On August
1st, about two weeks before the convention, he announced his
withdrawal:

> Governor Stevenson's delegate lead is such that he could be
> stopped only by throwing the convention into deadlock. I would
> not want to be a party to this. . . . Victory in November is
> more important than the victor in August. I am anxious that the

resources of the party, of myself and of Governor Stevenson not be dissipated by continuing the contest.

I would be less than honest if I said this was an easy decision for me to reach. It was not. It was painful. It necessitated prayerful soul searching.

So Estes Kefauver searched his soul and the presidential quest ended. But he was by no means done with politics. Less than a month after his withdrawal from the presidential race —and after Adlai Stevenson was nominated for the Presidency —he was chosen as Stevenson's running mate.

The vice-presidential balloting was more exciting than the race for the presidential nomination (Stevenson had swamped Harriman on the first roll call). Kefauver's rivals were Senators Kennedy of Massachusetts, Gore of Tennessee and Humphrey of Minnesota, and Mayor Wagner of New York City. The first ballot gave Kefauver 483½ votes; Kennedy 304; Gore 178; Wagner 162½; Humphrey 134½. On the second it was a neck-and-neck race between Kefauver and Kennedy. The South, the East and most of the party professionals were behind Kennedy; labor and the farms and towns of the Middle West, the Plains and the West backed Kefauver. During most of the roll call Kennedy led by a small margin, but at the crucial moment Gore and Humphrey delegates switched to Kefauver and others followed. The final vote was Kefauaver, 755½; Kennedy, 598. In the end Kefauver's victory proved to be worthless, while Kennedy had taken a step toward the Presidency.

Throughout the autumn Kefauver campaigned with his customary energy. When it was over he was "tired and almost voiceless." But despite the Eisenhower landslide he would not admit complete defeat. "We have lost an election," he conceded, "but the future belongs to true liberalism in this country." Howard McGrath, his 1956 pre-convention campaign manager, also issued a statement. Kefauver's ambition was still to be President. "He will take every honorable course to achieve that end."

But by 1960 he had apparently foresworn presidential am-

bition. His name was occasionally mentioned in early speculation, but he gave no sign of being interested. Instead he ran
for another Senate term. Once more he crushed determined
primary opposition. In the general election he won as usual,
although Kennedy lost Tennessee to Richard Nixon.

Like others among the unchosen—Webster, Calhoun, John
Sherman, Robert Taft—Estes Kefauver's career appears destined to be the United States Senate. For great Senators sacrifice
political expediency to the dictates of conscience. This may
well be the path to immortality—but it rarely leads to the
White House.

The Democrats

1960

AS the *1960 presidential campaign approached, Democratic confidence was diluted by a strong infusion of apprehension. Republicans were in the White House, Democrats would have to
storm the fortress, and in American politics the assaulting troops
have generally been repulsed. In the twenty-four elections between 1860 and 1960 the party in power has won sixteen times.
As a rule the ins stay in and the outs out.*

*Democratic fears were not induced solely by the reading of
past history. There were current problems. President Eisenhower could not run again but no one knew how potent his spell
was. He had been unable to transfer his personal popularity to
Republican congressional candidates but he had not tried very
hard. Would he extend himself for a successor? If so would he be
effective? Perhaps not, but the possibility of his influence was
disquieting. There were also the various factors summed up in*

the word communication—*the press, television, radio, public relation firms. The Republicans could be counted upon to have the money to utilize all the skills of "Madison Avenue," and most of the press would, as usual, support them.*

There was also the opposition candidate. From a very early date it was almost certain that the Republicans would nominate Vice-President Richard Nixon. After Governor Nelson Rockefeller's candidacy proved to be stillborn it was beyond doubt. Nixon had weaknesses—among Democrats he was the most unpopular Republican alive. Since there were more Democratic than Republican voters this was heartening. But he also had advantages. He had been skillfully groomed for the Presidency. His name and face were familiar to the electorate. He could justly claim legislative and administrative experience. He had represented America on good-will missions abroad; he was familiar with foreign affairs; he knew foreign statesmen. There had been a time when a large segment of the Republican press had questioned his fitness as a presidential candidate. But when it became evident that he was to be the party's choice the news lords knuckled under, rationalizing that a "new Nixon," cleansed of blemish, had risen phoenix-like from the ashes of the old. So he would have the support of about three-quarters of the country's newspapers and all the mass-circulation news and pictorial weeklies. Nixon also had a reputation as a shrewd political tactician and untiring, hard-hitting campaigner. Many Republicans believed, and some Democrats feared, that he would make mincemeat of any opponent.

Still, if Democratic liabilities were heavy, assets were substantial. The greatest of these was that President Eisenhower could not run again, and Democrats wishfully believed that his popularity was personal rather than an indication of Republican resurgence. Registration figures and state and congressional election results gave substance to their hope. More Democrats were registered than Republicans, and although they couldn't come close to beating Ike they could and more often than not did beat other Republicans. Moreover, with Eisenhower himself off the firing line the record of his administration could be attacked and there was an abundance of ammunition. He had gone to Korea and an uneasy truce prevailed there, but otherwise America's international position had worsened. Dien Bien Phu, Hungary, the rise of Nasser in Egypt and Castro in Cuba, the collapse of the Geneva conference, the U-2, Sputnik, had all damaged the country's prestige abroad, and raised doubts at home.

Nor was all well on the domestic front. There was unquestionably a recession in 1960 and all the wiles of Madison Avenue cannot convince a man out of a job—or a farmer who sees the spread between costs and income widening, or the merchant who depends upon both—that his woes are not real.

Finally, with Eisenhower would go any vestigial remains of the Eisenhower crusade. Nixon was in many respects a strong candidate but he would be extraordinarily vulnerable as a leader of the piously righteous. The necessity for a "new" Nixon had risen more from questions regarding the character of the "old" Nixon than from doubts of his capacity. Besides, vicuna had taken a place beside mink in the nation's political vocabulary and Dixon-Yates and conflict of interest had besmirched the great crusade. The Democrats could not make much of an issue over corruption in the Eisenhower administration, but neither could Republicans claim that they were a band composed solely of the pure of heart.

Summing it up, the Democrats had the arms and the ammunition to storm the White House. If the assault was to be successful they needed the best and the right leader, and although there were a number of capable aspirants for the job, none seemed to quite meet the requirements.

There was Adlai Stevenson—twice beaten and though available not a candidate. There was a quartet of United States Senators: Humphrey of Minnesota, Kennedy of Massachusetts, Symington of Missouri, Johnson of Texas. All but Kennedy had risen to positions of distinction in the Senate; each one save Symington suffered from crippling political disabilities. On the record as it read in 1960 Lyndon Johnson shaded his senatorial colleagues in political experience and achievement.

Johnson vs. Kennedy

I am a free man, an American, a United States Senator and a Democrat—in that order.

—LYNDON JOHNSON

LYNDON JOHNSON was born August 27, 1908, on a farm near Johnson City, a small Texas town about fifty miles west of Austin. His father was comfortably off but had more to boast of in the way of family than wealth. Among his ancestors was one of the founders of the Daughters of the American Revolution, a president of Baylor College and a signer of the Texas Declaration of Independence. His grandfather had founded Johnson City.

As a youth Lyndon attended the Johnson City public schools. After graduation from high school he went to California, presumably in search of adventure and fortune. He found adventure in such unromantic jobs as a teen-age boy can pick up; fortune eluded him. He hitchhiked home. After a period of varying jobs as a manual laborer, he decided on further education and in February, 1927, entered Southwest Texas State Teachers College. He made excellent grades, was a star debater, edited the school paper and was active in campus politics. He graduated in 1930. He was twenty-two years old. For a little over a year he taught in a Houston high school. His introduction to active politics was in 1931 when he campaigned for Richard Kleberg, one of the owners of the King Ranch, who was running for Congress. After the campaign Kleberg asked him to come with him to Washington as his secretary. He accepted and has been in public life ever since.

In Washington Johnson was in his element. He lived and learned politics. Sam Rayburn, an old acquaintance of his father's, befriended him. As Kleberg's secretary he was not much concerned with legislation but he learned how to serve the constituents back home, and to make his way through the maze of governmental agencies. He also found time to attend classes in law at Georgetown University, and, although he was a newcomer in Washington, to get himself elected president of the Congressmen's Secretaries organization.

In 1934 while in Austin he met Claudia (irretrievably nicknamed Lady Bird) Taylor, the daughter of a wealthy Texas businessman. They were married on November 17th. After a honeymoon in Mexico he returned with his bride to Washington. Lady Bird Johnson was to take an active part in her husband's political career.

These were the days of the New Deal and Lyndon Johnson threw himself into it with wholehearted zest. His admiration for Franklin Roosevelt was unreserved. It never diminished. After the President's death he said in the Senate, ". . . It is apparent to every American that [Roosevelt] was one of the giants of all times." When the time for Johnson's bid for the presidential nomination arrived, many of the early New Dealers supported him. He had not submissively accepted every measure demanded by President Roosevelt, but his voting record in the House and Senate is as favorable to the New Deal-Fair Deal as that of most Northern Democrats. Yet point to it as he may, he has never been able to project a national image of himself as a liberal. He is a Texan, and the shadow of Texas with its overtones of oil and gas and white supremacy envelops him. Few Texans are likely to admit it but there are circumstances under which it is a disaster to be from Texas. Had Lyndon Johnson been the Senator from New Jersey or California or Ohio he might now be the President of the United States.

In 1935 he was appointed Administrator for the Texas National Youth Administration. Not quite twenty-seven years old, he was the youngest State N.Y.A. administrator in the country. He did such a good job that he was recognized in Washington as one of the organization's most able men and in Texas as one bureaucrat who brought the pie out of the sky and gave substance to Washington promises. This trait was to characterize his political career. He never forgot Texas. In the capital he became known as an urbane and sophisticated statesman: in Texas he never quite abandoned the role of crossroad politician. The Austin (Texas) *Observer* reported on his "homecoming" to Blanco County after the 1960 Democratic Convention:

> Referring to cowhands who escorted him to the barbecue, he [Johnson] said, "I'm proud there are still some of 'em I can call by first names. . . ."
>
> "My grandfather practiced law here from 1887 into the 1900's. My mother spent her girlhood days in this town—she was always the greatest influence in my life," Johnson said. "Every time I make a decision affecting millions of people I think 'Would Mama agree with this?' or 'Would Daddy think this wise?'"

Early in 1937 the incumbent representative from Johnson's congressional district died. Johnson ran against nine other hopefuls for the seat. He campaigned as a New Deal candidate, declaring that if elected he would support Roosevelt including the court-packing plan. When the vote was in he had won.

In Congress Johnson fulfilled his pledge to support the President. He fought for extension of the Rural Electrification Authority, further government credit to farmers, including Negroes, and continuation of the National Youth Administration and Civilian Conservation Corps. He got a bill through the House authorizing an appropriation for a public housing project in Austin. Possibly no first-term Representative has ever gotten so many federal projects for his district. The district responded. He was re-elected without opposition in 1938 and again in 1940.

In 1941 Morris Shepherd, veteran Texas Senator, died. Johnson ran for the unexpired term. He had three opponents, former Governor W. Lee O'Daniel, Attorney General Mann, and former Congressman Martin Dies. All were veteran politicians. Johnson took the middle of the road on domestic reforms and pitched his campaign on support of F.D.R.'s preparedness program. In this he was following the President's lead. "Dr. Win the War" was beginning to supersede "Dr. New Deal." In the course of the campaign Johnson replied to charges of warmongering with the promise that if he voted to send Texas boys to war he would abandon his seat in Congress and accompany them. He ran second to O'Daniel by 1,311 votes. He returned to his seat in the House, and after Pearl Harbor did vote for a declaration of war. The same day, although congressmen are exempt from military service, he asked as a member of the Naval Reserve to be called to active duty. The navy obliged.

Johnson served with the navy for seven months before returning, by order of the President, with all other members of Congress, to his duties as a Representative. In the service he spent several months in Australia. He was in a flying fortress that crash-landed and a patrol bomber that had a motor shot out. General MacArthur decorated him with the Silver Star. While in the navy he was also re-elected to Congress without opposition.

Back in the House, he busied himself chiefly with problems related to the war. But of greater significance to his later presidential ambition was his vote for the Smith-Connally War Labor Disputes Act which required a thirty-day cooling-off period before strikes could be called in a defense industry. In 1947 he further alienated labor by voting for the Taft-Hartley Act, labeled by union leaders a slave-labor bill.

In 1948 W. Lee O'Daniel's Senate term expired and he announced that he would not try for re-election. Eleven candidates entered the field. Among them was Lyndon Johnson. His most formidable opponent was Coke Stevenson. Former associates in N.Y.A. helped him build a statewide organization. Organized labor, incensed at his support of the Taft-Hartley bill, backed Stevenson. In the primary Stevenson beat him by some seventy thousand votes, but with other candidates getting over three hundred thousand, no one had a majority. Texas law required a runoff. A tough, bitter campaign followed. Johnson won by an almost incredibly thin margin. Out of nearly a million votes he had a lead of 87. Not surprisingly Stevenson contested. There were suits and countersuits. In the end the Democratic State Executive Committee in a 29 to 28 vote certified Johnson as the winner. His enemies declared that he had stolen the election; unfriendly newspapers called him "land-slide Lyndon." He could bear their jeers philosophically. He had won. In the general election which followed—and in which Coke Stevenson supported the Republican candidate, Jack Porter, a Houston oil man—Johnson was elected by a two to one majority. He took his seat in the United States Senate in January, 1949.

In the House Johnson had been recognized by his colleagues as one of its most able men. He was not, however, one of its leaders. The seniority committee system, the rigid rules, and the vast size of the House make it almost impossible to join the top rank in a few terms. It takes long tenure. In the Senate, however, Johnson zoomed. In 1951 he was named Democratic whip. This carried with it membership on the Steering and Policy committees. After only two years he was among his party's Senate chieftains.

As a Southerner he supported Senator Russell of Georgia for the 1952 Democratic presidential nomination. But when Adlai Stevenson was nominated he pledged his support to the ticket and with Speaker Sam Rayburn led the Texas Democratic forces. He introduced Stevenson and Senator Sparkman, the vice-presidential candidate, to Texas political rallies and barnstormed through the state on their behalf. It was in vain so far as Stevenson's cause was concerned. Eisenhower's popularity and Stevenson's opposition to the Texas claim to tideland oil were too much. Ike won. But Johnson did not lose. When the smoke had cleared he and Rayburn retained their hold on the voters while erstwhile Democrats who had deserted to the Republicans were in the outer darkness. Among the curious phenomena of Southern politics is the fact that rank-and-file Democratic voters reserve the right to vote for Republican presidential candidates but are prone to politically execute the politicians who lead them in their heresy. It happened after 1928 and to some degree to Dixiecrats twenty years later. It happened in Texas when in the congressional election of 1954 all five of the state's congressmen who supported Eisenhower in '52, or said they would not vote for Stevenson, were replaced. Some did not try for re-election, others were beaten. All were gone.

Curiously, the result of an election in Arizona was to have greater significance for Lyndon Johnson than did Adlai Stevenson's defeat in Texas. There Senate leader Ernest McFarland was beaten by a political unknown—Barry Goldwater. As a consequence, when the 84th Congress convened in January, 1953, the Democrats had to select a new minority leader. The unanimous choice was Lyndon Johnson. He was the youngest man ever to be named to that position.

In 1954, he ran for a second Senate term. His primary opponent was Congressman Dudley Dougherty, rancher and oil millionaire. Doughterty's voting record in Congress was liberal, and he had been Texas's heaviest contributor to Adlai Stevenson, but he apparently decided he could beat Johnson as a conservative and super-isolationist. He advocated United States withdrawal from the United Nations and dug out an old House vote Johnson had cast in favor of abolishing the Dies Committee, the first of the House committees to investigate un-American activities. His campaign mas managed by Johnson's old and unrelenting adversary Coke Stevenson. Johnson did not bother to campaign in Texas, but in Washington he rallied Senate Democrats in a fight against an amendment to the Taft-Hartley Act which labor found even more intolerable than the act itself. Because of this—or because they disliked Dougherty—labor supported Johnson for the first time. This contributed to a victory in which he beat Dougherty by over half a million votes—a welcome contrast to his 87-vote margin over Coke Stevenson. In the November election he won handily.

The Democrats were also victorious nationally, so that when Johnson returned to Congress in January of 1953 his status was changed from minority to majority leader. Furthermore he and Sam Rayburn were now the top-ranking Democratic office-holders in the United States. They were keenly conscious of their position and insisted that it was they and the party in Congress that must make the record on which the Democratic voters should and would judge the Democratic party. Because of his age Rayburn could hardly aspire to the Presidency. Johnson was forty-six years old.

The case of Lyndon Johnson for the Presidency must rest on his record as Senate leader. On this record the bills he supported or opposed are of less significance than what they revealed about his views on government and his techniques as a politician and statesman. It has been said that politics is the art of the possible and that democratic politics are the politics of compromise—that the function of a major American party is to adjust diverse interests, relieve stresses, promote consensus. If these things are true, Lyndon Johnson is a past master in the art of democratic politics.

"I am a free man, an American, a United States Senator and a Democrat—in that order. I am also a liberal, a conservative, a Texan, a taxpayer, a rancher, a businessman, a consumer, a parent, a voter . . . and I am all of these things in no fixed order. . . . At the very heart of my own beliefs is a rebellion against this very process of labeling and filing Americans under headings. . . ."

Consistent with this rebellion against labels is a refusal to admit that the major American parties have deeply divisive philosophies. He sees congressmen as individuals exercising their judgment rather than as party automatons. He doubts the wisdom of a decision reached by a strict party vote. In the fields of foreign policy and national defense he has shown an almost total lack of partisanship. Unlike Robert Taft, his most distinguished opponent in the senatorial wars, he believes that party duels should stop at the waterfront. It is unlikely that he would endorse *in toto* the Taft dictum that the business of the opposition is to oppose. Naturally he was interested in making a party record and even a Johnson record. But they were to be based on legislative achievement rather than on the creation of partisan issues, and in legislative achievement no congressional leader since Henry Clay has been more adept. If Robert Taft merited the title Mr. Republican, Lyndon Johnson deserves that of Mr. Senator.

> He believed it possible to do anything that was worth the effort and the price, and so considered every problem from the standpoint of what was necessary to achieve the desired objective, and whether the objective was worth the cost. He learned early and never forgot the basic skill of the politician, the ability to divide any number by two and add one. But to find a ground on which a majority could stand, he did not regard as compromise.

Usually he would not bring a measure to the floor unless he could find such grounds. One veteran observer of the Senate writes: "As a political commander he is not interested in Charges of the Light Brigade. . . . Johnson is never happy to involve himself or his troops in gallant operations doomed in advance and useful only to those who love a lost cause." That he could so often find grounds upon which he could not only hold his own followers together but also work in reasonable harmony with the Republicans is the measure of his skill. He worked himself indefatigably and his staff relentlessly. He was never unprepared. He always knew the business at hand and what he proposed to do about it. Before an important measure came to the floor he discussed it with Democrats and Republicans alike. He did not always win support but he did find out what the situation was and what still had to be done. More often than not he found a way to do it. This sometimes took the form of pointing out the alternative. In 1957 he bluntly warned Southern Senators that they must forego a filibuster against a mild civil rights bill or have a stronger one pushed down their throats by a coalition of Republicans and Northern Democrats. The Southerners gave ground.

Naturally Johnson aroused opposition. Northern liberals in and out of Congress disliked his predilection for compromise; extreme Democratic partisans accused him of holding hands with Republicans; Southern Democrats could not quite welcome him as one of their own. He continued on his chosen path and the Senate generally followed. Political warriors of the middle ground are seldom acclaimed as heroes, but they are the generals most apt to win legislative battles. Even Johnson's opponents recognized this. There were mild Democratic rebellions in the Senate, but they were attempts on the part of liberals to nudge him farther to the left rather than to replace him. And they were largely abortive. They gained little support and he remained in the center.

By 1958 Lyndon Johnson was firmly entrenched as the leader of the congressional Democratic party. Other Democrats, notably Adlai Stevenson and Harry Truman, were more popular and enjoyed greater prestige, but none wielded such power. Naturally there was speculation among political experts—whose profession it is to speculate—on his presidential prospects. The general verdict was that he might be a kingmaker, and being Lyndon Johnson, could conceivably be the king. This, however, was judged extremely improbable. He was from the South; he was from Texas; he was a United States Senator.

Senate affiliation was regarded as a disability because of a recurrent pattern in American presidential politics. Since the time of the Civil War neither party has been inclined to invest its presidential hopes in congressmen. The Republicans nominated Garfield, Blaine, Harrison, McKinley and Harding over the whole span, but only Harding was the product of twentieth-century politics. For over fifty years the party had preferred candidates from almost anywhere else: governor's mansions, the ranks of business, the army. The Democrats have chosen even fewer candidates from among congressmen. Bryan served in the House of Representatives and Truman was in the Senate, but neither achieved the nomination primarily because of his distinction in Congress. With these exceptions Democrats have generally looked to state governors, though they tried, unsuccessfully, with a newspaper editor, a judge and a general. While few legislators from either party have been chosen, many have aspired—Republicans Robert La Follette the elder, Hiram Johnson, Arthur Vandenberg and Robert Taft, and Democrats Champ Clark, Oscar Underwood, Richard Russell and Estes Kefauver. The list is distinguished; the record of rejection is consistent.

There are reasons. Long service in the legislature results in commitments to issues or causes which alienate blocs of voters; a congressman becomes identified with a faction or wing of the party. William Seward was too antislavery for border-state Republicans and too pro-Catholic and alien for Know-Nothing Republicans. La Follette and Johnson were "progressives." Taft was "old guard." Vandenberg before his "conversion" was an isolationist. In other cases specific acts or words proved damaging. During his long career in the House, Champ Clark made intemperate statements that came home to roost; Kefauver's crime investigation made him a possibility but rendered nomination virtually impossible.

Lyndon Johnson was not immune from the dangers inherent in his exposed position. Nor was he able to escape unscathed. He offended labor by voting for the Smith-Connally and Taft-Hartley acts. Staunch liberals would not forgive his preference for compromise.

He did manage to emerge from the 1957 Civil Rights meat grinder fairly well. By compromise, persuasion and threats he shepherded a civil rights measure through the Senate. It was not very strong, but it did create a Civil Rights Commission and make possible stronger enforcement of the Fifteenth (Negro-suffrage) Amendment in the South. It was the first civil rights bill since 1875 to be enacted into law. The NAACP admitted that it marked some progress. On the school segregation issue Johnson was also spared excessive embarrassment when in deference to his position as Senate Leader his Southern colleagues refrained from demanding that he sign the manifesto attacking the Supreme Court's desegregation decision. Senator Kefauver was not so spared, and his refusal to comply branded him as a traitor to the South.

But if Johnson was a recipient of grace in these areas he had his own peculiar problem. He was from Texas, and in Texas oil and natural gas are important. He recognized this and although he knew it would hurt him nationally he supported oil depletion tax exemption and backed tideland oil and natural gas bills. In serving these powerful state interests he was doing what most congressmen do. It is no coincidence that farm support comes from agricultural states and labor legislation is pressed by representatives of industrialized areas. But somehow few causes are burdened with such a stigma as that attached to oil and, more recently, natural gas. Perhaps it is a hangover from the days of Harding and Teapot Dome and Secretary Fall and Harry Sinclair. Perhaps it is because millionaires, multimillionaires and a billionaire or two are involved, and the American people envy, admire and revere millionaires, multimillionaires and billionaires, and suspect their honesty. Perhaps it is rooted in the conviction that through ruthless use of power derived from wealth the oil and gas interests have obtained privileges denied to and at the expense of the rest of the country. Whatever the reason, an aura of evil enshrouds oil and gas and their champions, and Lyndon Johnson could not entirely escape it.

He had experienced and surmounted another disaster—a personal one. On July 2, 1955, without warning, he suffered a severe heart attack. Observers believed for a time that the duties of Senate leader—and certainly the Presidency—would be too heavy a burden for him to risk. But his recovery was so satisfactory that specialists assured him that his heart had suffered no permanent damage and that there was no reason to believe his health would impair his career.

By 1959 Lyndon Johnson was ready to consider the possibility of nomination for the Presidency of the United States. A *Newsweek* article in March quoted him as denying that he was running and declaring that he did not think a Southerner would be nominated for the Presidency in his lifetime. The article also predicted that when the convention met, Lyndon would be a candidate and might even be nominated.

The forecast concerning his candidature proved correct. On October 17, 1959, Sam Rayburn announced in Dallas that a Johnson for President committee had been organized. Rayburn and Texas Governor Daniel were co-chairmen. The committee was unofficial, meaning that Johnson had not given it his formal blessing, or officially admitted that he was a candidate. This fooled no one, nor did two such political realists as Sam Rayburn and Lyndon Johnson want it to. Johnson had entered the presidential race.

There was no favorite. Adlai Stevenson probably would have been, had he been willing to enter. He was as well known to American voters as Richard Nixon and could claim greater knowledge of world affairs and greater prestige abroad. Although he was clearly available should the party call him, he would make no move whatsoever for the nomination. This was his story and he stuck to it. His role in the pre-convention campaign was to be largely that of a spoiler who prevented a large number of almost fanatically devoted followers from supporting another candidate. They waited and hoped for Adlai.

The other leading possibilities for the nomination were, despite the taboo against congressmen, United States Senators. By early spring—in addition to Johnson—Humphrey, Symington and Kennedy were acknowledged candidates.

Of the congressional quartet John Fitzgerald Kennedy was the youngest and the least known to the public. His record in the House of Representatives had not been distinguished and he had made a slow start in the Senate. Toward the end of his first term, however, he picked up speed. He maneuvered a labor bill through the Senate and demonstrated a grasp of foreign affairs superior to that of most of his colleagues. Although not yet of the senatorial stature of Johnson, Humphrey or Symington, he was growing. He had other advantages. If his legislative record was not brilliant, his career out of Washington was. Although he made no attempt to capitalize on it, his war record marked him a hero. And it involved more than blind courage. He had proved himself resourceful and possessing a sense of responsibility. These are valuable qualities in a President. He had written *Profiles in Courage,* which received a Pulitzer prize, and *While England Slept,* which did not receive much notice when it first appeared in 1940 but did show a certain perception in the assessment of a political crisis. He had learned his politics in Boston, one of the hardest schools in America. He had proved his ability to get votes by winning elections. The charge that he was (and is) a better candidate than public official is not made out of admiration, but true or false it is not too great a fault in the eyes of politicians anxious to win.

He had further assets. Money was available and the costs of a major campaign embracing the presidential primaries are prohibitive to a candidate lacking funds. Kennedy had also worked harder and longer than any of his rivals for the nomination. Although he did not formally announce that he was a candidate until January, 1960, he began to run soon after the presidential campaign of 1956. While Lyndon Johnson wrote his record in the Senate, Kennedy played hooky in order to travel throughout the country making speeches and meeting people—at this stage mostly the right people, governors, mayors and men who held no office but possessed power. By midsummer of 1958 James Reston of *The New York Times* reported that Kennedy was engaged in a "conscious and well-planned campaign to meet the Democratic state leaders." In a prescient flash Reston added: "He has arrived, too, when political leaders analyzing President Eisenhower's political success are impressed with the power of personality in an age of television campaigning."

But John Kennedy had one liability. He was a Roman Catholic, a disability which appeared more fearsome because of the fate in 1928 of Al Smith, a far better known and beloved figure than was Kennedy in early 1960. To wipe out this liability Kennedy had to prove it was not fatal. The only way was the presidential primary. Public opinion polls would help, but they would not substitute for primary victories. This was not a new situation for candidates. Harold Stassen and Estes Kefauver had faced it. But there was this important difference. With each Stassen or Kefauver primary triumph the opposition hardened. Old-guard Republicans simply would not have Stassen, and Southern and Northern machine Democrats implacably opposed Kefauver. Kennedy, aside from his religion, was acceptable. He was generally regarded—though on the record inaccurately—as more liberal than Johnson. In Massachusetts he had lived amiably with machine bosses. Northern city organizations had no reason to fear him. To the South he was another Northerner, aside from his faith no worse than most and better than some. He had not played much of a role in the civil rights struggle. Overall, he was not the darling of city and county politicians throughout America but neither was he poison to them. If he could shake off the incubus of Catholicism they could take him. Many would even welcome him.

Senator Humphrey of Minnesota announced his candidacy on December 30, 1959. Three years younger than Johnson, he was born in Wallace, South Dakota. He went to school in Doland, another small South Dakota town, where his father owned a drugstore. He grew up in the era of Dakota crop failures, bank closings and dust storms. His father scraped through them all, though he did have to sell the family home and move into a smaller house.

Humphrey worked his way through three terms at the University of Minnesota before abandoning college to assist his father, who was opening a store in Huron, South Dakota. He married, quit the drugstore after six years, and resumed his studies. After earning an M.A. degree at Louisiana State University he returned to Minnesota where he worked toward a doctorate and taught political science.

In 1943 he ran for mayor of Minneapolis. He was second in a field of ten. Two years later he tried again and was elected. His political rise from this point was rapid. He was a leader of the movement to forge the alliance between the Democratic and Farmer-Labor parties that has dominated Minnesota politics since the late forties. Among the early triumphs of this combination was Humphrey's election to the United States Senate. He won re-election in 1954 and again in 1960. In 1948 he gained national attention by leading the fight on the floor of the Democratic National Convention for the civil rights plank that precipitated the revolt of the Dixiecrats.

As in Minnesota politics, Humphrey forged ahead rapidly in the Senate. He established himself as one of its liberal leaders and the unofficial emissary between the liberals and Lyndon Johnson. He and Johnson understood one another. This may be because Humphrey, too, believes in the art of the possible. He was steadfast in his principles to the point of damaging his chances for the Presidency, but when it comes to a vote he generally prefers a law that marks limited progress, to an issue. Nonetheless, his relations with the Farmer-Labor party, his advocacy of civil rights and a pro-labor voting record caused him to be branded by reactionaries of both major parties as a radical. Without revelation as to just what radicalism is, such charges possess no rational content. Two facts, however, emerge clearly from Humphrey's political career—including his voting record in the Senate. American democracy is not endangered by the principles or actions of Hubert Humphrey; he is an articulate, voluble, and on the whole effective leader of the left wing of the Democratic party.

In 1952 Humphrey supported Estes Kefauver for the Democratic presidential nomination, but when it became evident that he could not win, Humphrey urged the embittered Kefauver camp to support Stevenson. In 1956 he was for Stevenson from the beginning and hoped to be named as his running mate. In this he was disappointed. The race for the vice-presidential nomination fell to Kefauver and Kennedy.

On December 30, 1959, Humphrey formally announced his candidacy for the Democratic presidential nomination. Because of his identification as an extreme liberal he, like Kennedy, could only win by demonstrating great popular strength in the primaries. Unlike Kennedy, even this might not be enough. His "radicalism" made him unacceptable to the party right, and labor bosses doubted his capacity to beat the Republicans. Actually, nothing short of a disastrous depression would make Humphrey a formidable presidential candidate. Otherwise his position will probably remain that of an influential factional leader.

Johnson's third senatorial opponent was Stuart Symington of Missouri. Symington was recognized as a possible candidate as early as 1958 when he was re-elected to the Senate by an overwhelming majority. Unlike Kennedy and Humphrey, he had no disability which had to be dissipated for him to be judged available. On the contrary, he was the ideal compromise candidate. He was a Protestant. He had voted consistently for New Deal-Fair Deal measures, but had never led in the fight for social and economic reform. As a successful businessman he had the confidence of the business community, which finds it hard to believe that a man who makes a million dollars can be a threat to their interests.

He entered the public service in 1945 when President Truman called him to Washington to take charge of the disposal of surplus war property. During the next five years he served with distinction as Secretary of War for Air and (following the unification of the armed forces) Secretary of the Air Force, Chairman of the National Security Resources Board, and head of the Reconstruction Finance Corporation. As the first Secretary of the Air Force he fought hard for increasing its strength, with emphasis on long-range bombers. When the air force was cut back in the interest of economy he resigned in protest.

In 1952 he returned to Missouri to run for the United States Senate. He won in his first try. In the Senate he was noted for his continued fight for a bigger air force, and as the Cold War continued to grow hotter his efforts increased. Although not very effective in rough and loud political controversy, Symington showed greater courage than most of his colleagues, including the trio of presidential rivals, in criticizing Joe McCarthy and attacking President Eisenhower for cutting back the armed forces when Ike was generally regarded as sacrosanct. But somehow, perhaps because he avoided the spectacular, he remained relatively obscure outside of Washington.

In 1956 he was Missouri's favorite son for the presidential nomination, but refused to enter primaries or campaign. In 1958 he ran for re-election to the Senate and so swamped his Republican opponent that he became a serious presidential possibility. Once again he refused to enter primaries, but this time it was strategy. Kennedy was a Catholic, Humphrey was a "radical." Johnson was from Texas. Let them beat their brains out against one another and their own shortcomings. Then it would be Stuart Symington's turn. He was a Protestant; he was a Fair Dealer who, paradoxically, was regarded as "safe" by conservatives. Born in Massachusetts, he had engaged in business in Maryland and New York. He was a Senator from the border state of Missouri. He had administrative and legislative experience. He had proved he could win elections. Who possessed more to recommend him? Who among his major opponents had so few handicaps?

It would be brash to declare that Lyndon Johnson could not be nominated because he is from Texas. Experts said Kennedy couldn't win because he is a Catholic. But by teaming a Catholic and Texan the Democrats won the Presidency. Nonetheless one is tempted to say that Johnson's strategy for winning the nomination was foredoomed.

It would appear that as in the case of Humphrey and Kennedy his only hope lay in proving in the primaries that a Southerner could win outside the South. Johnson declined the challenge. Possibly he did so from prudence, possibly because as majority leader he could not spare the time and effort for an extensive primary campaign. Others could play truant from the Senate, be absent except for important roll calls; the Senate leader could not. His claim to the nomination rested largely upon his performance as a Senate leader. In a sense Kennedy, who on the record could not make a case that he was the best man, had to go after the nomination as the right man, while Johnson's strategy lay in forcing recognition that he was the right man because he was the best man. Of course, if a convention must choose between right and best it will choose the former. Johnson as an astute politician surely knew this. But there was a chance, and a good one, that Kennedy would fail in the primary test. Humphrey was almost certain to. Stevenson seemed determined to stay on the sidelines. Symington, favorite sons and dark horses would remain, but in this field Johnson would be a strong contender. So unlike Kennedy and Humphrey, he rejected going for broke in the primaries and stayed in Washington and tended shop.

Meanwhile, his camp was busy and Johnson himself was not inactive. He had strong congressional support. Senators and Representatives, friends, beneficiaries and those who hoped for future favors did what they could back home. As a rule they were dependents rather than masters of their state organization, so their influence was limited. But Texas supporters traveled far and wide extolling the virtues of L.B.J. He was well treated by the press. This was particularly true of Republican editors, who are always willing to pick Democratic candidates. Without much effort he won the support of an almost solid South.

The South, however, was not enough. A factional candidate cannot remain one and win. Knowing this, Johnson moved to identify himself with the West. Actually this did not involve a change of character. A Texan, he faced both ways but spiritually and psychologically he appears to be closer to the victory at San Jacinto than the defeat at Appomattox. He is more akin to a cowboy than a planter; he lives on a ranch, not a plantation.

Western strength was essential. He could not challenge Kennedy in New England; he could not make serious inroads in the industrial states of the East and Midwest; he could not vie with Humphrey for support among wheat and corn-hog farmers. But beyond the tier of states on the west bank of the Mississippi he had a chance. If he could pick up a hundred or so Western votes to add to the 350 he could count on from the South, he would not only be sure of a large first roll-call total; he could control between four and five hundred votes of the 763 needed to stop Kennedy.

The Johnson strategy led to a campaign on two levels. On one he picked up what pledged delegates he could, mostly from non-primary Western states; on the other he watched Kennedy.

Kennedy's problem was a hard one. He met it brilliantly. Victory dazzles the beholder, but even in retrospect it is difficult to perceive a single mistake in tactics. Kennedy started with a solid block of New England votes. His most important objective was the delegates from the Middle Atlantic and Great Lake states. In these regions two forces dominate Democratic politics—the city machines and organized labor. A candidate who gets the support of both is "in." But at least one of these elements is absolutely essential, as a fulcrum to win over the other. In the beginning Kennedy was not assured of either. It was not a matter of implacable opposition, but rather skepticism regarding his strength. They had to be shown.

Kennedy showed them. His first objective was Ohio, where Governor Mike Di Salle was running as a favorite son. Here the Kennedy command used brute force, taking advantage of factionalism among the state's Democrats. Di Salle received an ultimatum. Either he must promise to deliver the delegation to Kennedy or Kennedy would enter the primary against him.

He knew that a primary fight, win or lose, would split the party wide open. To the Kennedy camp such rule-or-ruin tactics were justified. Their aim was their man's nomination. Party unity in Ohio was of lesser consequence; Mike Di Salle was of no consequence at all. At worst the pieces could be put back together after the victory was won. (As a matter of fact, they were not. Contrary to the general voting pattern of the November returns, Kennedy lost Ohio to Nixon.) To Di Salle, Democratic unity in his state was of major consequence and so was his own political future. He could not risk a battle; he surrendered. The same tactics were employed in dealing with Governor Pat Brown of California. Kennedy agreed not to challenge his control of the delegation, providing control was used in Kennedy's interest. Brown's position was stronger than Di Salle's but he too backed away from a fight and was chained to the Kennedy chariot. In Indiana there was no outstanding Democratic boss with whom to deal, but there was a primary and no one else was entering it. Kennedy did and, unopposed, won. Indiana's votes were in the bag for at least the first roll call.

In other key states a soft sell was necessary. Party chieftains in New Jersey, New York, Pennsylvania and Illinois could not be intimidated. Kennedy had to convince them that he was the strongest man in the field. To do this he made use of the primary as a proving ground for his ability to win.

But if the test was to be convincing he had to beat someone. Throughout the campaign he was to challenge his opponents to stand up and fight. He got only one major response. The battle lasted only two rounds. The first was a draw with both fighters bleeding at the end. In the second Kennedy scored a knockout.

Hubert Humphrey was the victim. Humphrey chose Wisconsin as a fit place in which to demonstrate his own strength. He picked carefully. His Minnesota organization could operate in the neighboring state from its home base. He himself was well known there. He was strong with agriculture and had served labor faithfully.

Humphrey's decision gave Kennedy his opportunity. Or so Kennedy hoped. Both men campaigned hard. When it was over, it appeared that the anticipations of Johnson and other candidates that the primary opponents would knock each other out might be on the way to realization. Kennedy won both the popular and delegate contests by small margins. This was not too bad. The trouble was how he had won. Analysis indicated that his victory was a Catholic triumph. His popular majority came from heavily Catholic areas; he lost the heavily Protestant ones. This was exactly what wary and watchful Democrats all over the country had feared. He had won some delegates, but if anything his position was weaker than before.

Humphrey was hurt even worse. He had been unable to carry a neighboring state where the farm and labor votes were decisive. If he could not win under such circumstances, where could he win? Moreover, where were funds for future campaigning to come from? It's hard for a loser to raise money. But the picture was not all black. Humphrey rationalized—and there was statistical evidence in the election returns to back him—that he had been defeated not only by Catholics but by Republican Catholics who had taken advantage of Wisconsin's open primary to vote for their co-religionist. He would try again, this time in West Virginia which is over 90 percent Protestant. West Virginia was also severely stricken by the economic recession and Humphrey, "the radical," was presumably the poor man's candidate.

Kennedy was fully aware of the peril involved in challenging Humphrey in West Virginia. If he lost, opponents would insist that it was proof that a Catholic could not win. But if the risk was great so was the potential reward. If he could carry the "most Protestant" state in the Union it would be convincing evidence that Protestant religious bigotry was no longer a decisive force in American politics. Moreover, if he could win

Protestant as well as Catholic labor votes he could bargain with labor bosses. He entered West Virginia.

In the ensuing campaign the Kennedy camp complained that the religious issue was being raised and that Lyndon Johnson, afraid to enter the fight himself, was giving aid to Humphrey. Both charges were true, but Humphrey had nothing to do with stirring religious prejudice—and the action of the Johnson forces was entirely proper. If Kennedy had problems, however, he also had solutions. He was a tireless and effective campaigner; he had a magnificent staff and he had money. The Kennedy wealth was used legitimately but on a scale that Humphrey could not match. It gave Kennedy greater mobility, more publicity, more radio and TV time, and it was bait to local politicians hard up for funds to wage their own campaigns.

Kennedy won—this time decisively. Humphrey was through and knew it. He withdrew from the race, releasing delegates already pledged to him to vote according to their conscience. There was no immediate rush to the Kennedy bandwagon, but the opposition began to erode. He had proved he could win in a Protestant state. He was the front runner. He dared rivals to challenge his position. None did. Instead they waited, less hopefully now, for someone else to take on the champion, and intensified their work in non-primary states. Kennedy's momentum continued to pick up. He won a few more uncontested primaries and beat Senator Wayne Morse in Oregon, Morse's own state, but after West Virginia the battle shifted to the non-primary states. These ultimately would determine the nominee. Much has been made of Kennedy's primary victories and he probably could not have won without them. But he entered only seven and got only about one-hundred and thirty delegates. Seven hundred and sixty-one were needed to win. The purpose of the primary was to get the ammunition with which to storm other fortresses.

Kennedy's opponents were unable to devise means to stop the flow of the rising tide. They continued to hope. Kennedy was far ahead but he was not quite in. Toward the end it was conceded that he had some six hundred votes—a little over one hundred and fifty short of a majority. If he could be held there for one or two or at most three roll calls . . . If?

Johnson stepped up his efforts. He left the capital a little more frequently and stretched his absences by a few more hours. He issued an occasional statement, almost condescending in tone, pointed at Kennedy's youth, his relative lack of political stature. Others joined the attack. Truman, supporting Symington, also decried the Massachusetts Senator's inexperience and shortly before the convention lashed out angrily with the charge that Paul Butler, the National Chairman, was rigging it in Kennedy's favor. He added that under such circumstances he would not even attend. Eleanor Roosevelt suggested that Kennedy was young enough to defer his ambition— that he would make an excellent Vice-President. All of Kennedy's opponents thought he would make a good Vice-President.

The most serious threat, however, came from someone who did not join the active stop-Kennedy movement. Adlai Stevenson himself remained aloof, but throughout the spring and early summer a grass-roots trend toward him was manifest. But more menacing to Kennedy was the full-scale organization that was formed without Stevenson's blessing. Money was raised; Stevenson buttons reappeared; there were Stevenson ads in newspapers. Senator Mike Monroney of Oklahoma led the Stevenson army. He knew that without his candidate's active cooperation he could not get many pledged delegates, but he picked up half a hundred or so. These would serve as a base from which to launch a draft-Stevenson movement—after Kennedy was stopped.

The Kennedy campaign was fought ruthlessly. He did not hesitate to attack when it seemed advisable. But he did not attack Adlai Stevenson—the one rival that he appears to have genuinely feared. The others might stop Kennedy by joining forces. Stevenson, if he shook off his indecision and made a major effort, might do it alone. So he was left in peace—if he could find it in the equivocal position he had chosen to occupy.

The convention was scheduled to meet July 11th in the Sports Arena at Los Angeles. Arriving delegates experienced the customary reception. They were courted by the rival camps; their eyes and ears were bombarded with sights and sounds—balloons, slogans, bands, badges—designed to prove that this or that candidate was the people's choice. There is no weighty evidence that all this helps much, but because positive proof that it does not is lacking, it continues.

The major candidates had suites in the Biltmore Hotel. These were centers of varied activity. Conferences were held, information was collected and analyzed, plans were made and modified. The candidates themselves were in command. They had arrived in Los Angeles after proper notice so that impressive spontaneous demonstrations could be arranged. Even Adlai Stevenson arrived. He was more and more available each day. Throughout the convention more noise was made in his behalf than for any other candidate. Much of it was genuinely spontaneous. California's heart belonged to Adlai.

Johnson, who only a few days before the convention got around to announcing officially that he was a candidate, had headquarters in the Biltmore and another in a cottage near the Sports Arena. He expressed confidence that he would be nominated. He conferred with delegates and issued statements to the press. He did what he could, and since only Kennedy had more pledged delegates, his seemed to be the leading role in the move to block the front runner. Actually this was not true. His strength was a known quantity. It was substantial but it was not enough. It was obvious by now that if Kennedy was to be stopped it would be by a late ground swell for Stevenson epitomized by the demonstration that surged more or less continuously outside the convention hall from Monday night until the end of the first roll call. At its height thousands of people participated. Behind its façade the Stevenson organization was working desperately and to some effect. This did not shake the allegiance of pledged Kennedy delegates, but it did give pause to some who were uncommitted.

On the eve of the convention Kennedy still needed around a hundred and fifty votes. New Jersey, Pennsylvania, California, Minnesota and Illinois were the largest sources of uncommitted strength. In each of these the choice lay between Kennedy and Stevenson, and with the possible exception of Illinois no decision had been made when the delegates arrived in Los Angeles.

New Jersey was instructed for its favorite son, Governor Meyner. Kennedy had strength among delegates from the northern part of the state but Meyner would not release them. He himself leaned toward Stevenson. Pennsylvania's Governor David Lawrence had been a strong Stevenson man since 1952, and although Catholic he feared the issue in a presidential race. However, William Green, Philadelphia boss, was strong for Kennedy. Governor Brown of California was pledged to Kennedy but over half his delegation was pro-Stevenson and in open revolt. Minnesota, too, was split. Governor Freeman aligned himself with Kennedy, Senator Eugene McCarthy with the Stevenson leaders; Humphrey was undecided. The delegation caucused Monday and Tuesday without reaching a decision. Of the large key states, Stevenson was weakest in his own Illinois. Chicago mayor and boss Richard Daley controlled the Cook County delegation and Cook County dominates the Illinois Democratic party. On Sunday, the day before the convention convened, after a caucus, Daley announced that the bulk of the state's votes would go to Kennedy.

The battle was particularly fierce in two other states—Kansas and Iowa. Kennedy was not strong in either—the farm states opposed him in 1956 as a vice-presidential candidate and he lost them to Nixon in 1960—and both are normally Republican. However, they had elected Democratic governors, and visions of the vice-presidential sugar plum danced in their heads.

The visions were prompted by Kennedy emissaries. No promises were made but they were given to understand that they were receiving serious consideration. Presumably this was true. The weekend before the convention the two governors came out for Kennedy. Stevenson sentiment existed in both delegations, however, and there was some doubt if it could be suppressed.

The convention was called to order on Monday evening, July 11th. To millions of television viewers it appeared disorderly from beginning to end. The problem was not the emotion that disrupted the Democratic convention of 1912, or deep-rooted divisive issues such as split the 1924 Smith-McAdoo followers. It was simply inattention, due in part to poor acoustics. The delegates milled around, conferring with one another, giving interviews, doing anything but paying attention to the speakers on the platform.

It was bad manners and in view of the fact that millions were watching it was bad politics. But it was not quite the chaos that met the eye. Decisions were being made on the floor where representatives of the candidates were firming up their delegates, raiding those of their opponents, working on the uncommitted. Discussions between delegates were not always idle. They were trying to make up their minds.

Issues did not divide the Democrats in 1960. Ten Southern states protested the strongest civil rights plank ever presented to a Democratic National Convention but there was no walkout. The whole platform was adopted by a voice vote. Aside from civil rights, it was somewhat vague. It promised changes in American foreign policy, but these would deal with procedures rather than aims. It pledged efforts to "provide medical care benefits for the aged as part of the time-tested Social Security insurance system," and to "help in building the classrooms and employing the teachers that are essential if the right to a good education is to have genuine meaning. . . ." It side-stepped a direct declaration on the oil depletion allowance tax. Any of the candidates could run on it.

By Wednesday the convention was ready to choose a candidate for President. Alabama, first on the list of states, yielded to Texas. Speaker Sam Rayburn put Johnson's name into nomination. He emphasized Johnson's experience and his proven qualities as a leader: "This man can unite us. He will lead us to reason and to work together, for over many years he has proven that he possesses the magic gift of being able to lead men in a common cause." The customary demonstration, exceeding by three minutes the time limit permitted by convention rules, followed.

As in the 1952 Taft-Eisenhower contest, the first roll call was decisive. But this one was not a two-man fight. It was Kennedy against the field. If he failed to get the nomination on the first ballot he might still win on a second or even third. If he was stopped after three the convention would probably turn elsewhere. That would be Johnson's opportunity—or Stevenson's, or Symington's, or a favorite son's.

Kennedy was not stopped. Their governors delivered Iowa and Kansas; Pennsylvania gave him most of its vote. New Jersey held off, but he got almost half of California and part of Minnesota. With the fall or envelopment of such key citadels, lesser ones capitulated. Yet the roll call reached almost the end of the alphabet before the decision was reached. The spokesman for the Wyoming delegation, obviously excited to be cast for a few seconds in the role of a man of destiny, announced that the state's vote was "for the next President of the United States." At the time there was still doubt about that, but he had voted for the Democratic nominee, John F. Kennedy.

Lyndon Johnson received 409 votes. Of these, 335½ came from the South and border states, leaving only 73½ from the rest of the country. Outside the South only Delaware, New Mexico and the Canal Zone gave him a majority of their votes. Forty-three came from the West; the remainder were widely scattered. Though he had made dents elsewhere he remained primarily a sectional candidate.

Success breeds its own rationalization. In the case of presidential politics this includes the not unreasonable assumption that if a candidate is nominated and goes on to win he was the right man. This makes Kennedy the right man. He won. It cannot be proved that any other Democrat could have. He certainly was not the wrong man.

Yet there is an interesting, controversial and unprovable thesis that both parties nominated the wrong man and that Kennedy won not because he was a strong candidate but because Nixon was a weak one. The reasoning behind this is that Nixon, although popular with Republican politicians, is not particularly so with rank-and-file party members and independents, and among Democrats is the most unpopular of all possible Republican nominees; that under these circumstances all the Democrats had to do was to nominate someone who could get out the Democratic vote. But, faced with an easy way to win, Democrats made it hard by nominating Kennedy, who because he was a Catholic drove many Democrats to either vote for the unacceptable Nixon or stay at home.

Public opinion polls taken before the conventions tend to disprove this. They showed both Kennedy and Nixon leading their rivals. Moreover, both polled a heavy vote in the general election. So perhaps the thesis is fallacious. It remains interesting.

Lyndon Johnson was not the right man. He might have triumphed over his handicap as Kennedy did, but while Kennedy has demonstrated that a Catholic can be elected President, whether a Southerner can remains to be proved. Johnson was also opposed by big labor—most of whose leaders later fought his selection as Kennedy's running mate. Thus it is almost certain that he would have lost the industrial states of the East and Midwest. It was in these regions that Kennedy won the election.

Johnson would almost certainly have carried the South and the border states, including those lost by Kennedy. Outside the South and west of Missouri and Minnesota, Kennedy won only New Mexico, Nevada and Hawaii. Johnson couldn't have done much worse and might have done better. But the solid South and part of the West is not enough, and that appears to have been the limit of Johnson's strength. He would not have gotten the normal Democratic vote in the North, and unlike Kennedy he would not have gotten an abnormally heavy Catholic vote to make up the deficit. In 1960 he was the wrong man.

He had a strong claim to being the best man. He understands the office of the Presidency and its proper function in the American system. He understands American politics. He has proved he can get the possible. It is sometimes dangerous to reach for the impossible. Of course, his claim could be challenged by Stevenson's broader vision and greater capacity for inspirational leadership, by Symington's greater administrative experience, by Humphrey's equally rapid rise as a politician and statesman. On the record as it read on July 13, 1960, it could not be strongly challenged by John Kennedy. Kennedy may prove himself a great President—Andrew Jackson and Lincoln with less impressive pre-election records did—but in July, 1960, that lay in the future.

Overwhelmed by a daringly conceived and brilliantly executed campaign, the Democratic National Convention gambled on the right and best man. It won its gamble on the right man. The verdict on the best man will have to await history.

Lyndon Johnson remains a powerful force in the Democratic party and in America. To the surprise of his admirers—and in many cases the chagrin—he accepted second place on the Kennedy ticket. It may well be that by holding most of the South where Kennedy proved even weaker than anticipated he saved the ticket. His influence as Vice-President is hard to assess, but there is no doubt that he does exercise influence. He has divulged no plans for the future. One may wonder, however, if four or eight years as Vice-President of the United States might not make a man belong to the whole nation, rather than to just Texas, or the South. In 1968 Lyndon Johnson will be sixty years old.

The Republicans

1964

THE silly season for crystal gazing into a future presidential battle is the period between the last one and the intervening off-year elections. The future is obscure, the immediate past is not fully revealed and the present is deceptive. But the off-year elections begin to shed some light. Involving as they do state and local issues and personalities, this light illuminates the national political scene only fitfully. But it often reveals potential candidates and shattered prospects. Prospective nominees for the Presidency are broken by defeat, others increase in stature. New possibilities emerge. This seems particularly likely in the 1962 off-year elections when Richard Nixon and Nelson Rockefeller will presumably be candidates for governors of their respective states. A victory for either will enhance his presidential pros-

pects; defeat will remove him from the ranks of the available. If both triumph, the size of their majorities will be significant. If both lose, Senator Barry Goldwater will loom larger, while a search for alternative middle-of-the-road or liberal candidates will quicken. Perhaps some such possibilities will emerge from state gubernatorial battles; possibly the "Eastern," "liberal" wing of the party that nominated Wendell Willkie and Thomas Dewey and Dwight Eisenhower will recruit a champion from the ranks of business. The stock of generals seems to be somewhat low. If Rockefeller wins decisively, Goldwater's strength diminishes and the possibility that the party will be forced to resort to a Nixon draft recedes. If both Nixon and Rockefeller win comfortably but not overwhelmingly, the balance remains unchanged. But California and New York do not hold the only keys to the future. A national or regional pattern of voting may emerge as a decisive factor.

Whatever occurs 1964 will almost certainly be more predictable by the end of 1962 than at the beginning. Nonetheless, crystal gazing, even in the silly season, is an irresistible folly among the addicts of politics. If fruitless and bootless, it is probably harmless.

If there is a war—as distinct from a "police action"—nothing save death is predictable. If there is a deep depression the oracle must dissect and read entrails far different from those used while the economy maintains something akin to its present level. Discounting these two possibilities, the Democratic future is almost crystal clear. Almost, because human life and health are uncertain quantities. President Kennedy, however, due to his relative youth, is an excellent actuarial risk, and if he is available he will be renominated. Since 1884 when the Republicans chose James G. Blaine over President Chester Arthur who was serving out the assassinated Garfield's term, no party has rejected an incumbent who asked for renomination (unless the ailing Wilson was a serious candidate in 1920) . There are reasons for this. To re-

pudiate the President is to repudiate the party record. It is to say to the voter, "We misled you four years ago; trust us." Moreover, if there is a party insurrection a President and his allies can overcome it—if not quell it. Witness the renomination of William Taft over Theodore Roosevelt in 1912. So it may be assumed that Kennedy will be renominated.

The Republicans have no such ready solution. Ex-President Eisenhower is barred from another term by the Constitution and probably by age and inclination; Richard Nixon has said that he is not a candidate. He has said further that he will not be drafted; he has not said that he cannot be. There is a difference, and although the Republicans in over a hundred years of history have nominated only one loser for a second try—and he, Thomas Dewey, got beaten—Nixon remains a good possibility as the party's candidate in 1964. The others on the scene more than two and a half years before the event are Governor Nelson Rockefeller of New York and Arizona Senator Barry Goldwater.

Whoever the Republican nominee may be, he will face an uphill battle. The American people, like American parties, rechoose their Presidents. Since 1860 the incumbent has run for re-election fifteen times. Eleven times he has won. Of the other four, Grover Cleveland and Benjamin Harrison traded defeats, in 1888 and 1892; Taft was beaten in 1912 by the Republican party split, and Hoover in 1932 by the depression. Patterns of the past are not infallible guides to the future but neither are they senseless. The President in office is generally there because his party is the nation's majority party. Unless the loyalty of the electorate shifts in four years his challenger must get more than his own party's normal vote. This takes a jolting national experience of some kind, or an extraordinarily "right" man as the president's opponent. The incumbent has a positional as well as numerical advantage. Certain duties of his office are politically priceless. These include radio and television reports to the nation, press releases, widely reported and frequently broadcasted news conferences. He can and does use them—though by no means exclusively—to strengthen his position with the voters. The President of the United States is always news; a governor, even of California or New York, is so only occasionally; a Senator from Arizona, by virtue of his office, hardly ever. The President is also able to strengthen his party's organization by federal patronage, and he can propose legislative measures that promise to produce votes. Even if Congress rejects these he gets credit for trying. Naturally, he is responsible for failures, and the opposition party makes the most of them, but barring major blunders or disasters, the American voter forgives or forgets. Moreover the President, virtually certain of renomination, does not have to face civil war in his own party. He will not be wounded in fratricidal conflict; he has to train only for the main event.

President Kennedy has all these advantages and few Presidents have shown greater capacity to utilize opportunity. For the time being the omens favor him. The scattered 1961 elections indicate no significant change in the electorate, polls reveal him as personally more popular than Eisenhower was at the same period in his presidential career; polls and samplings show that the Democratic party remains, as it has been since 1932, the nation's majority party.

Beset with difficulties, the Republican future is not entirely hopeless. President Kennedy's first year has been a personal success; it has not been an overwhelming triumph of statesmanship. He has shown more vigor than Eisenhower, and a greater understanding of the responsibilities and potentialities of the Presidency. Perhaps because of this he has made blunders—notably in Cuba—that a policy of inertia would have avoided. He has had fair but not remarkable success in getting administrative measures through Congress. On his two most popular campaign promises—medical aid and education—he has thus far failed. On the whole, the record of the first Kennedy year is probably acceptable to his followers; it is not invulnerable to attack from his opponents.

Republicans are further fortified by the closeness of the 1960 election. Only a few more votes, only two or three more key states—and Nixon would have won. It was heartbreaking, but it was also a heartening augury for the future. Still, if rays of hope are to burst into a November sunrise in 1964, the Republicans must find the right man.

Goldwater and Rockefeller
Unchosen?

They equate the Democratic Party with the welfare state, the welfare state with socialism and socialism with communism.
— PRESIDENT JOHN F. KENNEDY

I am not one to mold nature to try to fill preconceived plans.
— NELSON ROCKEFELLER

PRESIDENT KENNEDY may or may not have had Senator Barry Goldwater in mind when on November 18, 1961, he struck out against the "discordant voices of extremism." There can be no doubt, however, that Barry Goldwater, on the following day, equated Americans for Democratic Action with socialism, and President Kennedy with members of this organization who are in, or close to, his administration. He has also equated socialism with Communism. It is the same technique by which some liberals equate the John Birch Society with fascism and Senator Goldwater with the John Birch Society and it has the same validity: none at all. Barry Goldwater no more advocates fascism than John Kennedy advocates socialism. He is an archconservative and since 1956 has become the most articulate voice of the right wing of the Republican party, a wing which is still firmly within the framework and historical tradition of American democracy. It is the old guard, and it has its philosophic roots in nineteenth-century liberal laissez-faire doctrine. Not the laissez-faire of Jefferson and Andrew Jackson but of Social Darwinism and the Gospel of Wealth. Governor Nelson Rockefeller's grandfathers, John D. Rockefeller and Senator Nelson W. Aldrich of Rhode Island, were of this persuasion; so were Andrew Carnegie, Mark Hanna, and Presidents Harrison and McKinley. In the 1940's, Senator Robert A. Taft, more liberal than his predecessors, assumed leadership of the old guard. When he died Senator Knowland took command. Goldwater followed Knowland. Characteristically he was not chosen but took over. While other conservative leaders floundered between their principles and loyalty to the President he boldly called for the Republican party to set its course to the right—his more severe critics say to the rear. In a sense they were right, but not wholly so. Goldwater speaks for the old guard and he may still be its candidate for the Presidency, but he does not quite belong. The conservatism of the old guard is the smug conservatism of complacency, even when there seems little about which to be complacent; Barry Goldwater's is the angry reaction of the counterrevolution. It is less the materialistic conservatism of Wall Street than the nostalgic conservatism of the frontier. He is nearer to Paladin or Wyatt Earp than to McKinley. If he is nominated for the Presidency his campaign song might well be "Don't Fence Me In."

Barry Goldwater's grandfather, Michael Goldwater, was a Polish Jew who left Poland in 1848. He went first to Paris and then to London, where he married Sarah Nathan. In 1852, accompanied by his brother, he migrated to America. Landing in New York, the two headed for California and the gold rush. Failing to find gold they started a store in Sonora, California. The Goldwassers—changed somewhere along the way to Goldwater—have been Western merchants ever since.

The Sonora store failed. Michael sent his wife and children to San Francisco and joined his brother who had already abandoned Sonora for Los Angeles. In 1862, responding to news of a gold strike on the Gila River, he loaded wagons with merchandise and recrossed the desert to Arizona. During the next two decades he and his brother opened general merchandising stores in Ehrenberg, Prescott, Tombstone, and Phoenix, Arizona. They also supplied United States Army posts with wheat.

Meantime, Sarah remained in San Francisco where in 1866 Baron Goldwater, Barry's father, was born. In 1882, at the age of sixteen, Baron left San Francisco for Prescott, Arizona, where he joined his father and older brother, Morris. Ten years later Michael Goldwater sold his business interests to his sons Baron and Morris. In 1894 Baron took charge of the partnership's business in Phoenix.

The Goldwaters prospered. When Baron, at the age of forty, met Josephine Williams, a descendant of Roger Williams, founder of Rhode Island, he was one of Phoenix's leading businessmen. Miss Williams had come to Arizona suffering from tuberculosis. She and Baron were married January 1, 1907. On their second wedding anniversary their first child was born. He was named Barry. Two more children, another son and a daughter, followed. All were reared as Episcopalians—their mother's faith.

As a youth Barry lived the life of the son of an affluent citizen of a small but growing Western city. He was part of Phoenix society, such as it was, and all the advantages it offered were his. In school he was an indifferent student with little interest in study. It was the era before progressive education, but he learned by doing. His fascination with mechanics and electronics made him an early convert to do-it-yourself. When he was fifteen he went to Staunton Military Academy at Staunton, Virginia. After graduating he entered the University of Arizona. A year later, upon his father's death, he quit college to go into the family business. He was twenty years old. At the age of twenty-eight he became president of Goldwaters, Inc., a position he was to hold until 1953 when he entered the United States Senate.

Three years before he became president of Goldwaters he married Margaret Johnson of Muncie, Indiana, daughter of an official of the Borg-Warner Corporation. The couple have four children, two sons and two daughters. But a growing business and growing family have not wholly absorbed the apparently inexhaustible energy and roving interests of Barry Goldwater. He has found time for activities embracing almost every phase of Arizona life—its Indians, its mountains and canyons, and its history. He has continued to learn by doing. He visited the Indian reservation and took such excellent photographs that he has been admitted as an associate member of the Royal Photographic Society of London. He has a magnificent collection of Hopi Kachina dolls. He went with a party down the almost unnavigable Colorado River from Utah to Lake Mead at the Arizona-Nevada border. Flying over the Grand Canyon he observed a shadow which he suspected was that of an uncharted natural bridge. He hired a helicopter, found the bridge and named it the Margaret Bridge after his wife.

He learned to fly in 1930. At the outbreak of the war he was rejected by the army air corps because he was too old (thirty-two) and afflicted with astigmatism. He rejected rejection. First he managed to get himself accepted as a ground-school instructor in gunnery. In his off time he photographed training pilots in flight. They in turn, during their off time, accompanied him on flights until he had accumulated enough flying time to qualify as a ferry pilot. From August, 1943, to the end of the war he served with the air transport command. Today he is a brigadier general in the air reserve and the only United States Senator to pilot jet planes. This accounts in part for his intense interest in the air force. More significantly, it illuminates his demand for a tough foreign policy backed by a readiness to use force. The civilian soldier is frequently more militant than the professional.

At the end of the 1940's Barry Goldwater was one of Phoenix's leading citizens. He was president of a sizable corporation; he had been cited by the United States Chamber of Commerce; he had been voted Phoenix's man of the year; he was a director of the Association of American Indian Affairs. He was a member of the American Legion and Veterans of Foreign Wars. He was a Shriner, an Elk, a Woodman of the World. He was everything but a statesman. Although he had acted as adviser to the Commissioner of Indian Affairs during President Truman's administration he had shown no particular interest in politics. This changed in 1949 when he ran for the Phoenix city council. The ticket of which he was a part was non-partisan and pledged to better civic housekeeping rather than ideology. He was elected. So although in public life, he was not very far in, and not as a party partisan. He took the next step a year later when he managed Howard Pyle's campaign for governor. Pyle won—the first Republican governor in the history of Arizona. And Barry Goldwater had tasted blood. In 1952 he ran for the United States Senate.

His Democratic opponent was Ernest W. McFarland, the majority leader of the Senate. This position, one of the nation's high seats of power, enabled McFarland to tend quite effectively his constituency's interests. This is particularly valuable to a state such as Arizona, that has few electoral votes to snare presidential support and few congressional votes to bargain and barter.

The campaign saw the Goldwater political personality take shape. He possessed those intangible qualities that make politicians personally popular with the voters. He was plausible, energetic, and effective—and he was handsome. Although few men have tried harder to sell their principles, it seems probable that he is more successful in selling himself. His political techniques also emerged in 1952. He argued in terms of black and white. The method is simple. He starts with value judgments which he presents as incontrovertible facts and builds his case on these foundations. In 1952 he asserted that he represented the American idea—that was one incontrovertible fact. McFarland's ideas were socialistic ideas—that was another incontrovertible fact. So the voter must choose between Americanism and socialism. That was the final incontrovertible fact. Truman and the Democrats were soft on Communism; the national government spent too much money; it was robbing the states of their constitutional rights. He, Barry Goldwater, was against Communism, against big government, against big labor and for states' rights. The technique worked. It was a close election—Goldwater needed Ike's coattails—but he won by 6,752 votes. Eisenhower had a majority of over 40,000.

In his first five years in the United States Senate Goldwater stood to the right of the Republican center, but not yet on the extreme right. He had supported Eisenhower against Taft for the Republican presidential nomination, and thus was regarded as an Eisenhower rather than old-guard Republican. But clearly he did not accept the "modern Republican mystique." When he was so inclined, he opposed the President. In 1954 he refused to join in the movement blessed by Eisenhower to censure Senator Joseph McCarthy. He did not go all the way with McCarthy, but he did say that his mistakes were those of excessive zeal in a worthy cause, and that the Republicans were committing "cannibalism" in censoring him. In this opposition to party "cannibalism" he has been consistent. He criticizes the views of liberal Republicans, but he never forgets that they are Republicans, and as such preferable to Democrats—at least to Democrats running against them. This—combined with the fact that he seldom makes personal attacks on his opponents—helps explain why he remains popular with colleagues of both parties.

His first-term voting record reveals his orientation. He was for bills giving tideland oil to the states and providing for the sale of government-owned rubber plants to private industry. He was against the use of federal revenues from oil leases as grants to aid education; he was opposed to public power. He was opposed to tax relief for small business—although he himself would probably have benefited from it—and against a tax cut to families with incomes of not more than $5,000 a year. A seemingly inconsistent note was a vote in favor of a salary increase of $7,500 for congressmen. Possibly he regards Senators and Representatives as entrepreneurs entitled in a free enterprise system to all they can get. He is opposed in principle to any governmental aid to farmers, believing that agriculture is better off operating in a free market. But he did vote for the

Agricultural Act of 1954 which provided flexible price supports for basic farm products. Presumably he regarded it as the least of alternative evils.

From the beginning he has been an extremist in his opposition to organized labor. His position is forthright. He believes in the right of labor to organize and to bargain collectively. But he insists that union membership should be purely voluntary and wants right-to-work laws in every state. He would weaken collective bargaining by eliminating the "evil" of industry-wide bargaining. He also wants federal legislation banning political activities by unions. In this he retreats somewhat from his usual insistence on states' rights; perhaps he justifies it on the grounds of a national emergency. He is reported to have said that Walter Reuther and the United Auto Workers are a greater menace than the Soviet Union.

Given his premise, Senator Goldwater is perceptive in making Reuther the cloven-hoofed beast of the labor movement. It is not labor's abuse of power that most disturbs him. It is its possession of power. So he characteristically strikes at the jugular vein; vitiation, not reform, is his chief goal. With the possible exception of the John Birch Society, which he seems afraid to condemn, labor appears to be the only thing in America that does frighten Barry Goldwater.

Goldwater's attitude towards foreign policy also emerged during his first five years in the Senate. On the whole it is consistent. He favored penalizing nations that traded with Communist China; he was against confirming Charles E. Bohlen as Ambassador to Russia; he urged a proposed half-billion-dollar cut in foreign aid. He supported the Bricker amendment which would limit the treaty-making power of the President and in effect give the states a voice in determining treaties.

In 1955 Goldwater was chosen Chairman of the Republican Senatorial Campaign Committee. It was a show of confidence in him, and it gave Goldwater an opportunity to make himself known outside Arizona and Washington. He worked hard in the campaign, making no distinction between right, center and "modern" Republicans. When the elections went against the party's candidates—except for President Eisenhower, Republicans fared badly—no one held Goldwater responsible.

Upon his return to the Senate in 1957, he assumed a new role. When or why he made his decision is not generally known. Perhaps he was keenly conscious of the Republican old guard's lack of leadership. Robert Taft was dead; Knowland of California was in political limbo; the "new" Nixon was of necessity a modern Republican; Senator Everett Dirksen of Illinois lacked stature. Goldwater stepped in.

On April 8, 1957, he attacked the Eisenhower administration. It was with the "deepest sorrow," but it was "a matter of conscience." Maybe he would be "among the missing" after the next election but he would not betray the taxpayer by voting for an Eisenhower-backed foreign aid bill which in his opinion constituted fiscal irresponsibility. It was by no means a party bolt, but he had crossed the Rubicon. He was no longer the President's man. He made this abundantly clear when he proceeded to denounce modern Republicanism as in conflict with sound party philosophy. No Senate Republican replied. So by design or accident less than ten years after he ran for the Phoenix city commission, Barry Goldwater had seized leadership of the right wing of the Republican party. It did not make him a presidential possibility. That awaited the 1958 elections.

Although Goldwater spoke dramatically of the political danger he risked in attacking the Eisenhower administration, he probably was not really too worried. Whatever effect his move to the right might have nationally, it was almost certain to prove popular in Arizona. Always conservative, the state grows more so as Tucson and Phoenix become an increasingly popular Mecca for those who have enough money to retire. This is particularly true since a large proportion of the immigrants are from the Midwest, heartland of the Republican old guard.

In 1958, as in 1956, Goldwater's opponent was Ernest W. McFarland. After the 1952 defeat, McFarland had run and been elected the state's governor. Once again Goldwater's cam-

paign was tireless. This time he won without benefit of the
Eisenhower coattails. His majority was decisive, and it was the
more impressive because 1958 was a bleak year for Republicans.
Throughout the country they fell before the Democratic onslaught. A G.O.P. victory was memorable.

Yet even Goldwater's 1958 triumph did not make him a presidential candidate overnight. In fact his 1960 presidential
boom was late and lean. In April South Carolina pledged its
convention votes to him. Arizona's were his for the asking and
he could unquestionably pick up additional support—princi-
pally from the South, a little from the West. He did not try.
Instead he attempted to force Nixon and the Republican party
to the right. His formula for America at mid-century, and the
Republican party for November, was forthright:

> If [Nixon] would come out with a strong statement of "con-
> servative" principles relating to these problems [federal aid to
> education and security for the aged] you couldn't beat him with
> a club. People are desperately looking for a man who will give
> them "conservative" leadership, tell the farmers to get back
> under the law of supply and demand, get the chiselers off the
> welfare roles, tell people that their welfare depends on them-
> selves, not on the Federal Government.

This sort of thing pleased conservatives, and as the convention approached he had considerable backing for the vice-
presidential nomination. He did not, however, have that of
Nixon. There were strategic reasons for this. Although Nixon
had gravitated to the party center and was assured of its vote,
he had entered politics as the candidate of the right and he still
retained strong conservative support. Therefore Goldwater,
as a running mate, could only strengthen him where he was
already strong. There were other reasons for rejecting Goldwater. In the approaching campaign the Republican candidates would have to defend the Eisenhower record. Goldwater
had attacked it. Finally, Nixon could not accept the Goldwater
program. So Goldwater's vice-presidential chances were no

brighter than those for the presidential nomination. He probably didn't care.

But if he was not in the convention limelight as a possible nominee, he did emerge from the Chicago meeting with measurably greater influence. This was the result of unabashed espousal of reactionary principles, and stubborn refusal to be awed by Nixon, the new leader of the party. When Nixon came to terms with Rockefeller he called it a betrayal. He made no secret of his disappointment at the platform.

Goldwater's was the only name, other than Nixon's, to be placed in nomination. He did not request it, but when dissident Louisiana delegates wished to do it he did not protest. But he immediately withdrew. In doing so he gained the national television audience that was watching the convention proceedings. Millions of Americans were seeing and hearing Barry Goldwater for the first time. They saw a pleasant, if deadly earnest, speaker. He was "photogenic." They heard what may have been the best speech of the convention. He did not strike his conservative colors, but he did affirm his party loyalty and, in a far more convincing fashion than Rockefeller, he pledged support to the Republican ticket. He pleaded for other conservatives to join him. He demanded they not only support the party's nominee but that they work for him—no sulking, no leaning on the oars, no fishing on election day.

In the campaign he followed his own advice. He worked for Nixon unstintingly—mostly in the South where he emphasized the similar views of conservative Republicans and Southern Democrats. He urged Southerners to try voting Republican just to see how good it would make them feel. He ridiculed Kennedy, attacked Lyndon Johnson. He did not endorse the Republican party platform, but insisted that it was better than the Democrats'. Although a school integrationist in principle, he gave comfort to segregationists by championing states' rights. It is impossible to know how many votes he got for Nixon— religious bigotry probably accounted for more—but he undoubtedly got a great many. And he emerged from the cam-

paign as the Southern Republicans' presidential candidate for
1964.

Although Barry Goldwater's 1958 election triumph was duly
noted, his was not the image that most soothsayers, gazing into
the crystal ball to detect prospective candidates for the Presidency, saw. Far across the continent from Arizona another Republican had won. In New York, as politically potent as Arizona
is anemic, Nelson Rockefeller, a newcomer to politics, had
beaten the incumbent Averell Harriman for governor. The
Republican left as well as the right had found a leader.

Nelson Rockefeller was born at Bar Harbor, Maine, in July,
1908. He was reared after the fashion of the very rich. He spent
his childhood in town houses, on country estates and in American and European travel. He was educated in private schools
and at Dartmouth College, where he was initiated into Phi
Beta Kappa, America's premier honorary scholastic society.

During his teens he met Mary Todhunter Clark at Bar Harbor. Her mother was the daughter of George Roberts, a president of the Pennsylvania Railroad; her father belonged to an
old and socially prominent Pennsylvania family. The young
couple became engaged while Rockefeller was at Dartmouth
and were married soon after his graduation. Following a honeymoon that included a world tour they settled down in New
York. Although Mrs. Rockefeller seems to be somewhat more
liberal politically than her husband (at one time she was a
member of the Liberal party) she is a registered Republican,
and has accompanied him on speaking campaigns throughout
the state. She was generally regarded as a political asset before
the collapse of the marriage in 1961.

For ten years Rockefeller engaged in activities related to the
family business. In 1940 President Roosevelt appointed him
Coordinator of Inter-American Affairs. It was his first entry
into public life. In the Washington jungle he proved himself
tough and shrewd in bureaucratic infighting. His was an independent agency and before long crossed swords with State

Department officials. This was over policy matters but there was also the dog-eat-dog kind of struggle that almost always goes on in such situations, and which was especially virulent in the New Deal days. During 1944 he moved up, becoming Assistant Secretary of State in charge of Latin-American affairs. But when James Byrnes became Secretary of State (1945) and Dean Acheson undersecretary, the independent Rockefeller was relieved of his position. In 1946 he founded the American International Association for Economic and Social Development (the AIA), a nonprofit organization designed to assist Latin-American governments in programs aimed at improvement in underdeveloped areas.

During the early years of the Eisenhower administration he served first as undersecretary in the Department of Health, Education and Welfare, and then as special assistant to the President. In these positions he was apparently less at home than during the earlier days of government service. In the Department of Health, Education and Welfare he was content to echo the ideas of his chief, Oveta Culp Hobby. As foreign policy adviser to the President he fought—without mobilizing all his potential resources—an unsuccessful battle for greater foreign aid. In 1955 he returned to private life.

He left the government service convinced that the American people should be better informed concerning the problems facing them. This was in conformity with the Rockefeller family pattern of support to education as a means of contributing to the nation's well-being. But his approach was new. He suggested studies of national problems. These would be financed privately by the Rockefeller Brothers' Fund. His brothers approved. Dr. Henry Kissinger was appointed Special Studies Director. The project is characteristic of Nelson Rockefeller —it is concerned with data to be used in understanding specific problems rather than with an overall program for America. He is a social technician rather than a social planner. In this— critics notwithstanding—he is neither to the right nor the left, but in the central current of the American tradition.

Early in 1958 the Rockefeller Fund made its first report. It indicated a need for greater expenditure on national defense. This and subsequent reports have been acclaimed as significant analyses of the nation's problems. Were Nelson Rockefeller to be nominated for the Presidency, they might well contribute to the Republican party platform.

In 1957 a group of New York City Republicans launched a drive to draft Rockefeller for governor. Averell Harriman, the Democratic incumbent, unintentionally contributed to the movement by suggesting, perhaps, facetiously, that the Republicans should oppose him with a candidate such as Rockefeller. G.O.P. party professionals did not at first accept Rockefeller as a gift from heaven. He was not one of their own; he was an amateur, and so far as anyone knew not even a politically talented one; his orthodoxy was suspect among conservatives. But New York Republicans do not ignore a Rockefeller. It was suggested that he run for the Senate. He wasn't interested, and after conferring with Westchester County leaders and the Chairman of the State Republican Committee, he canvassed the state, rounding up delegates. When the state party convention met it nominated him as its candidate for governor.

It is possible that Rockefeller was not opposed more vigorously from within the party because the nomination did not appear to be worth much. Harriman had been a good governor, was a national figure who had twice been a candidate for the Democratic presidential nomination, and had proved that he could get votes and win elections. The campaign that followed attracted as much national attention as any other gubernatorial race of the century. It was a news natural—a battle of multimillionaires. The heirs of two of America's largest fortunes were struggling not to monopolize an industry or control a railroad, but for public office. But it was more than this. The political stakes were high. Averell Harriman was no longer young, but if he could carry New York again in 1958 he might make one more try for the Presidency. With Adlai Stevenson shopworn from defeat and no other outstanding candidate in sight, it might be his year. For Rockefeller it was in all probability do or die. Victory would propel him in one mighty leap to the forefront of presidential possibilities; defeat would banish him to private life, or at best public service confined to appointive positions.

The Republican New York City machine was not very strong and the upstate bosses were not enthusiastic. However, what Rockefeller lacked in organization he atoned for in energy. He made over a hundred speeches in over a hundred towns. Not only New Yorkers but all America saw him. Newsreels, television, newspaper photographs, pictured him eating hot dogs and pizza. He talked to Puerto Ricans in Spanish; he posed in Harlem with Count Basie's orchestra. He grinned, quipped and shook hands. This was window dressing, and as good window dressing does, it helped to sell the product. But behind it was a hard-driving campaign designed to appeal to the reason of the voter. As is customary with Republicans, he accused his Democratic opponent of being soft toward Tammany Hall, and promised to rid the state of bossism. But he did more. He challenged the Democratic claim that it alone was concerned with the well-being of the common man. He pledged himself to improve public health and welfare programs, to combat juvenile delinquency, to aid education. So while in Arizona Barry Goldwater, the grandson of an immigrant, preached the laissez-faire gospel of wealth, in New York the grandson of John D. Rockefeller espoused the cause of the democratic welfare state.

Nelson Rockefeller, however, was still fundamentally a Republican businessman in politics. He believed as strongly as Goldwater in fiscal responsibility; he believed in governmental measures that would create conditions favorable to industry, commerce and agriculture. It was expansion of the economy which was to furnish the revenue to pay for social services. He did not attack free enterprise, or propose to shackle or enfeeble it. He did propose to harness it to the service of the community.

He won the election by an overwhelming majority of 557,000

votes. The victory was rendered even more significant by analysis. Rockefeller carried upstate Republican New York by about the usual G.O.P. majority, but in New York City he cut heavily into the customary Democratic majority. Democrats and Independents had voted for him. Moreover, he had carried the Republican ticket with him—a feat which even Eisenhower could not match.

In his first few months of office Rockefeller proved to be a hard-working, hard-driving chief executive. He also demonstrated that he could handle the state legislature. Despite ideological hostility of some Republican legislators and Democratic opposition, he shoved most of his program through. This included an increase in taxation which many political experts declared—gleefully or regretfully—would doom him. The winning political formula, they said, is to promise more for less, and give as much as you can without an increase in costs, or at least in payments. It was not Rockefeller's formula. Services were not to be bestowed on the citizenry, they were to be bought by them. Furthermore they were to be paid for, not charged.

As an administrator he met the high standards set by such New York predecessors as Al Smith, Herbert Lehman and Thomas E. Dewey. His appointments were good; there were no scandals. The first-year record was good, if somewhat brief, when presidential ambitions became manifest.

Potentially he had been a possible presidential candidate since his election; his name, with Vice-President Nixon's, had been in the forefront of speculation concerning Eisenhower's successor. But while Nixon lined up support Rockefeller hesitated. Even after the August announcement that a Midwest headquarters would be opened and Rockefeller for President clubs had been organized in various parts of the country, he would only commit himself so far as to say that he would wait for the November public opinion polls before making up his mind. These prognostications proved unfavorable. He appeared to have substantial strength in New England and New York but little elsewhere. He lagged far behind the Vice-President.

This was not surprising. He suffered from disadvantages that could not be overcome in a few months. He was not personally known to politicians throughout the country; the old guard everywhere distrusted him; the South feared him as an integrationist; he had no national organization; he lacked President Eisenhower's blessing. Outside of New York only one politician with a strong state following, Senator Homer Capehart of Indiana, endorsed him. The Republican National Committee favored Nixon.

Rockefeller made one more move. He visited the hinterland. In November he went to the West Coast, in December to the Midwest and South. In some places he was received courteously, in others indifferently or rudely. The Republican politicians had made up their minds. They wanted Nixon. Just after Christmas, Rockefeller announced that he was not a candidate for the presidential nomination.

> . . . Any quest on my part for the nomination would entail a massive struggle in primary elections throughout the nation demanding so greatly of my time and energy that it would make impossible the fulfillment of my obligations as governor of New York. . . . I am not, and shall not be, a candidate for the nomination for the presidency. This decision is definite and final.

The statement had implications that went beyond mere withdrawal. Rockefeller acknowledged the fact that six months before the party convention Republican leaders had decided to nominate Nixon; he did not express approval of the decision by endorsing their choice. He forswore seeking the nomination; he did not say that he was unavailable. A few months later, in May, he said that he would accept a draft.

The Nixon camp was worried. They were not afraid that Rockefeller would be drafted. They knew that they had the convention sewed up. But recent polls showed Nixon running behind Kennedy. The November election would require a solidly united party. So those who had treated Rockefeller shabbily in the winter turned to courting him in the spring. He was cold to their blandishments, even to hints of a vice-presidential nomination, and busied himself in New York where, among other things, he obtained enactment of a law that would help the aged pay for health insurance. When on June 8th he did return to the national arena it was not to give aid and comfort to Vice-President Nixon.

The Rockefeller June 8th statement is in some respects comparable to Barry Goldwater's April, 1957, Senate speech. Goldwater had broken with the President and seized the leadership of the Republican right. Rockefeller praised President Eisenhower while criticizing aspects of his administration. His real target, however, was those "now assuming control of the Republican party"—Richard Nixon, although the Vice-President was not mentioned by name.

> We have come to a time that calls for plain talk. . . . The vitality and integrity of the Republican party, at so critical a time as the present, become matters of national concern. Without a two-party system that works with candor and courage, the American Republic—the very processes of Democratic government—cannot work responsibly. . . . I am deeply convinced, and deeply concerned, that those now assuming control of the Republican party have failed to make clear where the party is heading and where it proposes to lead the nation. . . . We cannot and must not confuse taking pride in the past with taking measure of the future. . . .
>
> I cannot pretend to believe that the Republican party has fully met this duty. . . . I find it unreasonable—in these times —that the leading Republican candidate for the presidential nomination has firmly insisted upon making known his program and his policies not before, but only after nomination by his party. . . .
>
> We cannot as a nation or as a party, proceed—nor should anyone presume to ask us to proceed—to march to meet the future with a banner aloft whose only emblem is a question mark. . . .

The path of great leadership does not lie along the top of a fence. . . . The people want and need one thing above all others: a leadership of clear purpose, candidly proclaimed.

This was essentially a political manifesto. It was aimed at Richard Nixon, not Barry Goldwater. Nonetheless, if 1964 brings a choice between Rockefeller and Goldwater it may be profitably reread. For in it Rockefeller makes clear that he would use the Republican party as a creative instrument of national policy that would take "the measure of the future." This is in sharp contrast to Goldwater's objective, the restriction of national policy to functions deeply embedded in the past.

The Nixon camp's reaction to the statement was sharp. The Republican National Chairman, a ruthless Nixon partisan, said the statement was an attack on the Eisenhower administration. Goldwater called Rockefeller a "rich man's Stassen." Nixon himself recalled that the New York governor had said that he would not accept a vice-presidential nomination and ironically assured the country that he would not try to draft him. *Time* speculated that Rockefeller wanted Nixon to lose so that he himself could be nominated in 1964.

Rockefeller remained unruffled and unrepentant. He said that as a loyal Republican he would support the party nominee, but he did not concede that as of that time—June—Nixon could carry New York. He repeated that though not a candidate, he would accept the nomination if it were offered.

His real motives can be known only to himself, but it seems probable that by this time he had forsworn ambition for 1960 and was trying to force the party to accept his program for America rather than himself. In fact, that is precisely what happened some six weeks later. His triumph is a strange episode in the history of intraparty politics.

It was July. The Republican convention was about to convene. Richard Nixon, the nomination clinched beyond reasonable doubt, was already in Chicago. The Resolutions Committee controlled by his supporters had produced a middle-

of-the-road platform. It commended the Eisenhower administration and promised that Nixon would carry on. It was a good
enough platform. Its authors hoped it was one upon which all
elements of the party could stand. Everything was set for a convention that would place Republican dignity and unity in
sharp contrast to the squabbling confusion exhibited by the
Democrats during their recent Los Angeles meeting. Rockefeller, aloof in New York, tossed a bomb. He found the platform lacking in strength. His supporters in Chicago, weak in
numbers but fortified by the righteousness of their cause,
threatened a platform fight on the convention floor.

Nixon took command. Without consulting his advisers or
the Resolutions Committee, he flew to New York for a conference in Rockefeller's East Side apartment. The result was a
fourteen-point program—the "Fifth Avenue Treaty"—which
met Rockefeller's demands. Republican party leadership had
abandoned the banner emblazoned with a question mark.

The conference over, Nixon flew back to Chicago to quell
any storm his action might generate. There was a storm. Barry
Goldwater was part of it. He branded the agreement "a
Munich." Republican politicians, however, had so committed
the party to Nixon that by the time the convention met it had
no real power of decision. It could only register its chosen
leader's will. Muttering and grumbling, it did so. The Rockefeller platform became the Republican platform. It is possible
that Nixon was not altogether unhappy. Necessity had compelled him to move a little to the left of Eisenhower—a thing
he had hesitated to do for fear of offending the sometimes iras-
cible general. And he had pulled Rockefeller's teeth—or at
least blunted them. A few days later when the convention nominated Nixon, Nelson Rockefeller was present, duly decorated
with Nixon buttons. He expressed approval of the platform.

On the whole the 1960 election did not do much to aid prophecy for 1964. Had Nixon been severely drubbed he would
have been politically dead. He almost won and remains alive.

The Democrats triumphed by carrying most of the industrial and urban states and holding the greater part of the South. This leaves the Republicans with two alternatives. They can try to regain their onetime supremacy in such states as New York, New Jersey, Pennsylvania, Illinois and Michigan (potential Rockefeller country) or they can try to make up their deficit in the South (potential Goldwater country). In either case they must hold the Plains and the West (Nixon country). So the three—Nixon, Rockefeller, Goldwater—remain. Dark horses are undoubtedly overflowing the stables, but none as yet has entered the running.

As of the dawn of 1962 two of the three most discussed possibilities for the 1964 presidential nomination, Nixon and Goldwater, declare that they are not candidates, while it is rumored, and denied, that Rockefeller may abandon politics. Speculation, then, centers on which of the coy bridegrooms—if any—will be dragged to the altar.

Any choice of the best man in a current or future race involves the choosers' political principles and prejudices. Extreme right-wing Republicans and Southern Democrats prefer Goldwater; middle-of-the-roaders probably still like Nixon; liberal Republicans and some Democrats support Rockefeller. Leaving principles and programs aside and judging purely from "job training," Rockefeller appears on the record to be the best man. He has been a strong and adroit governor; as a bureaucrat he learned his way around Washington and how to deal with national administrative agencies. His knowledge of world affairs is certainly broader and deeper than Goldwater's, probably than Nixon's. He is liberal, but not so far to the left that the gap between him and the modern Republicans cannot be bridged. On fiscal responsibility and armed might he should be acceptable to conservatives.

Goldwater is not the best man. A zealous enemy of Communism, he rallies public opinion against it within, but seems totally unable to comprehend the problem of mobilizing international resistance to the menace from without. He advocates cutting foreign aid to all countries who will not toe our own policy line, breaking off diplomatic relations with all Communist countries, discontinuing attempts to reach an agreement on disarmament. Such a policy would probably alienate all our allies except Nationalist China. Having thus weakened the United States, he would have it get tougher and tougher in its attitude. For a man who suspects starry eyes, all this seems amazingly unrealistic.

On the domestic front he lacks administrative experience. He has proved himself as a business executive, but business and political leadership require different skills. The businessman is his own master; he can determine and carry out a policy of his own choosing. Cooperation from his subordinates is highly desirable; it is not imperative. He can discharge them. The democratic statesman must somehow engineer consent. He cannot "fire" a recalcitrant Congress; he must persuade or lead it. Goldwater has not soothed tempers or calmed troubled waters. He emphasizes rather than blurs differences of opinion. He creates dissension rather than unity among Americans. Such men have value, but not as President of the United States.

Nelson Rockefeller might be the right man. *If* he is reelected governor of New York by a comfortable majority; *if* he is willing to make the massive effort in 1964 that he shunned in 1960; *if* Nixon is by choice or mandate of the California voters out of the running; *if* no new rival springs up overnight —as he himself did in 1958—his chances are bright. But there would still be obstacles.

He has not yet been accepted by Republican politicians outside New York. This does not prove that he never will be. His rejection in 1960 may have been because party leaders, committed to Nixon, resented his late bid as damaging to harmony. A convincing win in New York could rally Eastern regulars to him. With such a base the industrial states in the Midwest and on the Pacific Coast might fall into line. However, the old guard everywhere and the South will probably fight him to the end.

The political effect of his divorce from his wife is speculative. James Cox, the 1920 Democratic candidate, was divorced. Warren Harding beat him. Adlai Stevenson is divorced; he has been beaten twice. But it is unrealistic to attribute their defeats to divorce. They would have been snowed under anyway, though the smothering blanket might have been lighter. As with the Rockefeller candidacy generally, the divorce disability will be judged by the 1962 election. If he wins, his supporters will declare the issue harmless; if he loses, his family problems will cease to be of public interest.

Rockefeller has assets as well as liabilities. He will be a nationally known figure. His record as governor includes a tax rebate, a rare phenomenon in American politics. It points to fiscal responsibility, economy and good housekeeping. In late 1961 he summoned a special session of the legislature and pushed through a program providing fallout shelters for state schools and institutions. The fallout shelter controversy will probably continue to rage, but meantime while others talk, the New York governor has acted. He has won an election in the nation's most populous state. He has an affirmative program for America at the mid-century.

While his position is exposed it is strategically strong. In a September, 1961, meeting, the Executive Committee of the Republican National Committee surveyed Nixon's 1960 defeat. It found his greatest weakness had been in urban centers, with labor and minority ethnic groups—that is, in the big cities of the North. If G.O.P. strategy is to be directed towards remedying these weaknesses Rockefeller is the right man for 1964.

It is almost inconceivable that Barry Goldwater might be. He may come to the convention with a large block of votes garnered from the South and Arizona and a scattering elsewhere, but it is improbable that he will have significant second-choice support. He has taken a position so far to the right that the stronger he grows the more he will frighten politicians eager to build the party appeal on the broadest possible base.

No major party can afford to nominate a presidential candidate who is completely unacceptable to a large bloc of American voters. Goldwater has waged unrestrained war on organized labor; labor will reciprocate. He claims that he is actually trying to protect the workers from their own power-hungry leaders. He is an honest man; he probably believes it. Labor does not. American workers do not accept the archconservative's claim that he, rather than their natural leaders, is their true friend. No matter how good it might be for the character of the whole man, he simply won't accept the proposition that a dollar earned as the result of his own bargaining is better than a dollar and a quarter derived from collective bargaining or a minimum wage law. Most of the labor vote is now Democratic; with Goldwater as the Republican presidential nominee the remainder would be. Few Republican candidates for congressional or state office in an industrial state can afford the loss.

Goldwater wants to free agriculture so that the law of supply and demand will force inefficient operators off the land. He says that the farmers want to be thus freed. Maybe they do, but in their crop referendums they continue to vote overwhelmingly for price supports. Nixon carried the farm states. He did not do it by promising to withdraw federal support from agriculture. Candidates from agricultural states—including the South—do not run on platforms pledged to reducing agricultural aid. They know their farmers.

Goldwater believes in protection of civil rights, including racial integration, for all Americans. In Phoenix he has supported antidiscrimination. There can be no question of his sincerity. But he believes more strongly in states' rights. He says that he is not ready to force his judgment on the people of the South. Further, he holds that the Supreme Court decision on school integration is not the law of the land, thus substituting Goldwater for the Court as an agency of judicial review. The Goldwater decision is that the Constitution *"does not* require the states to maintain racially mixed schools." This binds the South to him. As a Republican presidential candidate he might carry it, or at least the greater part. But it would be at the expense of the party in the North. He has said that the duck hunter should go where the ducks are. There are undoubtedly ducks where he is hunting, but there are more elsewhere that his blasts will flush toward Democratic blinds.

Goldwater has attacked the graduated-income, inheritance and gift taxes, and compares them unfavorably with sales, excise and property taxes which are proportionally equal for rich and poor. He would cut taxes in general by having the government "begin to *withdraw* from a whole series of programs that are outside its constitutional mandate—from social welfare programs, education, public-power, agriculture, public housing, urban renewal and all the other activities that can better be performed by lower levels of government or by private institutions or by individuals." He believes that Social Security legislation deprives the individual of his rights to spend his money as he pleases during his productive years. Thus he would repeal the administrations of Franklin Roosevelt, Harry Truman and Dwight Eisenhower as well as the 1960 Republican party platform. Unless America is ready for revolution from the right, he will, as a presidential candidate, remain unchosen.

Acknowledgments

The authors wish to acknowledge the direct quotations, listed below, that have been used with the permission of authors, publishers, or copyright holders, given as written authorizations.

Page 7, Epigraph.

From *The Making of the President 1960* by Theodore H. White. Copyright © 1961 by Atheneum House, Inc. Reprinted by permission of the publisher.

The Republicans—1860: *Seward vs. Lincoln*

Page 28, line 15, "Now there is neither Whig party nor Whig . . ." William H. Seward cited in Reinhard H. Luthin, *The First Lincoln Campaign* (Cambridge, Massachusetts: Harvard University Press, 1944), p. 26.

Page 32, line 24, "The New Yorkers here . . ." Murat Halstead cited in William B. Hesseltine, ed., *Three Against Lincoln: Murat Halstead Reports the Caucuses of 1860* (Baton Rouge: Louisiana State University Press, 1960), p. 159.

Page 37, line 4, "They have gambled me all around . . ." Abraham Lincoln cited in James G. Randall, *Lincoln the President* (New York: Dodd, Mead & Company, 1945-1955), Vol. 1, p. 170.

Page 38, line 29, "Make no contracts that will bind me." Endorsement on the margin of the *Missouri Democrat* [May 17, 1860] cited in Roy P. Basler, ed., *The Collected Works of Abraham Lincoln* (New Brunswick, New Jersey: Rutgers University Press, 1953), Vol. 4, p. 50.

Page 38, line 31, "Dubois: 'Damn Lincoln' . . ." Cited in William E. Baringer, *Lincoln's Rise to Power* (Boston: Little, Brown and Company, © 1957), pp. 266-267.

Page 42, line 8, "To believers in the hand . . ." Eugene H. Roseboom, *A History of Presidential Elections* (New York: The Macmillan Company, 1957), p. 180.

Page 44, line 15, "Greeley slaughtered Seward and saved the party." John Defrees, cited in Glyndon G. Van Deusen, *Horace Greeley: Nineteenth Century Crusader* (Philadelphia: University of Pennsylvania Press, 1953), p. 247.

The Republicans—1876: *Bristow vs. Hayes*

Page 55, line 27, "I still think Blaine is so far ahead . . ." Hayes diary, May 19, 1876, cited in Charles Richard Williams, ed., *The Diary and Letters of Rutherford Birchard Hayes* ([Columbus, Ohio]: The Ohio Archaeological and Historical Society, 1922-1926), Vol. 3, pp. 319-320.

Page 57, line 18, "A baser, more villainous and unmitigated *lie* . . ." Benjamin H. Bristow cited in E. Bruce Thompson, "Benjamin Helm Bristow, Symbol of Reform" (Ph.D. dissertation, University of Wisconsin, 1940), p. 16.

Page 58, line 24, "In 1870 . . . I invited him into our law firm." John M. Harlan cited in David G. Farrelly, ed., "John M. Harlan's One-Day Diary, August 21, 1877, An Interpretation of the Harlan-Bristow Controversy," *Filson Club History Quarterly*, Vol. 24 (April, 1950), p. 163.

Page 68, line 20, "His war on the whiskey thieves . . ." Hayes diary, March 21, 1876, cited in Williams, ed., *Hayes Diary and Letters*, Vol. 3, p. 309.

Page 70, line 24, "He had no fear of Morton . . ." Jeremiah S. Black cited in David Saville Muzzey, *James G. Blaine, A Political Idol of Other Days* (New York: Dodd, Mead and Company, 1934), p. 109.

Page 72, line 21, "If any man nominated by this convention . . ." Robert Ingersoll cited in E. Bruce Thompson, "The Bristow Presidential Boom of 1876," *Mississippi Valley Historical Review*, Vol. 32 (June, 1945), pp. 25-26.

Page 74, line 14, "There is a man in this section . . ." Howard cited in Charles Richard Williams, *The Life of Rutherford Birchard Hayes* (Boston and New York: Houghton Mifflin Company, 1914), Vol. 1, p. 450n.

Page 75, line 18, "Also your articles . . ." Hayes to Major W. D. Bickham, April 26, 1876, cited in Williams, ed., *Hayes Diary and Letters*, Vol. 3, p. 317.

Page 79, line 14, "It is only in the contingency . . ." Hayes diary, May 19, 1876, cited in *ibid.*, p. 320.

The Republicans—1880-1888: *Sherman vs. Garfield, Blaine, Harrison*

Page 95, line 3, "studied the popular current . . ." James A. Garfield cited in Matthew Josephson, *The Politicos, 1865-1896* (New York: Harcourt, Brace and Company [1938]), p. 281n.

Page 95, line 7, "the chief characteristics of his life . . ." James A. Garfield diary cited in *ibid.*

Page 97, line 22, "apparently the thought of his trust . . ." James Ford Rhodes, *History of the United States* (New York: The Macmillan Company, 1920-1928), Vol. 8 (*History of the United States From Hayes to McKinley, 1877-1896*), p. 126.

Page 99, line 24, "I will not accept if nominated . . ." William T. Sherman cited in Lloyd Lewis, *Sherman, Fighting Prophet* (New York: Harcourt, Brace and Company [1932]), p. 631.

Page 108, line 6, "A great many colored delegates from the South . . ." Joseph Benson Foraker cited in Herbert David Croly, *Marcus Alonzo Hanna: His Life and His Work* (New York: The Macmillan Company, 1923), p. 136.

The Democrats—1912: *Clark vs. Wilson*

Page 124, line 16, "I say there is no such training-school . . ." Champ Clark, *My Quarter Century of American Politics* (New York: Harper and Brothers, © 1920), Vol. 2, p. 13.

Page 127, line 8, "because at the time the Democrats . . ." *Ibid.*, p. 27.

Page 131, line 6, "If we had not made the rules fight . . ." *Ibid.*, p. 260.

Page 136, line 18, "a man who will be . . ." Woodrow Wilson, *Constitutional Government in the United States* (New York: Columbia University Press [1908]), p. 65.

Page 137, line 3, "This strenuous objection . . ." William Gibbs McAdoo, *Crowded Years: The Reminiscences of William G. McAdoo* (Boston: Houghton Mifflin Company, © 1931), p. 143.

Page 139, line 9, "William Randolph Hearst . . ." Clark, *Quarter Century*, Vol. 2, pp. 264-265.

Page 140, line 23, "The majority of House Democrats . . ." *Ibid.*, pp. 397-398.

Page 142, line 2, "[Bryan] treated me with scant courtesy . . ." *Ibid.*, p. 398.

Page 146, line 35, "Give me no political dilettante . . ." James Reed cited in Arthur S. Link, *Wilson: The Road to the White House* (Princeton: Princeton University Press, 1947), p. 446.

Page 151, line 28, "I lost the nomination . . ." Clark, *Quarter Century*, Vol. 2, p. 392.

Page 151, line 32, "Bryan was dishonest . . ." *Ibid.*, p. 424.

Page 152, line 11, "The concensus of world opinion . . ." *Ibid.*, p. 443.

The Republicans—1920: *Lowden vs. Harding*

Page 164, line 4, "His political associations . . ." Walter Lippmann, "The Logic of Lowden," *New Republic*, Vol. 22 (April 14, 1920), p. 206.

Page 167, line 5, "There is a logic to Lowden . . ." *Ibid.*, p. 204.

Page 171, line 26, "fell into a doze . . ." Mark Sullivan, *Our Times: The United States, 1900-1925* (New York: Charles Scribner's Sons, 1926-1935), Vol. 6, p. 39.

Page 171, line 32, "Believing as I do in political parties . . ." Warren G. Harding cited in "A Marionette for President," *The Nation*, Vol. 110 (June 26, 1920), p. 842a.

Page 174, line 19, "My motto for the Reds is S.O.S." Cited in "Was General Wood Misquoted?" *New Republic*, Vol. 22 (May 19, 1920), p. 371.

Page 176, line 17, "You don't have to hire 'em . . ." The Chicago *Herald and Examiner* cited in William Thomas Hutchinson, *Lowden of Illinois: The Life of Frank O. Lowden* (Chicago: University of Chicago Press [1957]), Vol. 2, p. 456.

Page 176, line 29, "The real cause of my defeat . . ." Frank O. Lowden to John Campbell, Denver, June 17, 1920, cited in *ibid.*, p. 470.

Page 179, line 3, "the Senate group . . ." William Allen White, *Masks in a Pageant* (New York: The Macmillan Company, 1928), p. 404.

Page 179, line 15, "Any good Republican can be nominated . . ." Boies Penrose cited in Charles A. and Mary R. Beard, *The Rise of American Civilization* (New York: The Macmillan Company, 1930), p. 674.

Page 182, line 32, "Oh, there's going to be a deadlock . . ." Senator Reed Smoot cited in Sullivan, *Our Times*, Vol. 6, p. 58.

Page 184, line 16, "They were like a lot of chickens . . ." Senator Wadsworth cited in *ibid.*, p. 61.

Page 186, lines 4, 5, 8, "no world beater," "impressive appearance," "best of the bunch," "go along." Cited in Wesley M. Bagby, "The 'Smoke-Filled' Room and the Nomination of Warren G. Harding," *Mississippi Valley Historical Review*, Vol. 41 (March, 1955), pp. 663-664.

Page 188, line 3, "The next morning, uneasy delegates . . ." Harold L. Ickes, *The Autobiography of a Curmudgeon* (New York: Reynal & Hitchcock, p. 232.

Page 188, line 20, "I could not understand then . . ." Frank O. Lowden cited in Hutchinson, *Lowden*, Vol. 2, p. 466.

The Democrats—1924: *McAdoo vs. Smith*

Page 197, line 17, "Reflecting on the possibilities . . ." William G. McAdoo, *Crowded Years: The Reminiscences of William G. McAdoo* (Boston and New York: Houghton Mifflin Company, 1931), p. 53.

Page 197, line 31, "Day after day I sat . . ." *Ibid.,* p. 55.

Page 198, line 26, "It was dead indeed . . ." *Ibid.,* p. 65.

Page 198, line 30, "It was not a ghost . . ." *Ibid.,* p. 73.

Page 199, line 2, "The weakest spot in it . . ." *Ibid.,* p. 74.

Page 203, line 10, "Say 'McAdoo!' . . ." John W. Owens, "The Dilemma of the Democrats," *New Republic,* Vol. 39 (June 4, 1924), p. 36.

Page 206, line 21, "Just what Mr. Doheny . . ." "The Week," *ibid.,* Vol. 38 (March 5, 1924), p. 28.

Page 207, line 8, "They whitewashed an innocent man . . ." "The Week," *ibid.* (February 27, 1924), p. 2.

Page 220, line 3, "Nothing was charminger . . ." William Hard, "Davis the Double-Edged," *The Nation,* Vol. 119 (July 23, 1924), p. 94.

The Republicans—1952: *Taft vs. Eisenhower*

Page 230, line 28, "My husband is not a simple man . . ." Martha Taft cited in Caroline Thomas Harnsberger, *A Man of Courage, Robert A. Taft* (Chicago: Wilcox and Follett, 1952), pp. 129-130.

Page 231, line 13, "all the glamour of a pint of branch water." Cited in *ibid.,* p. 142.

Page 235, line 31, "Upon foreign policy . . ." William Allen White, "Republicans Act 'Like Democrats,'" *The New York Times,* June 25, 1940.

Page 237, line 34, "The Democrats said my bill . . ." Congressman Knutson cited in Malcolm Moos, *The Republicans* (New York: Random House [1956]), p. 433.

Page 240, line 18, "She identified these factions . . ." Doris Greenberg, "Mrs. Luce Attacks Truman and Party," *ibid.,* June 22, 1948.

Page 244, line 20, "confided in him that he was 'a good Kansas Republican.'" Roy Roberts cited in Paul T. David, *et al., Presidential Nominating Politics in 1952* (Baltimore: Johns Hopkins Press [1954]), Vol. 1, p. 27.

Page 244, line 30, "a candidate to the full limit . . ." Henry Cabot Lodge cited in Clayton Knowles, "Lodge to Enter Eisenhower in New Hampshire Primary," *The New York Times,* January 7, 1952.

Page 248, line 20, "mother, home and heaven." B. Carroll Reece cited in David, *et al., Presidential Nominating Politics,* Vol. 1, p. 52.

Page 252, line 18, "backroom schemings." Dwight D. Eisenhower cited in Russell Porter, "Eisenhower Says He'll Take Delegate Fight to the Floor," *The New York Times,* July 4, 1952.

Page 252, line 21, "a straight-out issue between right and wrong." Dwight D. Eisenhower cited in Russell Porter, "Eisenhower Scores Taft 'Chicanery,' " *The New York Times*, July 5, 1952.

Page 252, line 36, "amid flickering candles . . ." "The Eye of the Nation," *Time*, Vol. 60 (July 14, 1952), p. 22.

Page 253, line 15, "There will be no compromise . . ." Henry Cabot Lodge cited in "Crucial Decisions at Chicago," *Newsweek*, Vol. 40 (July 14, 1952), p. 22.

Page 258, line 17, "I came over to pay a call . . ." Dwight D. Eisenhower cited in William S. White, *The Taft Story* (New York: Harper and Brothers, 1954), pp. 180-181.

Page 260, line 4, "On the issues, Taft and Eisenhower . . ." "Taft Has Edge in Delegates; Ike Leads in Popular Polls," *Newsweek*, Vol. 39 (June 23, 1952), p. 21.

Page 262, line 11, "[The Eisenhower program] certainly isn't all I'd like it to be . . ." Robert A. Taft cited in Richard H. Rovere, "What Course for the Powerful Mr. Taft?" *The New York Times Magazine*, March 22, 1953, p. 32.

The Democrats—1952: *Kefauver vs. Stevenson*

Page 268, line 19, "dress designer, book illustrator and interior decorator." Jack Anderson and Fred Blumenthal, *The Kefauver Story* (New York: The Dial Press [1956]), p. 60.

Page 269, line 36, "a liberal who does not antagonize the conservatives." Jay Walz, "A Tennessee Crusader Tackles Crime," *The New York Times Magazine*, July 30, 1950, p. 22.

Page 270, line 11, "Specifically, Kefauver and his staff . . ." "Antitrusters on the Ropes," *Business Week*, October 19, 1946, p. 17.

Page 271, line 5, "seventy-three-year-old monarch of Memphis," "No Free Riders," *Time*, vol. 52 (August 16, 1948), p. 22.

Page 271, line 6, "I have been elected 26 times without being defeated . . ." Ed Crump cited in *ibid*.

Page 271, line 19, "The machine was so powerful . . ." Charles Edmundson, "How Kefauver Beat Crump," *Harper's Magazine*, Vol. 198 (January, 1949), p. 81.

Page 272, line 36, "This is a pedigreed West Tennessee coon . . ." Estes Kefauver cited in *ibid*., p. 82.

Page 273, line 5, "revival of the independent frontier spirit." Estes Kefauver cited in "Estes Kefauver in Tennessee," *New Republic*, Vol. 119 (October 11, 1948), p. 9.

Page 274, line 25, "I don't want to master-of-ceremony a circus." Estes Kefauver cited in Walz, "Tennessee Crusader," p. 10.

Page 274, line 35, "The television viewers at home . . ." Jack Gould, "Video Captures Drama of Inquiry," *The New York Times*, March 13, 1951.

Page 290, line 1, "Smear Stevenson day." James Reston, "Stevenson Stays Out of the Limelight," *The New York Times*, July 24, 1952.

The Democrats—1960: *Johnson vs. Kennedy*

Page 304, line 19, "It is apparent to every American . . ." Lyndon B. Johnson cited in Booth Mooney, *The Lyndon Johnson Story* (New York: Farrar, Straus and Cudahy [1956]), p. 64.

Page 309, line 24, "I am a free man . . ." Lyndon B. Johnson, "What I Believe —and Why," *The Texas Quarterly* cited in *Reader's Digest*, Vol. 74 (April, 1959), p. 75.

Page 310, line 12, "He believed it possible to do anything . . ." Ralph K. Huitt, "Democratic Party Leadership in the Senate," *American Political Science Review*, Vol. 55 (June, 1961), p. 337.

Page 310, line 22, "As a political commander . . ." William S. White, "Who Is Lyndon Johnson?" *Harper's Magazine*, Vol. 216 (March, 1958), p. 53.

Page 315, line 33, "conscious and well-planned campaign . . ." James Reston, "Honors for Kennedy," *The New York Times*, August 18, 1958.

Epilogue. The Republicans—1964: *Goldwater and Rockefeller—Unchosen?*

Page 347, line 15, "If [Nixon] would come out with a strong statement . . ." Barry M. Goldwater cited in "The Goldwater Formula for a Nixon Victory," *U.S. News & World Report*, Vol. 48 (April 25, 1960), p. 81.

Page 356, line 16, "rich man's Stassen." Barry M. Goldwater cited in "Banner With a Strange Device," *Time*, Vol. 75 (June 20, 1960), p. 10.

Page 361, line 34, *does not* require the states to maintain . . ." Barry M. Goldwater, *The Conscience of a Conservative* (Shepherdsville, Kentucky: Victor Publishing Company, 1960), p. 34.

Page 362, line 10, "begin to *withdraw* from a whole series of programs . . ." *Ibid.*, p. 61.

INDEX

Index